SAGE was founded in 1965 by Sara Miller McCune to support the dissemination of usable knowledge by publishing innovative and high-quality research and teaching content. Today, we publish over 900 journals, including those of more than 400 learned societies, more than 800 new books per year, and a growing range of library products including archives, data, case studies, reports, and video. SAGE remains majority-owned by our founder, and after Sara's lifetime will become owned by a charitable trust that secures our continued independence.

Los Angeles | London | New Delhi | Singapore | Washington DC | Melbourne

OPENINGS for PEACE

Thank you for choosing a SAGE product!
If you have any comment, observation or feedback,
I would like to personally hear from you.
Please write to me at **contactceo@sagepub.in**

Vivek Mehra, Managing Director and CEO, SAGE India.

Bulk Sales

SAGE India offers special discounts
for purchase of books in bulk.
We also make available special imprints
and excerpts from our books on demand.

For orders and enquiries, write to us at

Marketing Department
SAGE Publications India Pvt Ltd
B1/I-1, Mohan Cooperative Industrial Area
Mathura Road, Post Bag 7
New Delhi 110044, India

E-mail us at **marketing@sagepub.in**

Get to know more about SAGE

Be invited to SAGE events, get on our mailing list.
Write today to **marketing@sagepub.in**

This book is also available as an e-book.

OPENINGS for PEACE

UNSCR 1325, Women and Security in India

Edited by
Asha Hans
Swarna Rajagopalan

Los Angeles | London | New Delhi
Singapore | Washington DC | Melbourne

First published in 2016 by

 SAGE Publications India Pvt Ltd
B1/I-1 Mohan Cooperative Industrial Area
Mathura Road, New Delhi 110 044, India
www.sagepub.in

SAGE Publications Inc
2455 Teller Road
Thousand Oaks, California 91320, USA

SAGE Publications Ltd
1 Oliver's Yard, 55 City Road
London EC1Y 1SP, United Kingdom

SAGE Publications Asia-Pacific Pte Ltd
3 Church Street
#10-04 Samsung Hub
Singapore 049483

Published by Vivek Mehra for SAGE Publications India Pvt Ltd, typeset in 10.5/12.5 pt Times New Roman by Diligent Typesetter India Pvt Ltd, Delhi and printed at Sai Print-o-Pack, New Delhi.

Library of Congress Cataloging-in-Publication Data Available

ISBN: 978-93-859-8566-9 (HB)

SAGE Team: Shambhu Sahu, Saima Ghaffar, Shobana Paul, and Ritu Chopra

Contents

List of Abbreviations

ABAI	Agricultural Biosecurity Authority of India
AFSPA	Armed Forces Special Powers Act
APDP	Association of Parents of Disappeared Persons
APHC	All Parties Hurriyat Conference
AR	Assam Rifles
ATT	Arms Trade Treaty
BD	Bajrang Dal
BPFA	Beijing Platform for Action
BJP	Bharatiya Janata Party
BSF	Border Security Force
CAFI	Control Arms Foundation of India
CBI	Central Bureau of Investigation
CEDAW	Convention on the Elimination of All Forms of Discrimination Against Women
CJP	Citizens for Justice and Peace
COWF	Conflict Widows Forum
CrPC	Code of Criminal Procedure
CSCOHRM	Civil Society Coalition on Human Rights in Manipur
CSO	Civil Society Organizations
CSPSA	Chhattisgarh Special Public Safety Act
CSW	commercial sex worker
DAWN	Development Alternatives with Women for a New Era
DDR	Demobilization, Disarmament, Reintegration
DPKO	Department of Peacekeeping Operations
DRC	Congo
ECOSOC	United Nations Economic and Social Council
EEVFAM	Extrajudicial Executed Victims Families' Association, Manipur
FASPA	Freedom [to] Assume Special Powers [with] Arms

FIR	First Information Report
GBV	Gender-based Violence
GNWP	Global Network of Women Peacebuilders
HAP	Hague Appeal for Peace
IAY	Indira Awas Yojana
ICC	International Criminal Court
ICCPR	International Convention of Civil and Political Rights
ICPPED	International Convention for the Protection of All Persons from Enforced Disappearance
ICTJ	International Centre for Transitional Justice
ICTR	International Criminal Tribunal for Rwanda
IDP	Internally Displaced Person
IDRC	International Development Research Centre
IEA	Indian Evidence Act
IFCD	Irrigation and Flood Control Department
IGNWPS	Indira Gandhi National Widow Pension Scheme
IHL	International Humanitarian Law
IL	International Law
ILO	International Labour Organization
IPC	Indian Penal Code
IPRA	International Peace Research Association
IRB	India Reserve Battalion
ISAF	International Security Assistant Forces
JKPSA	Jammu and Kashmir Public Safety Act
LAPs	local action plans
LoC	Line of Control
LTTE	Liberation Tigers of Tamil Eelam
MDACTO	Mapithel Dam Affected Ching-Tam Organisation
MDAVO	Mapithel Dam Affected Villages Organisation
MGNREGA	Mahatma Gandhi National Rural Employment Guarantee Act
MHA	Ministry of Home Affairs
MISA	Maintenance of Internal Security Act
MKM	Muslim Khawateen-e-Markaz
MLA	Member of the Legislative Assembly
MPs	Members of Parliament
MSCW	Manipur State Commission for Women

MSF	Médicins Sans Frontièrs
NAP	National Action Plan
NATO	North Atlantic Treaty Organisation
NAWO	National Alliance of Women's Organisations
NDC	National Development Council
NE	North East
NEN	North East Network
NFHS	National Family Health Survey
NFSA	National Food Security Act
NGO	Non-governmental Organization
NHRC	National Human Rights Commission
NMA	Naga Mothers Association
NNC	Naga National Council
NPC	Naga People's Convention
NPMHR	Naga People's Movement for Human Rights
NREGA	National Rural Employment Guarantee Act
NSCN	National Socialist Council of Nagaland
NSCN-IM	National Socialist Council of Nagaland—Isak Muivah
NSCN-K	National Socialist Council of Nagaland—Khaplang
NWUM	Naga Women's Union Manipur
PDA	Preventive Detention Act
PDS	Public Distribution System
PHC	Primary Health Centre
PLA	People's Liberation Army
PMGSY	Pradhan Mantri Gram Sadak Yojna
POTA	Prevention of Terrorism Act
PREPAK	People's Revolutionary Party of Kangleipak
PUDR	People's Union for Democratic Rights
RAY	Rajiv Awas Yojana
RPF	Revolutionary People's Front
RTI	Right to Information
R2P	Responsibility to Protect
SALW	Small Arms and Light Weapons
SAARC	South Asian Association for Regional Cooperation
SAR	South Asian Region
SCR	Security Council Resolutions
SEWA	Self Employed Women's Association

SHG	Self-help Group
SIT	Special Investigation Team
SLP	Special Leave Petition
SPF	Secular Progressive Front
SRVAW	Special Rapporteur on Violence Against Women
SSZ	Special Security Zone
TADA	Terrorist and Disruptive Activities Act
TSL	Tangkhul Shanao Long
UAPA	Unlawful Activities (Prevention) Act
UDHR	Universal Declaration of Human Rights
UNICEF	United Nations Children's Emergency Fund
UNLF	United National Liberation Front
UNMIL	UN Mission in Liberia
UNPK	United Nations Peacekeeping
UNSCR	UN Security Council Resolution
UTs	Union Territories
VDB	Village Development Board
VDF	Village Defence Force
VDFs	Village Defence Forces
VHP	Vishwa Hindu Parishad
WAD	Women's Action for Development
WID	Women in Development
WIGJ	Women's Initiatives for Gender Justice
WILPF	Women's International League for Peace and Freedom
WinG	Women in Governance
WIPNET	West African Women in Peacebuilding Network
WISCOMP	Women in Security, Conflict Management and Peace
WPS	Women, Peace and Security

Foreword

In the 15 years since the adoption of UN Security Council Resolution 1325, we have seen a tremendous enthusiasm among civil society at all levels in raising awareness, engaging in advocacy and building capacity for its meaningful implementation. It is my pleasure to write the foreword to this publication which is a meaningful endeavour to move the agenda forward on the occasion of the 15th anniversary of the adoption of this groundbreaking resolution.

All of us need to remember that the adoption of 1325 has opened a much-awaited door of opportunity for women. To trace back, on International Women's Day in 2000, I had the honour of issuing on behalf of the UN Security Council, in my capacity as its President, a statement that formally brought to global attention the unrecognized, underutilized and undervalued contribution women have always been making towards the prevention of wars, peace-building and engaging individuals, communities and societies to live in harmony. All 15 members of the Security Council recognized in that statement that peace is inextricably linked with equality between women and men, and affirmed the value of full and equal participation of women in all decision-making levels. That is when the seed for Resolution 1325 on women and peace, and security was sown. The formal resolution followed this conceptual and political breakthrough on 31 October of the same year, giving this issue the long overdue attention and recognition that it deserved.

My own experience particularly during the last quarter century has made it clear that the participation of women in peace-making, peace-keeping and peace-building assures that their experiences, priorities and solutions contribute to a long-term stability and inclusive governance. I have seen time and again how women—even the humblest and the weakest—have contributed to building the culture of peace in their personal lives, in their families, in their communities and in their nations.

The contribution and involvement of women in the eternal quest for peace is an inherent reality. Women are the real agents of change in refashioning peace structures ensuring greater sustainability.

In choosing the three women laureates for the 2011 Nobel Peace Prize, the citation referred to 1325 saying: 'It underlined the need for women to become participants on an equal footing with men in peace processes and in peace work in general'. The Nobel Committee further asserted: 'We cannot achieve democracy and lasting peace in the world unless women obtain the same opportunities as men to influence developments at all levels of society'.

The main inspiration behind 1325 is not to make war safe for women but to structure the peace in a way that there is no recurrence of war and conflict. Research and case studies consistently suggest that peace agreements and post-conflict rebuilding have a much higher chance of long-term success when women are involved. That is why women need to be at the peace tables; women need to be involved in the decision-making and in the peacekeeping teams to make a real difference in transitioning from the cult of war to the culture of peace.

The driving force behind 1325 is 'participation' in which women can contribute to decision-making and ultimately help shape societies where violence in general, more so against women, is not the norm. 1325 marked the first time that such a proposition was recognized as an objective of the UN Security Council.

'Women in every part of the world continue to be largely marginalized from the political sphere'. This is unfortunate and unacceptable. Empowering women's political leadership will have ripple effects on every level of society and consequently on the global condition. When politically empowered, women bring important and different skills and perspectives to the policymaking table in comparison to their male counterparts.

When women have been included in peace negotiations, they often have brought the views of women to the discussions by ensuring that peace accords address demands for gender equality, human rights, good governance and rule of law in new constitutional, judicial and electoral structures. We would not have to be worrying about countering extremism if women have had equality in decision-making, enabling them to take measures which would prevent such extremism. Ensuring equality and inclusion, mutual respect and fairness in international relations is essential to weed out roots of extremism.

I recall Eleanor Roosevelt's words saying: 'Too often the great decisions are originated and given shape in bodies made up wholly of men, or so completely dominated by them that whatever of special value women have to offer is shunted aside without expression'. It is a reality that politics, more so security, is a man's world.

Unfortunately, the challenges to women's rights and their equality not only continue, but also mutate and reappear, undermining any hard-earned progress—of course, in the process, those become more and more complex, complicated and difficult to overcome.

The ever-increasing militarism and militarization have made the situation even worse. The global patriarchy's encouragement to the voluminous arms trade has made it easier for extremists of all kinds in obtaining the arms to impose on others their extremist world views. Ending the arms trade and serious steps toward disarmament should be part of the prescription for reducing and eliminating extremism and all militarized violence.

Recognition that women need to be at the peace tables to make a real difference in transitioning from the cult of war to the culture of peace, I believe, made the passage of 1325 an impressive step forward for women's equality agenda in contemporary security politics. The slogan of Global Campaign on Women, Peace and Security which we launched in London in June 2014 reiterates: 'If we are serious about peace, we must take women seriously'. Of course, achieving real gender equality requires 'transformative change'. In this conceptual reorientation, the politics of gender relations and restructuring of institutions, rather than simply equality in access to resources and options, should become the priority.

Fifteen years after the adoption of 1325, the governments are still trying to get their acts together on its effective implementation by preparing respective National Action Plans (NAPs) as called for by the Security Council. Civil society, on its part, should systematically monitor and evaluate its implementation to hold all sides accountable. Also, countries should work towards the elimination of violence against women and ensure that victims have full access to justice and that there is no impunity for perpetrators. Some countries boast that they do not need a national plan as their countries are not in conflict. To that, I say emphatically that no country can claim to be not in conflict where women's rights are not ensured. Very relevant in this context is the civil society initiative to prepare a People's Action Plan as cogently articulated by Betty Reardon in her persuasive contribution in this publication.

In general, NAPs should be designed to coordinate and strengthen the implementation of 1325. They should contain a catalogue of measures and clear targets and benchmarks for full and meaningful implementation. The creation of an action plan provides an opportunity to initiate strategic actions, identify priorities and resources, and determine the responsibilities and timeframes. The whole process of developing a plan is also a process of awareness raising and capacity building in order to overcome gaps and challenges to the full implementation of 1325.

In real terms, NAP is the engine that would speed up the implementation of Resolution 1325. So far, only 48 out of 193 UN member States have prepared their plans—what a dismal record after 15 years. There are no better ways to get country-level commitment to implement 1325 other than NAPs. I believe very strongly that only NAPs can hold the governments accountable. There has to be an increased and proactive engagement of the UN secretariat leadership to get a meaningfully bigger number of NAPs—for example, setting a target of 100 NAPs by 2017.

In case of India, for both the government and civil society, preparation of its NAP is particularly important. NGOs (non-governmental organizations) should persistently continue to pressure and demand that the government develops the country's NAP for the implementation of 1325.

At the global level, the UN secretary-general needs to take the lead in setting up six-monthly inclusive consultative process for 1325 implementation with the civil society organizations at all levels for all relevant UN entities. Also, all relevant NGOs are to be mobilized at country level by the 1325 national coordination body supported by the UN resident coordinator.

Again, to recall my message in 2011, I welcomed the focus of Sansristi's workshop,

> on the significance of and need for human-centred approach to security. Security can no longer be understood in purely military terms or in terms of state security. Rather, it must encompass economic development, social justice, environmental protection, democratization, disarmament, and respect for human rights and the rule of law. To attain the goals

of human security, the most essential element is the protection and empowerment of people. As 1325 deals with peace & security with special attention to the half of the global population, it is crucially important that the human security concept becomes the key to the resolution's implementation at the national, regional and global levels.

The existing international policies and practices that make women insecure and deny their equality of participation, basically as a result of its support of the existing militarized inter-state security arrangements, are disappointing. We need to realize that the world is secure when we focus on ensuring human security with a feminist perspective and full and equal participation of women at all decision-making levels, in all spheres of human activity and at all times.

1325 is a 'common heritage of humanity' wherein the global objectives of peace, equality and development are reflected in a uniquely historic, universal document of the UN. As we look ahead, what is called for is an ever-growing global movement involving more and more women and, of course, men.

This publication is a concrete and determined step towards the objective of contributing meaningfully to the emerging global movement for women's equality and empowerment. It reflects our common eagerness, energy and enthusiasm to move forward. With wonderfully articulated presentations, skilfully authored by experts from various background and experiences, and brilliantly put together with accomplished editing by Asha Hans and Swarna Rajagopalan, the book deserves wide-ranging attention and global readership.

Ambassador Anwarul K. Chowdhury
former Under-Secretary-General of the United Nations
former Permanent Representative of Bangladesh to the UN
President of the UN Security Council in March 2000 and June 2001
Initiator of the UNSCR 1325
September 2015.

Acknowledgements

Fifteen years after the UN Security Council adopted Resolution 1325, we reflect on what we as feminists have achieved in organizing around issues of peace, security and justice. We realize that while the resolution has been adopted in many countries, women continue to struggle against patriarchal and state violence in conflict zones. The increase in armaments and State-controlled laws has contributed to the violence against women in particular and pose profound challenges for women.

While writers across the globe on peace and security have been variously successful, we inherit many old challenges of global masculinist militarism and patriarchy, and new challenges of economic militaristic action. This volume testifies to the deeply committed feminist writing and activism. The writings cover a range of critical essays with an urgency to reflect on UNSCR 1325. As we reach this 15th year mark, the authors have voiced the vision of agency and justice.

This is an important collection in the context of peace and grew out of two conferences held in Bhubaneswar, India in 2011 and 2013 organized by Sansristi. Bringing together women both from academia and activists to initiate the discourse on NAP for India, it extended to militarism and suppressive laws being maintained. We are thankful to Navsharan Singh of IDRC (International Development Research Centre) who had the faith that supporting the two conferences would bring about radical change in global thinking.

We are also grateful to Betty Reardon, who has not only been promoting UNSCR 1325 at the UN and across many countries of the world but also mentoring us on how to take this issues forward. Betty Reardon's presence and our collective wish for peace facilitated a discussion of a fresh thinking on women, peace and security and development of People's Action Plan. We also are thankful to Anwarul K. Chowdhury, former Under-Secretary- General of the UN—the main figure behind the adoption of UNSCR 1325 and who kindly consented to writing the foreword to the volume.

We are grateful to the writers who have contributed to this volume, most of them activists and academics. They have brought their experience, insight and scholarship to our collective effort, and we are very grateful to them for their patience and graciousness as they waited for feedback and went through rounds of revision. We are sad that in the process of putting the volume together, we lost Ila Pathak, an activist with both radical thought and action. Unfortunately, she died while the volume was in progress but Saumya Uma stepped in and added a postscript. We are grateful to Saumya for taking on this challenge with so much generosity. We would like to thank other colleagues also who have contributed to our discussions and writings, although they were not a part of this project.

September 2015.

1

Openings for Peace:
An Introduction to the Volume

Swarna Rajagopalan

This book, *Openings for Peace: UNSCR 1325, Women and Security in India* has evolved over two meetings organized by Sansristi in Bhubaneswar. The first, in March 2011, was centred on brainstorming People's Action Plan to implement the UN Security Council 1325, but the discussions placed the spotlight on the limitations of the 1325 framework for India. A second meeting, in April 2013, brought the focus squarely to a critical appraisal of 1325 as well as a constructive conversation about alternative strategies of adoption and adaptation. This anthology thus twins a discussion of the WPS (women, peace and security) resolutions with a discussion of militarism, exploring the relevance of the resolutions in settings that are not deemed 'conflict'.

Fifteen years ago, the UN Security Council adopted Resolution 1325, which turned out to be the first of the many WPS resolutions it has since passed. A central instrument specified in 1325 and reiterated in subsequent resolutions is the National Action Plan (NAP). For a decade, the efforts of civil society and the UN system centred on getting nation-states to adopt NAPs to address the various 'pillars' of 1325.

NAPs are seen by UN agencies as a public commitment to implement 1325 (UN Women 2012). NAPs adapt global ideas to local contexts. They are expected to describe what has been accomplished and to detail what it hopes to do within clear time frames. The process of drafting an NAP can be inclusive so as to create awareness and facilitate a consensus-building debate on gender issues in peace and security. NAPs, thus create ownership of WPS priorities. The NAP strategy gives government efforts visibility (although from the government point of view, this may not be a selling-point); as a corollary, they make it easy to monitor and evaluate government actions and hold governments accountable. NAPs facilitate and clarify coordination between government agencies.

Around the time that we began planning this book in 2011, the idea of the NAP was losing appeal and momentum. To nation-states, especially in South Asia, to adopt an NAP was seen as an admission that there were conflicts within the State—an admission that would invite unwanted international attention to internal issues. For long-standing peace activists, the prospect of a State-authored plan for inclusion held out very little hope for true inclusion of women and their concerns into conflict resolution and peace processes.

The 2011 meeting was supposed to brainstorm the elements of People's Plan as also to consider the process whereby we might arrive at such a plan. Instead, as we assembled, it was clear that if some of us were sceptical that any of our governments would, in fact, adopt an NAP. The two South Asian States that have done so, did it with a considerable amount of UN support. For others, coming from a lifetime of peace activism, this seemed like just another faddish idea when older issues remained unresolved. There were questions about effectiveness and utility, and also whether the NAP framework would allow us to address the deeper problem of militarization. We never really discussed a People's Plan but the idea lingers in this volume. What we would all agree upon is that peace must be sown at the ground-level and will not trickle down from an NAP.

Insofar as this book is a collective rumination about 1325, women, peace, security and militarization, the NAP remains important to it as a key referent. We return to it occasionally, only to walk away again. The 12 chapters included herein reflect the trajectory of this conversation that has drawn on history, activism, case studies and theoretical discussions in equal part. The conversation moves forward in stages.

The next three chapters offer an exploration of the WPS resolutions—what they provide, their intellectual and political genesis and their rationale. The next chapter by Swarna Rajagopalan explicates 1325 and its sister resolutions that variously address the problems of participation, impunity for sexual violence in conflict and institutional measures to sensitize UN fieldworkers and peacekeepers. She recounts the evolution of ideas on security and feminist critical scholarship in international relations as part of the genesis of the WPS resolutions. The chapter closes speculating about other contexts where the 1325 pillars could serve as an advocacy tool.

Soumita Basu wonders why Indian women's groups, which have engaged with other international conventions, have not been enthused by 1325, even though the WPS resolutions reflect a feminist agenda on peace and security. She argues that civil society organizations have an important role to play in creating awareness about the resolutions, at least given India's significant contribution to UN peacekeeping.

Next, Anuradha Chenoy argues that the fact that women have not been included in prevention, management and resolution of conflicts makes 1325 necessary. She points out however, that 1325 does not address militarization and violence in society. Chenoy suggests that when awareness about 1325 is more widespread at the grass roots, and we are able to extend and apply 1325 to the broader context of militarization, civil society will be able to hold the government accountable for its own commitments and rhetoric on women, peace and security.

Emergency laws that limit civil rights are the concern of the next two chapters. A colonial legacy in South Asia, laws may be enacted or invoked for special circumstances that centralize the State, limit civil liberties and expand the powers of State agencies to include arbitrary preventive detention. They usually facilitate and foster a climate of impunity that has special gendered consequences.

Amrita Patel begins by describing the colonial origins of these coercive laws. She then surveys what is a veritable supermarket of such instruments, meant to address 'disturbances' or 'terrorism'. At the core of her chapter is her description of the Armed Forces Special Powers Act (AFSPA). In the words of the minister who introduced the legislation in 1958, as quoted by Patel, 'It only seeks to protect the steps the armed forces might have to take in the disturbed areas'. This facilitation of impunity has enabled decades of militarization and human rights violation, especially in North Eastern India. Patel discusses the growing support for the abolition of this particular coercive law. Like other writers in this volume, she contends that invoking or implementing 1325 is meaningless without a repudiation of such militaristic laws.

Ritu Dewan's very short chapter—almost just a note—is a sharp critique of three other measures that appear innocuous, but offer the State a means of extending its control and limiting the freedom of ordinary citizens. She discusses the Agricultural Biosecurity Bill (2013), the Jammu and Kashmir Police Bill (2013) and the creation of special security zones. An activist tract, it points to 'the context of rising violence, of the increasing culturalization of especially gender and sexual violence, and of the institutionalization of State violence', and hopes to elicit democratic protests against these. Dewan's note presages the economic militarization that Asha Hans describes in her chapter on Manipur.

The next three chapters look at the 'conflict' context in which these laws have mostly been enforced: North East India more generally, Nagaland and Manipur in particular and Jammu and Kashmir. Although the Government of India (GoI) uses 'disturbed areas' rather than conflict areas to describe these places, it is commonly accepted that these have been conflict zones for a long time.

Paula Banerjee draws on her many years of research to offer this volume insights about the impact of conflict on women, women's agency as peacemakers and the salience of 1325, especially in Nagaland and Manipur. She points out that as a consequence of women's agency as mediators and peace activists, women end up being marginalized by the community leadership. She flags this potential problem that could be reinforced by 1325. On the other hand, women's demand for 33 per cent reservation in legislatures is at odds with the political establishment. She says that women can be allies and adversaries of both the State and the human rights communities.

Asha Hans' chapter takes a deeper and comprehensive look at Manipur. Most notably, it extends our understanding of this militarized society by explicating and describing the relationship between global capital, militarization and economic security. Into this mix, add the consequences of a porous border and India's Look East policy. Without the right to property, assets or decision-making even of their own income, Hans points out that women are far from well-placed to thrive in this environment. Rather, it has created its own vulnerabilities— women who trade in the border area, for instance, face demands for sexual favours from security personnel. The 1325 story is taken further—not just women at the peace table; not just coercive laws; not just traditional conflict situations, but this entire universe of conflict and militarization consequences that ensues.

The absence of institutional platforms has, in the view of Rekha Chowdhary and Vibhuti Ubbott, worked in favour of Kashmiri women. Circumstances have forced them out of their homes, to enter police stations and other formal spaces, to search for their family members and negotiate their release. They have had to fend for themselves amid curfews and violence. They are well-prepared to be politically active and to serve as bridge or pressure group for peace. 1325 would mandate the opportunity to absorb this talent and experience.

The longest chapter in the book is about the riots and the violence. This was written by the late Ila Pathak, edited by us and updated with a postscript by Saumya Uma. The chapter draws on civil society fact-finding reports to build a case for implementing international regimes and covenants (including 1325) to such situations. These cases are a bit of a departure from the others in this book—they were episodic and lasted days—but their impact remains. Justice, as Ilaben points out, is yet to be done. Women have borne the brunt of violence in both locations, facing brutal sexual and gender-based assaults, and the delays in justice hurt them the most. Saumya Uma sees 1325 being most useful as an advocacy and negotiation tool at the level of the district and State administration, while seeking justice and punitive action.

Betty Reardon, who contributed to sustained activism at the UN that got 1325 passed, reflects that perhaps the best prospect for making the ideas enshrined in 1325 a reality lies not with government NAPs but local peace and women's rights activism. She takes the conversation back to the resolutions and points out that as later resolutions focus time and again on sexual violence, they partly undo the most important aspect of 1325—women's participation and agency. She offers tools to enable local civil society groups to come up with their own 'People's Action Plans'.

Asha Hans' conclusion reiterates the importance of local activism by civil society—making both People's Plan with a larger canvas and Local Action Plans to respond to crises like the violence in communal riots. She describes 1325 as a paradigm shift that would be reinforced by civil society building alliances to promote its pillars and by thinking of it not as institutional changes but building a culture of peace.

The chapters in this book reflect the scholarship, activism and political consciousness of the authors. Working in different spheres, they share some concerns. First, while UNSCR 1325 began as a women's peace movement initiative that sought to challenge thinking about security and about women's empowerment, discussions about implementation have largely been confined to promoting the NAPs, although top-down initiatives are elitist and rarely as inclusive as they need to be. Second, they acknowledge that making women visible has to mean making all women visible and also not making victimhood the central condition of that visibility. Third, if UNSCR 1325 reflects a moment of global consensus on women's participation in peace-making, the contributors to this volume would like to see this consensus translated into local action. The authors seek to place the WPS resolutions in very local, specific contexts without assuming they will always be relevant as is. Fourth, there is some concern that the later WPS resolutions have focused heavily on sexual violence in conflict. While this is important, such a focus can lead to protection-centred solutions rather than to finding ways to end the culture of impunity around violence. Finally, weaving in and out of the various chapters is the desire to anchor women's security not in State security policies but in the transformation of State structures and social attitudes.

Preventing Conflict, Transforming Justice, Securing the Peace: A Global Study on the Implementation of United Nations Security Council Resolution 1325, a report prepared in 2015 by a special high-level expert panel to mark 15 years since the adoption of 1325, echoes these themes (UN Women 2015). Pointing out that 1325 had its origins as a human rights resolution, it argues for both punitive justice for women and a serious effort to change structural iniquity. Like most authors in this book, the experts writing the global study express grave concern not just about conflict settings but militarism, extremism and militarization. The global study also reinforces what the authors in this book suggest: that implementing 1325 should not be left to governments alone. There is a role for civil society and the media in this work.

A word about the diversity of approaches, styles and lengths within the volume: We value this diversity as a reflection of the authors' own background and experience. Although many of the authors have trained as scholars, their work is animated by a wish to see social transformation, including peace. Accordingly, while we did not solicit policy recommendations, to intertwine the description of a problem with an exploration of its solutions is instinctive to them. Some chapters are written with the relative detachment of academics; some are passionate, even anguished. Our editorial interventions have not sought uniformity. We have been committed to letting author's voices come through, while merely seeking clarity.

This book is our analytical contribution to the activist task of taking 1325 as an instrument and making it work for each of us in our contexts. We believe those local interpretations and adaptations will enrich and further the participation of women, the prevention of conflict and the protection of women in conflict (or conflict-like situations and emergencies). 1325 got us talking, but the authors in this book have taken the discussion from State-centric NAPs to people-driven local agendas for action. Fifteen years since the adoption of the resolution, the world has come around to this view.

References

UN Women. 2012. *Women and Peace and Security: Guidelines for National Implementation/Guidelines for the Development of a National Action Plan on Women, Peace and Security.* New York: UN Women.

————. 2015, October. *Preventing Conflict, Transforming Justice, Securing the Peace: A Global Study on the Implementation of United Nations Security Council Resolution 1325.* Available at: http://wps.unwomen.org/~/media/files/un%20women/wps/highlights/unw-global-study-1325-2015.pdf (Accessed on 18 February 2016).

2

The 1325 Resolutions: From Thought to Action

Swarna Rajagopalan

I have written three avatars of this chapter from 2011 till date (21 September 2015).

The first ambitiously sought to delineate the historical and discursive factors that made possible the adoption of UNSCR 1325 (2000). I wrote in that introduction, the following:

> Something important has shifted in the way the world thinks, when thinking collectively, about gender relations. Patriarchy thrives in most communities and households. States are still paternalistic and insensitive to gender inequity. Families still prefer and favour boys and men in most places. But at the most distant stratum of contemporary human experience, something has shifted, and UN Security Council Resolution 1325 (2000) reflects this shift.

This was in February 2011.

The second was just less ambitious but as I wrote it, something kept slipping away from me—conviction, I suspect. I have dreaded sitting down to this third avatar. When you revisit a writing project at intervals, there is no flow of thoughts or words and that is dispiriting. But finish this, I must. This third avatar retains some shadows and some substance of the first two, but the journey moves on, using this discursive history to push the 1325 envelope and expand its scope and agents. How can we take this marvellous set of tools (1325 and its sister resolutions) and put them to good use?

The chapter begins with a review of 1325 and its 'sister' resolutions. It maps thinking in feminist and security studies circles that made consensus on the principles behind 1325 possible. The resolutions themselves draw attention to issues such as sexual violence that were always part of war but never part of the conversations about peace.

This chapter suggests that UNSCR 1325, read actually as a rubric that includes subsequent related resolutions, is the product of more than four decades of discursive interventions that have engaged the theoretical and policy universes. These changes pushed to open up and include new referents, new issues and new actors. They were democratizing in intent and impact. Women's participation and involvement is one of the means to end the gendered iniquities of war.

In its third incarnation, this chapter also doubles as an opening reflection on themes that have emerged in the evolution of this book. The first of these is the idea that while UNSCR 1325 primarily engages with and addresses governments, there is a role that civil society, especially the transnational women's movement, has played and retains in its articulation and implementation. The second theme relates to what is revealed when one employs a gender lens and how what we learn about women's experiences and agency reinforce the case for implementing 1325 to several kinds of conflict and militarized situations.

The Security Council Resolutions refer mainly to the context of conflict and primarily address their instructions to member States and UN personnel. But States are limited by both will and capacity and the insistence on National Action Plans (NAPs) could limit the substantive reach of the resolutions. This chapter continues the 'opening up' process by looking (albeit briefly) at other contexts to which the values of 1325 are relevant and at the role of civil society in promoting these values—which are also the values of the women's movement and of every human rights and women's rights convention we have adopted. The paper closes by speculating what it would mean to extend the context of 1325 beyond conflict and to extend the responsibility for acting on it beyond States.

I. 1325

On 31 October 2000, the UN Security Council passed a resolution that enjoined member States to include women at every level of decision-making and at every stage of a conflict timeline. 1325 was preceded by a number of laws and protocols to which it refers explicitly and it was also followed by other resolutions with similar intent. In this paper, '1325' is used as a rubric for UNSCR 1325 itself and the related resolutions that followed its passage. In this section, the provisions of UNSCR 1325 will first be summarized, followed by brief descriptions of other resolutions in this rubric.

UNSCR 1325

The prefatory clauses of UNSCR 1325 remind us that this landmark resolution did not appear in a vacuum and that at least five years of debate and resolve preceded it. A reconstruction of the history they recall begins with the Beijing Platform of Action.

The Fourth UN World Conference on Women held in Beijing in 1995, negotiated the Beijing Declaration and Platform for Action that devoted an entire chapter to women and armed conflict. In 1999–2000, the UN Security Council passed resolutions on the themes of children in armed conflict and the protection of civilians. The Windhoek Declaration (May 2000) at the 10th anniversary meeting of the UN Transitional Assistance Group made several suggestions for mainstreaming gender in peacekeeping and peace support operations.

The political declaration of the special General Assembly session to mark the fifth anniversary of the Beijing Platform included sections on the same. Elsewhere, UNSCR 1325 also refers to the UN Charter, the Geneva Conventions and their Additional Protocols, the Refugee Convention, the Convention on the Rights of the Child, the Rome Statute of the International Criminal Court and the Convention on the Elimination of All Forms of Discrimination Against Women (CEDAW). In other words, this resolution was the culmination of many debates, pulling together and very clearly giving inclusive and gender-sensitive peace-making the status of an accepted norm.

UNSCR 1325 addressed the UN Secretary General, member States and conflict parties while committing itself to factoring in gender concerns in its decision-making and actions.

UNSCR 1325 begins by urging 'increased representation of women at all decision-making levels in national, regional and international institutions and mechanisms for the prevention, management, and resolution of conflict' (S/RES/1325 [2000] Article 1). This is the provision with which the resolution is most identified. Member

States are asked to provide good women candidates for a roster to be maintained by the secretary general for appointments. They are asked to increase 'financial, technical and logistical support' for gender sensitivity training (Article 7).

All conflict parties are asked both during peace talks and in a post-conflict phase to adopt a gender perspective. UNSCR 1325 identifies three elements of such a perspective. First, the special needs of women and girls in a post-hostilities phase should be recognized. Second, local women's peace initiatives should be supported and women should be involved in every aspect of peace-building. Third, post-conflict political and constitutional arrangements should guarantee the human rights of women and girls. It is further suggested that women's groups, local and transnational, be suggested to gain an understanding of what women's special needs are. Conflict parties are reminded to respect international law's protections for women and children and to remember that refugee camps and settlements are civilian spaces for humanitarian action.

UNSCR 1325 also takes on the issue of gender violence in two very important provisions. Article 10 calls on all conflict parties to protect women and girls from 'gender-based violence, particularly rape and other forms of sexual abuse'. Article 11 is addressed to member States, asking that they put an end to impunity for those responsible for genocides, crimes against humanity and war crimes 'including those relating to sexual and other violence against women and girls'. There is to be no amnesty for such crimes.

The secretary general is asked to carry out studies of the impact of armed conflict on women and girls, their role in peace-building and gender dimensions of peace-making (S/RES/1325 [2000] Article 16). He is asked to report to the Security Council, which in turn makes a commitment to taking cognizance of gender issues in its decision-making and mandating a gender perspective to actions it initiates.

1325's 'Sister' Resolutions

Other recent UN Security Council Resolutions have signalled a fast-diminishing tolerance towards gender violence in conflict situations. Read together with 1325, they make a very strong statement about women, peace and security.

UNSCR 1820 (S/RES/1820 [2008]) begins by noting that

> [C]ivilians account for the vast majority of those adversely affected by armed conflict; that women and girls are particularly targeted by the use of sexual violence, including as a tactic of war to humiliate, dominate, instil fear in, disperse and/or forcibly relocate civilian members of a community or ethnic group; and that sexual violence perpetrated in this manner may in some instances persist after the cessation of hostilities.

It also notes that 'rape and other forms of sexual violence can constitute a war crime, a crime against humanity, or a constitutive act with respect to genocide' (Article 4).

The essence of UNSCR 1820 is the call to all concerned parties to put an end to sexual violence in armed conflicts (Article 2). The resolution offers examples of appropriate measures that might be taken: military disciplinary measures; upholding command responsibility; troop training; careful selection of personnel based on previous history; 'debunking myths that fuel sexual violence'; evacuation of women and children if there is a threat that they may face sexual violence (Article 3); excluding sexual violence and rape from post-conflict amnesties (Article 4); and building punishment for sexual violence into post-conflict regimes (Article 5).

The resolution then trains attention on the role that peacekeeping operations can play in the prevention and elimination of sexual violence (Articles 6–11). Training, zero-tolerance policies, pre-deployment screening, 'in-theater awareness training' (Article 7) and deployment of more women peacekeepers are suggested.

UNSCR 1888 (S/RES/1888/ [2009]) takes forward the point that UN peacekeepers and humanitarian interventions have an important role to play in protecting women and girls from sexual violence. The resolution reminds member States that the responsibility for ending impunity for perpetrators of 'genocide, crimes against humanity, war crimes and other egregious crimes perpetrated against civilians' rests with them. Ending impunity in such cases is essential if societies are to come to terms their past conflicts and move on. The political will of civilian and military leadership needs to be demonstrated; 'inaction can send a message that the incidence of sexual violence in conflicts is tolerated'. The resolution expresses concern that there are so few women in formal peace processes, that mediators and ceasefire monitors do not know how to deal with sexual violence, and that few women lead UN-sponsored talks and mediation efforts.

Much of UNSCR 1888 reiterates the instructions of UNSCR 1820. Its distinctive contribution lies in the view it takes of domestic laws relating to sexual violence.[1] States are urged to undertake legal and judicial reforms so that sexual offenders and rapists can be punished and victims treated with dignity as justice takes its course. The UN is instructed to work with experts and governments to ensure that the rule of law prevails. In effect, the resolution is pointing out that international norms will not be effective if national and local laws do not conform to them. There can be no justice for conflict victims of sexual violence, if there is none for other victims of sexual violence in that society.

UNSCR 1888's concluding provisions refocus attention on its peacekeeping and humanitarian missions. One of the specific recommendations here is that there should be a women's protection adviser attached to each operation, in addition to gender and human rights advisers (Article 12). Emphasizing the importance of local support and adoption of the UN view of zero-tolerance for sexual violence, the resolution also encourages

> leaders at the national and local level, including traditional leaders where they exist and religious leaders, to play a more active role in sensitizing communities on sexual violence to avoid marginalization and stigmatization of victims, to assist with their social reintegration, and to combat a culture of impunity for these crimes. (Article 15)

UNSCR 1888 also sets a timeline for compliance with setting up a UN 'composite gender entity' within two years—which is what UN Women is.

UNSCR 1889 (S/RES/1889 [2009]) reaffirms the importance of bringing women to the peace table. It reprises most of the themes that all the 1325 resolutions sound: more women at the peace table; a better understanding of how women and girls experience conflict; gender sensitization of UN humanitarian and peacekeeping personnel; zero-tolerance for sexual violence during the conflict, UN operation or peace process; the creation of special offices and services; working with local civil society and government; getting sexual violence on the peace agenda from the beginning; and the end of amnesty for sexual violence and rape.

UNSCR 1960 (S/RES/1960 [2010]) reaffirms the Security Council's view that sexual violence in conflict exacerbates the conflict and impedes the prospects for peace. The most powerful provision is arguably the 'naming and shaming' provision. The resolution 'encourages' the inclusion in the secretary general's annual reports of information about those conflict parties believed credibly to have committed or been responsible for rape or other sexual violence in conflict situations. It suggests a separate list in the annex of the report. Moreover, it announces the Security Council's intention to act on this list with sanctions or other measures. (Article 3)

UNSCR 2106 (S/RES/2106 [2013]) opens with an expression of concern about the slow implementation of Resolution 1960 and remains focused on the problem of sexual violence in conflict and post-conflict situations. The resolution reiterates that protection and ending impunity is essential to peace (Article 1). The resolution is first and foremost addressed to UN missions and field offices and urges the use of women's protection advisers and gender advisers, for instances. Article 21 points to the role of women's organizations and other civil society organizations and networks in enhancing community-level protection against violence as well as ensuring access to justice. Article 20 of the resolution identifies HIV and AIDS prevalence as affecting women and girls disproportionately in conflict zones and mandates UN agencies and States to make provisions to support them.

UNSCR 2122 (S/RES/2122 [2013]) has been hailed as a return to the broader thinking on 1325. It evokes the ideals of women's and girls' empowerment and gender equality and points out that barriers to full participation are inimical to peace and security. It calls for the 'consistent implementation' of 1325, for regular informational inputs and briefings on the issue and the inclusion of women, peace and security concerns across all reports. The resolution acknowledges that conventional weapons are used to perpetrate violence against women and girls and calls for women's participation in ending the illegal arms trade (Article 14). While several recent women, peace and security resolutions focused on sexual and gender-based violence (GBV), UNSCR 2122 restores some balance by returning equal and full participation to the agenda.

UNSCR 2242 (S/RES/2242 [2015]), was passed the month of 1325's 15th anniversary and is notable for its recognition of the role that civil society, especially women's organizations, can play in the implementation of 1325. It also takes cognizance explicitly of the impact of counterterrorism on women's lives and of the role women can and do play in facing both terrorism and violent extremism. In this, the Resolution mirrors the recommendation of the global study on 1325 that also underscores the importance of protecting women human rights defenders and not involving them in counterterrorism work (UN Woman 2015; Rajagopalan 2015).

II. New Thinking for a New World

For centuries, women featured in war chronicles either as victims or spoils or as exceptional warrior-queens. The last six decades, however, have seen an unprecedented, impossible to predict, normative shift in international society. This shift lies in the growing recognition that women are the proper subjects for study and policy and that they matter in social and political life—a recognition that is as transformative as it sounds redundant. The evolution of ideas in two areas is reflected in the provisions of the 1325 resolutions: feminist scholarship in international relations; and the post-Cold War changes in security studies. This part of the chapter outlines some of these ideas.

Feminist Scholarship in International Relations

Feminist scholarship in international relations is more engaged with the activist and practitioner worlds than other mainstream scholarship in that discipline. It would not be a stretch to say that feminists have learnt from the work and the struggles of the global women's movement. Five issues may be said to form the pivot around which feminist writing in international relations revolves. These are: the twin questions of invisibility and silence; violence; the breaking down of binaries; and patriarchy. In the conflict and post-conflict settings for which the 1325 resolutions are intended, these five issues manifest in a variety of ways.

The point of departure for feminist international relations scholarship, and for many scholars, is the question, 'Where are the women?' (Enloe 1989). Searching for ourselves, our lives and our voices in the canonical literature of the discipline and searching in vain the identification and enumeration of women in different international relation settings and the description of the roles they play, remain the most common research agenda (Rajagopalan 2005). The search for women has three corollaries. First, you notice that women play far more complex roles in conflict and other settings than stereotypes and simplified theoretical frameworks allow. Second, you notice that the interactions that are relevant to international relations extend far beyond the traditional scope of the field, to include trade, migration, development and cultural practices. Finally, the search for women and the inclusions of new transactions and interactions brings into the purview of our analysis all kinds of State and non-state actors.

Conflict and post-conflict settings are already complex and when you choose to look for and notice women's experiences they are further complicated. 'Women and children' (Enloe 2000 cited in Cohen 2004) appear first as victims of war, then by and by they appear as combatants, as auxiliary workers, as peace activists, among the displaced and even, and as Amena Mohsin describes, as those who stay behind to 'homestead' family property (Mohsin 2005). The absence of all these roles from the traditional discourse of war and peace is inexplicable, but their absence from the actual process of peace-building is inexcusable.

The other side of invisibility is silence. Even after we have looked for, listed, counted and described women and what they do, scholars are still speaking for them. The question of silence has two parts. The lesser but easier to fix part might be the weight that feminist scholarship carries in the mainstream of international relations, which is the subject of several interesting interviews with pioneering scholars in the field. The larger, more challenging issue is getting women whose lives are enmeshed in this web to speak for themselves. This is true for both scholarship and policy. Development practitioners have been developing a variety of participatory approaches. But in security policy-making there is still a huge disconnect between those who make the decisions and those who live with them. The disconnect should be easier to remedy in scholarship, but the first person accounts or the reports that use a lot of voices from the field are still generated more by grass roots projects and practitioners. The documentation of women's experiences, diverse as they are, as narrated and framed by the women who have those experiences, thus remains an important research priority.

One consequence of this silence has been that conflict analysis and peace processes do not hear about women's experiences and are insensitive to their needs. This, in turn, has resulted in accords and post-conflict development plans that overlook the same, reinforcing some of the inequities of the pre-conflict status quo.

When we start taking into account women's experiences, it is impossible to ignore the experience of violence. This experience begins with the use of rape and sexual violence as weapons of war, but actually extends well beyond the battlefield to the gendered impact of insecurities generated by a conflict setting (trafficking, livelihood and displacement) and the rising levels of violence in a society experiencing a long drawn-out conflict, including rising levels of domestic violence. In other words, women's experiences of violence in a conflict setting are not restricted to violations of the Geneva Conventions, but to the structural impact that conflict has on society and economy. Speaking about violence experienced by women holds a trap: Will we once more portray them as passive victims, depriving them first of individuality and then of voice? The feminist challenge is to see not just the trauma of violence, but also the agency exercised by women in the face of this violence—in rebuilding their lives, in helping others heal, in being complicit in the silence and, indeed, in perpetrating violence.

Sustained activism by women's organizations reflected and reinforced the normative climate in which condemnation of wartime sexual violence was institutionalized (Pietilä 2007, 33). The use of rape and sexual violence is now seen as a form of torture and a crime against humanity.

The discussion of violence reduces to rubble the imagination of barriers between the private and the public, domestic and international, and inside and outside. For women who experience violence within the home, and we know this is an inexcusably large percentage of women, it's always war. The worlds of home and outside, social policy and foreign policy, and policing boundaries and policing behaviour are completely entangled. Regarding them as separate effaces, the problem of pervasive violence also obfuscates the many connections between our private interactions and the world of markets, diplomacy and war. Blood diamonds are a good example; the decision to buy a diamond ring could be a decision to finance a militia. Feminist thought removes the screens that prevent scholars and policymakers from joining the dots to understand better how all-encompassing the consequences of conflict can be.

As a result of feminist writing and activism, the connection is now being made between militarization and GBV as well. The proliferation of arms, demobilization of combatants without disarmament and an uneasy socio-economic climate all appear to create higher levels of violence within the home and outside.

Almost all societies are patriarchal, placing men and boys at the centre of all relationships and power equations. And in almost all societies, while gender violence cuts across sex, women and girls, experience it much more than men. Feminists have long read gender violence as the exercise of power and the expression of control (or the desire to control). Patriarchy underpins the culture of tolerance that allows perpetrators of violence to get away with impunity. It sets up a value-system where victims of gender violence have to handle both trauma and culpability for their experience. On the other hand, it is always possible to find extenuating circumstances within this value-system that explain (and justify) the perpetrator's compulsions. For feminists, post-conflict situations offer an opportunity to rework at least the rules for the public sphere (of work and political participation) in order that they may in turn have a long-term impact on patriarchal relationships.

Post-Cold War Security Studies

When the Soviet Union collapsed and the Berlin Wall fell, many international relations scholars began to wonder what they had missed. Why had none of their theories or calculations predicted this cataclysmic change? One result: Definitional debates have animated security studies for the last few decades. As early as 1991, Emma Rothschild captured the essence of this new thinking with one word: expansion. As she pointed out, it was about stretching the concept of security laterally to include many dimensions of policy making, and stretching upward and downward to include other actors and levels of analysis (Rothschild 1995, 53).

In the post-Second World War period, with the global proliferation of the nation-state system, perhaps it was natural that the newly won nation-state of Asia and Africa or the recently restored nation-state of Europe became the cynosure of security scholars and policymakers. Foreign policy and military strategy (including for some, nuclear weapons policy) made up the subject matter of 'security'. 1945 arguably marks a departure from the past in many ways: the first use of atomic bombs; decolonization and the formation of new nation-states, European in mould but non-European in every other way; the twinning of reconstruction and development as part of the international agenda; and the creation of a new international forum for collective security, the United Nations, whose mandate extended far beyond matters of war and peace. Allied unity did not last much beyond the end of the war and the creation of post-war regimes, however, and the 'golden age' was marked by Cold War politics (Walt 1991, 213). Ideological and strategic poles emerged: democratic/capitalist on one side and totalitarian/communist on the other, naming them a political act in itself. As a corollary, one meaning of security was to maintain the equilibrium between the two poles (overlooking the vast majority of 'non-aligned' States). All international interactions mattered if they were relevant to this global drama, or else they were virtually non-existent. Development and political stability too were handmaidens to this purpose. However, as it turned out, the end of the Cold War was precipitated by all the factors that were not included in this view of security.

The disjuncture between academics studying security and those actually working in the real world was never greater than in the 1970s and 1980s. A series of global commissions were convened to study and deliberate the big issues of the time. A trilogy of reports was particularly influential, their titles articulating a worldview when strung together: *Common Crisis* (1980); *Common Security* (1982) and *Our Common Future* (1987).

The Independent Commission on International Development Issues (Brandt Commission) was convened from 1966 to 1983, its members including former premiers and experienced technocrats from around the world. The Commission produced two reports, *North-South: A Program for Survival* (1980) and *Common Crisis: North-South*

Cooperation for World Recovery (1983) that drew attention to the reality of global interdependence. The Independent Commission on Disarmament and Security Issues, chaired by Swedish Prime Minister Olof Palme, published their report, *Common Security*, in 1982. The Commission rejected the utility of nuclear weapons and nuclear war, making the case for global disarmament and a collaborative approach to security. The timing of the argument was wrong for Cold Warriors, but the idea that we should seek security not against but with others, resonated with peace activists in and outside academia. In 1987, when the World Commission on Environment and Development published *Our Common Future*, and spelt out the concept of 'sustainable development' it quickly became a norm. It was defined as 'development that meets the needs of the present without compromising the ability of future generations to meet their own needs'. The Brundtland Commission wove into its analysis and recommendation a perspective that made the connection between economic development, security and the everyday lives of people, reiterating the Brandt and Palme Commissions' plea for cooperative action.

At the end of the 1980s, a decade of North-South dialogue and consultation had taken place, making the linkages and arguments that were to characterize the 'new security thinking'. In 1990, the UNDP began to publish its annual Human Development Report and in 1994 the report theme was 'human security'. The idea of 'human security' is generally attributed to the authors of the 1994 *UNDP Human Development Report*, that is, 'not just security of their nations', 'not just security of territory', and 'not in the weapons of our country'. Mahbub ul Haq wrote in 1994 of a new concept of human security whose referent would be 'people' (ul Haq 1994, 1 cited in Bajpai 2011, 11). The UNDP Report stated:

> In the final analysis, human security is a child who did not die, a disease that did not spread, a job that was not cut, an ethnic tension that did not explode in violence, a dissident who was not silenced. Human security is not a concern with weapons-it is a concern with human life and dignity. (UNDP 1994, 22)

It defined increasing human security in terms of prioritizing human development over weapons development and acquisition, using the money saved by reducing the latter for sustainable development

(UNDP 1994). Freedom from fear and freedom from want—phrases that entered this discourse from the despatch of the US representative at the San Francisco Conference—were identified as the two major components of human security (UNDP 1994, 24). The big distinction made both by the UNDP and by Canadian and Norwegian officials who took up the concept was that human security put people at the centre. Much of the early effort was to list all the threats that could be classified as 'human security' and they included drugs, HIV/AIDS, environmental degradation and state repression among them.[2]

What was murky in the real world began to get murky in academic writing as well. The fact that they could not predict the fall of the Soviet Union prompted international relations and security studies scholars to introspect about the shortcomings of their field as it was. Neorealism had posited a universe of airtight, sealed units but it was their internal dynamic that had caused a cataclysmic change in the system. In 1983, Barry Buzan's now classic *People, States and Fear* recognized that while States might be the primary referent of security, they were not alone. He considered the security of individuals and of clusters of nation-states as well. Moreover, he stepped beyond the traditional association of security with politics and the military, to include economic, societal and environmental dimensions in his consideration (Buzan 1991, 19–20). In less than a decade after this, these questions were no longer marginal to the field. This introspective moment made long-standing critiques and concerns more visible. These took on the assumptions of realism and neorealism; the centrality of the State; the unitary, 'airtight' depiction of the unit; the elision of differences, especially inequalities between units; and even the meanings of 'peace' and 'security'. Scholars such as Mohammed Ayoob pointed out that traditional security thinking ignores the centrality of State-building to the security challenges faced by Third World States. But the architects of the idea of 'human security' are concerned also with the consequences of State making, among other things, for the lives and survival chances of human beings, citizens or otherwise.

In sum, the scope of the field has been enlarged to take cognizance of new issues, new actors and the undermining of the domestic-international divide once the field admits 'new' challenges such as ethnic conflict and terrorism.

New issues and new considerations were added to the security agenda. Feminists attributed insecurity to fundamentally unjust systems such as patriarchy and placed structural violence and violence against women on the agenda. Others made the connection between ecological degradation, distribution of natural resources, disasters, conflict and survival. The impact of structural adjustment and then globalization both added concerns about livelihood security, displacement and gender justice to the security agenda. The scope of the field was stretched to include foeticide and fisheries, land rights and landslides. Just as their priorities had influenced the research agendas of the Cold War era, grant-making agencies facilitated this stretching by funding large, multi-year projects that saw the evolution of the 'new security thinking' from common and collective security to human security to non-traditional security.[3]

Moving well beyond replicating J. David Singer's three levels of analysis—the individual, the State and the system, which were reflected even in Buzan's book—security scholars began to recognize the significance of non-state actors, whether civil society groups, multi-national corporations or terrorist groups. It has now become impossible to ignore the porosity of nation-state borders. Financial transactions, people, weapons and most lethal, ideas move fluidly across the tightest of controls and even States with a great capacity and will for coercion have found that harder to sustain.

1325 as a Mirror

Feminist thinking and changes in security studies are in themselves reflections of a democratizing push to make theory and policy more reflective and responsive to complex reality. Where feminists insist on making women visible and on a gendered understanding of reality, the margins of security studies are yielding to include more issues and an array of human experiences of insecurity. The 1325 resolutions in spelling out a mandate for the UN and for member States specifically mention consultations with civil society, thereby recognizing the role of civil society in promoting this 'women, peace and security' agenda.

It should be noted that even as academics and activists continue to discuss where 1325 is relevant and who should promote and implement its values, in 2013, the Committee on the Elimination of

Discrimination against Women passed a general recommendation on women in conflict prevention, conflict and post-conflict situations (United Nations Committee on the Elimination of Discrimination against Women 2013). General Recommendation No. 30 expands on every aspect of the 1325 resolutions, adding background, highlighting problems, recommending solutions and offering a segue to new situations where 1325 applies (for instance, writing about conflict displacement allows us to also talk of 1325 in other displacement situations). Perhaps most usefully, it offers a reporting procedure for 1325, something presently lacking at the national level, suggesting that the national (and shadow) CEDAW reports include information about 1325 implementation as well.

III. Moving Forward: Implementing 1325

The 1325 resolutions throw open the question of the referent. They answer the question, 'Whose security?' by clearly pointing to individuals and communities. The two most important points they make pertain to the inclusion of (individual) women in deliberative and decision-making processes and to taking cognizance of the experience of women and girls who experience sexual and GBV, by virtue of gender and by virtue of belonging to a particular group or ethnicity. The two questions that I want to raise and discuss in this section are:

1. Do the 1325 resolutions have relevance beyond the context of conflict?
2. Who has agency with regarding to the implementation of the resolutions?

Beyond Conflict

The UNSCR resolutions confine themselves strictly to the context of conflict, conflict transformation and peace-building. However, the priority areas for 1325—participation, prevention, protection, and relief and recovery—apply well beyond the conflict context. Is there a sphere to which they are not relevant? And given that these ideas echo the CEDAW, they have really always been meant to be applied to every sphere—the difference is that the 1325 resolutions have the backing of the Security Council's enforcement mandate. The question then is how far can we stretch that mandate? After all, 1325 cannot be implemented in a vacuum. This section suggests three contexts other than traditional conflict settings for which the 1325 resolutions have relevance. Reintegrating 1325 into the broader normative framework of CEDAW, General Recommendation No. 30 underscores the place of women, peace and security concerns as part of a gender equality and human rights framework, making it possible to interpret the scope of 1325 broadly.

For instance, that women experience disasters differently from men is now axiomatic among a growing section of disaster relief practitioners. The difference extends through every aspect of the disaster—in the anticipation, preparation and cleaning up; in experiences at temporary shelters; in the content and distribution of relief supplies; in lack of documentation; and in consequent lack of access to entitlements.

The *Hyogo Framework for Action 2005–2015: Building the Resilience of Nations and Communities to Disasters*, which lays out widely accepted guidelines on how and which actors should help communities strategize to face disasters, mentions gender in two ways. First, it recommends that a gender perspective should be integrated into all disaster risk management plans and policies. This includes taking gender concerns into account at all times and providing for special needs. Second, it recommends gender sensitization training be a part of all disaster risk reduction training and education.[4]

Operationalized through the four 'pillars', the 1325 resolutions now offer practical ways in which to implement and monitor the gender dimensions of any framework of analysis and action. Participation, prevention, protection, and relief and recovery offer a checklist of gender priorities within every priority area of the Hyogo Framework. In the ongoing Hyogo Framework 2 process, women's groups are emphasizing the importance of gender-disaggregated data collection. Women's leadership is to be promoted across all policies and projects.

Displacement increases women's vulnerability to physical threats such as sexual and GBV through the loss of homes, separation of families, the breakdown of community, poor housing and living conditions, livelihood insecurity, lack of access to health-care or even nutrition, and poverty.

The Sphere Project is a collective effort by voluntary organizations to improve the quality of humanitarian assistance delivered to affected populations.[5] Gender is one of the cross-cutting themes of the Sphere Project, but it stops with recommending gender analysis of crisis situations in order to understand the gendered vulnerabilities of both women and men. To invoke the 1325 resolutions would be to expand this idea into a practical road map for gender equity in humanitarian situations.

The *Guiding Principles on Internal Displacement* are a framework for the protection of internally displaced persons (IDPs).[6] They take cognizance of gender in a variety of ways, including explicitly mentioning the protection of refugees against sexual and GBV. In addition, the Guiding Principles recommend the full participation of women in decision-making and planning and that their access to education is assured. They also acknowledge the right of all IDPs to have correct documentation and recognize the health needs of women. The 1325 resolutions reinforce these principles and recommendations, and as Security Council Resolutions, speak the will of the international community.

In recent years, non-violent and violent transitions from authoritarian to democratic regimes have dominated the news—especially what has come to be called 'Arab Spring'. In the rallies, marches and demonstrations that have preceded the fall of these regimes, women have marched, sometimes led, the protests.

The hard-won democratization does not extend to women. Seldom are women prominent members of the new government. The constitutions that are written anew still entrench patriarchal institutions. The sexual and GBV committed on the previous regime's watch as well as during the campaign for regime change are often relegated to the sidelines as the new dispensation settles down. This is not very different from disaster or conflict settings where amid the destruction lies an opportunity to rewrite some fundamentals, but the opportunity is quickly lost. The 1325 resolutions offer civil society a standard to which they can hold new regimes and transitional authorities.

Conflicts abound in every society and the vision behind 1325 is not as limited as the reach of a UN Security Council Resolution. Conflicts occur at the level of usage of shared utilities; who gets to park, whether buses or pedestrians have right of way or who gets first access to a shared water source. They occur locally between communities and between employers and employees, and over the question of who gets to decide the use of land or natural resources. States sometimes mediate, sometimes intervene to take sides and sometimes choose to turn a blind eye (which is also a form of intervention).

The utility of identifying these other contexts lies first, in being able to take advantage of 1325 even where governments are hesitant to admit the existence of conflict contexts and second, in being able to draw from the pool of women, stories and lessons learned in these contexts, for adaptation to conflict contexts. It also offers actors multiple entry points to achieve what are the common goals of all these resolutions and regimes—gender justice. What 1325 brings to these other contexts is the edge—in terms of resources and priority—offered by securitizing any issue, but with those come loss of accountability and transparency and, ironically, the very democratization and inclusion that 1325 stands for.

In all these instances, the 1325 resolutions apply. In all these instances, it is important to take into account the experiences of women and their participation in peace-making and peace-building is a necessary pre-condition for peace. Sexual and GBV are instruments of control in any of these settings, which may offer different degrees of opportunity and different levels of impunity. Finally, recovery and reconstruction that does not factor in women's needs simply creates the conditions for the recurrence of conflict.

Agency for All

The Security Council Resolutions have instructions for member States, for the UN and for the secretary general, but suggests that local and international women's groups be consulted and included in these processes.

In 2004, the Security Council called on member States to implement 1325 through the adoption of NAPs, a strategy that UN Women has been promoting since then.[7] NAPs are meant to be a platform for member States to articulate their priorities, set targets and outline strategies for implementing the resolutions. A casual survey of countries that have adopted plans shows that most of them are not directly affected by conflict; adopting a NAP has to be politically much harder in States actually engaged in conflict. Not surprisingly, one response has been to deny the existence of conflicts within the State.

Given that States have been the focus of the UN's 1325 activism, it would seem that a key to having 1325 implemented would be to focus on lobbying the State. But is that the only way to promote the values and objectives of the resolutions, the only interventions that civil society can make? Women's organizations may be presumed to have the greatest interest in promoting 1325 and they, in addition to or at least instead of the State, have the capacity to give root to the values and ideals of the 1325 resolutions.

CEDAW's General Recommendation No. 30 has this to say about 'women':

> II.6. Women are not a homogenous group and their experiences of conflict and specific needs in post-conflict contexts are diverse. Women are not passive bystanders or only victims or targets. They have historically and continue to have a role as combatants, as part of organized civil society, human rights defenders, members of resistance movements and as active agents in both formal and informal peacebuilding and recovery processes. (United Nations Committee on the Elimination of Discrimination Against Women 2013)

Better than a top-down NAP drafted by a handful of experts for the government, locally drafted agendas that reflect the needs of different groups of women can hope to capture and represent this diversity. This reinforces the case for local civil society to take the lead on promoting 1325 and its implementation.

Participation

There is a chicken-and-egg issue with the participation pillar of the 1325 resolutions. The purpose of the resolutions is to draw women into the public sphere and engage them in every aspect of public life. But if there are not already women in the public sphere, visible and vocal, it becomes very easy to say, 'We cannot find the women. Where are the women? This is why we cannot include them at the peace table'.

Engagement in the public sphere could take any form, but it is very important for women to take on political work. It is important for women's organizations everywhere to engage with conflict and security discourses; this engagement should not be contingent on their location. This is the pool from which peace processes have to draw. To this end, it is important that the work that women do in the public sphere is made visible—not just through documentation for the record but also in practical terms—with the creation of publicly accessible directories.

It is important to create awareness about women, peace and security issues, and to create platforms where communities can fill in their own details, fashioning multiple local agendas and, sometimes, reinterpreting ideas to suit their own circumstances. The 1325 agenda will not work in broad brush-strokes, painted by a few on behalf of everyone else.

Prevention

Involving women in early warning or prevention activities is an important aspect of the 1325 resolutions. How is this possible without the support of civil society? Networked at various levels from the grass roots to cyberspace, the drawing and sharing of information is an integral function of civil society groups, no matter the specific concern they work on. With a little training and coordination, this is a very useful point of intervention towards implementing the 1325 agenda.

The prevention of sexual and GBV is the second part of this 'pillar'. While the concern of the 1325 resolutions is with violence during and as a part of conflict, the very States and societies that are asked to end impunity for conflict-time sexual and GBV unfailingly have a bad track record for the same in other times and contexts. The 'trickle-down' potential of 1325 standards is what makes them a powerful tool for society. The description of violence against women that takes place outside conflict contexts as 'the violence of normal times' or 'a war against women' neatly captures the lived reality that for most individuals, the fear and experience of sexual and GBV in 'peace' or conflict exist on a single continuum. Victim care and support service providers outside the conflict context are well-placed to shape the strategies and projects that would further this agenda.

Protection

The physical safety of citizens and others within its jurisdiction remains one of the primary functions of the State and the protection mandate is best served by its agencies. But where the State alternates between protector and predator—as it does—civil society acquires the responsibility to monitor, inform and hold the State accountable for its failure to protect citizens. The protection mandate extends to creating awareness about laws and services, and work where the reach of civil society can augment efforts by State agencies.

Relief and Recovery

The experience of women's organizations extends across every sphere of reconstruction activity—legal and institutional change; livelihood; housing; and health care and education. There are things civil society organizations could do during the conflict and in the post-conflict phase that facilitate the integration of 1325 values into relief and recovery programmes.

One essential input in the conflict phase is to integrate the thinking of 1325 into all peace activities. It is often the case that in very bitter conflicts, gender issues are relegated to the backburner, set aside to be revisited when everything is over and there is peace. By then, it is too late to make structural changes. It is therefore important that all development activity and all peace activism during the conflict be engendered, that advocacy agendas include women, peace and security issues, such as ending impunity for sexual and GBV, and that women's rights and gender equality be factored by debate and discussion into all competing visions of the future. This is something that only civil society organizations can do and that women's organizations have a particular stake in.

The second is in building the platforms or fora for communication within communities, so that when time comes to give inputs and feedback on relief and recovery programmes, women are able to articulate clearly what they need, what puts them at peril and what is redundant. It is too easy to dismiss people's voices by saying that some issues are too technical for them. It is the task of civil society to make sure that people have the language they need to make their voices heard.

IV. Conclusion

In Clemenceau's words, 'War is too important to be left to the generals'. Peace is certainly too important to be left to States, especially to reluctant States. The concerns that animate the 1325 resolutions emerged from feminist thought and activism on the one hand and evolving security ideas that also reflected changes in the real world on the other. The sustained efforts of the transnational women's activism made 1325 a reality and the UN system has played an important part in its promotion. However, the primary instrument for the implementation of 1325 has so far been the NAP, which must be formulated by States—whose role in creating the same crisis situations is also acknowledged by the resolutions. This chapter, and the rest of this book, point to the work civil society and individual women are doing and can do to further the women, peace and security agenda—with or without the partnership of States. Both the global study on 1325 and the most recent WPS Resolution 2242, reinforce this view. With expanding agency and expanding scope, we come full circle and recommit to the full menu of gender equality and human rights regimes we have crafted in the last century.

Notes

1. The effacement of the domestic–international divide completely reflects feminist thinking.
2. Kanti Bajpai's paper records all the various lists that were generated as a prelude to suggesting a way to conduct a human security audit.
3. Also, see the website of the Consortium of Non-Traditional Security Studies in Asia (NTS-Asia), http://www.rsis-ntsasia.org/index.html (Accessed on 7 June 2016) and the webpage of the Women in Security, Conflict Management and Peace (WISCOMP) project on engendering security, http://wiscomp.org/programs/gender-and-nts-south-asia/ (Accessed on 7 June 2016).
4. *Hyogo Framework for Action 2005–2015: Building the Resilience of Nations and Communities to Disasters*, available at: http://www.unisdr.org/we/coordinate/hfa (Accessed on 7 June 2016).
5. The Sphere Project, available at: http://www.sphereproject.org/about/ (Accessed on 7 June 2016).
6. *Guiding Principles on Internal Displacement*, available at: https://documents-dds-ny.un.org/doc/UNDOC/GEN/G98/104/93/PDF/G9810493.pdf?OpenElement (Accessed on 7 June 2016).

7. PeaceWomen, National Action Plans, available at: http://www.peacewomen.org/member-states (Accessed on 7 June 2016).

References

Bajpai, Kanti. 2000, August. 'Human Security: Concept and Measurement'. Kroc Institute Occasional Paper No. 19: OP: 1, 11. University of Notre Dame, USA: Kroc Institute for International Peace Studies.

Buzan, Barry. 1991. *People, States and Fear: An Agenda for International Security Studies in the Post-Cold War Era*, 2nd ed., 19–20. Boulder, CA: Lynne Rienner Publishers.

Cohen, Carol. 2004. 'Mainstreaming Gender in UN Security Policy: A Path to Political Transformation?' Working Paper No. 204, Boston Consortium on Gender, Security and Human Rights. Available at: https://www.amherst.edu/media/view/92331/original/mainstreaming+gender+in+UN+security+policy.pdf (Accessed on 29 January 2015).

Enloe, Cynthia. 1989. *Bananas, Beaches and Bases: Making Feminist Sense of International Relations*. Berkeley, CA: University of California Press.

———. 2000. 'Women and Children: Making Feminist Sense of the Persian Gulf Crisis'. The Village Voice, 25 September. In Mainstreaming Gender in UN Security Policy: A Path to Political Transformation? Working Paper No. 204, 2004 by Carol Cohn.

Haq, Mahbub ul. 1994. 'New Imperatives of Human Security'. RGICS Paper No. 17, Rajiv Gandhi Institute for Contemporary Studies (RGICS), Rajiv Gandhi Foundation, New Delhi.

———. 2000. 'New Imperatives of Human Security'. RGICS Paper No. 17. In Kanti Bajpai, 'Human Security: Concept and Measurement,' Kroc Institute Occasional Paper No. 19: OP: 1. Indiana: University of Notre Dame.

Mohsin, Amena. 2005. 'Silence and Marginality: Gendered Security and the Nation-State'. In *Women, Security, South Asia: A Clearing in the Thicket*, edited by Farah Faizal and Swarna Rajagopalan, 134–53. New Delhi: SAGE Publications.

Pietilä, Hilkka. 2007. *The Unfinished Story of Women and the United Nations*. NGLS Development Dossier. New York, NY and Geneva: UN Non-Governmental Liaison Services, United Nations.

Rajagopalan, Swarna. 2005. 'Women and Security: In Search of a New Paradigm'. In *Women, Security, South Asia: A Clearing in the Thicket*, edited by Farah Faizal and Swarna Rajagopalan, 11–88. New Delhi: SAGE Publications.

———. 2015. '15 Years of Resolution 1325: All about Women, Peace and Security'. *DNA India*, October 14. Available at: http://www.dnaindia.com/india/standpoint-15-years-of-resolution-1325-all-about-women-peace-and-security-2134722 (Accessed on 18 February 2016).

Rothschild, Emma. 1995. 'What is Security?'. *Daedalus*, 124 (3): 53. The Quest for World Order (Summer, 1995).

United Nations Committee on the Elimination of Discrimination Against Women (CEDAW). 2013. 'General Recommendation No. 30 on Women in Conflict

Prevention, Conflict and Post-conflict Situations', CEDAW/C/GC/30, Advance unedited version. Available at: http://www.ohchr.org/Documents/HRBodies/CEDAW/GComments/CEDAW.C.CG.30.pdf (Accessed on 20 September 2015).

UNDP (United Nations Development Programme). 1994. 'New Dimensions of Human Security'. In *Human Development Report 1994*. Available at: http://hdr.undp.org/en/media/hdr_1994_en_chap2.pdf (Accessed on 28 June 2016).

UN Women. 2015. *Preventing Conflict, Transforming Justice, Securing the Peace: A Global Study on the Implementation of United Nations Security Council Resolution 1325*. Available at: http://wps.unwomen.org/~/media/files/un%20women/wps/highlights/unw-global-study-1325-2015.pdf (Accessed on 18 February 2016).

Walt, Stephen M. 1991. 'The Renaissance of Security Studies'. *International Studies Quarterly*, 35 (2): 213. Available at: http://www.jstor.org/stable/2600471 (Accessed on 7 June 2016).

3

Civil Society Actors and the Implementation of Resolution 1325 in India

Soumita Basu

Introduction

Resolution 1325 is possibly the only UN Security Council Resolution whose passage on 31 October 2000 has been celebrated every year—with one exception in 2012—with an open debate at the Security Council during the anniversary month.[1] Even though this practice was found to be highly unusual when first suggested in 2001, the anniversary celebrations have become a much-anticipated event in the calendar of women, peace and security (WPS) advocates at the UN. Carol Cohn writes that if Resolution 1325 had included a date for the UN Secretary General to submit his/her report, the theme–WPS–would have become a regular item on the Security Council agenda: 'In the absence of this commitment, advocates make the most of the anniversary' (Cohn 2004, 5 [fn12]). This is just one example of the creative ways in which actors engaging with the resolution, especially from the civil society, have sought to fill the gaps in the document and address the lag in its implementation.

In its legislative constitution, Resolution 1325 is an international policy mechanism with many institutional constraints–it is a Security Council Resolution with limited understanding of gender, peace and security (Shepherd 2008). In terms of its ideational energies and momentum for mobilization (the case outlined above being one example), however, the Resolution is driven decisively by the 'global constituency'[2] led by civil society organizations (CSOs) in particular, including at the time of its passage in the Security Council in 2000. In light of their role at the UN and in diverse local and national contexts across the world, this chapter examines the significance of CSOs in employing Resolution 1325 and the follow-up resolutions in India. These international policy instruments are understood here to be additions to the existing toolbox used by WPS communities in the ongoing conflict resolution processes in the country and could be relevant to their work in at least two ways. On the one hand, the resolutions may be seen as normative inspirations–a global symbol of solidarity on WPS issues. And, on the other hand, the resolutions have specific recommendations for States, the UN and indeed all relevant actors in its operational paragraphs that may be used by CSOs in India as advocacy and monitoring tools that have international recognition. As Prügl and Meyer point out, international documents–in this case, Security Council Resolutions–are significant not because 'governments will automatically implement them but [because]…national and local groups can use them to hold their governments accountable' in specific local contexts (1999, 13). For instance, operational paragraph 8(b) of Resolution 1325

> calls on all actors involved, when negotiating and implementing peace agreements, to adopt a gender perspective, including, inter alia…. Measures that support local women's peace initiatives and indigenous processes for conflict resolution, and that involve women in all of the implementation of the peace agreements. (UN 2000; emphasis in original text)

This can be used in the calls for greater inclusion of women in governmental efforts to resolve the situation in 'disturbed areas' (the official classification of conflict regions within India).

The broad research puzzle that informs this chapter is the apparent lack of interest in drawing upon the WPS resolutions towards taking forward the WPS agenda in India, specifically by women's groups because it is they who generally work on these issues in the country. More than a decade after its adoption in the UN Security Council, Resolution 1325 may be increasingly referred to in academic and policy debates on gender and security in India but, with some exceptions (Banerjee 2013; Chenoy 2012),[3] there has been little direct engagement so far with what the employment, if not implementation, of 1325 in India might entail—the 'nuts and bolts' of local usage. Against this background, the question that the chapter seeks to address first is: Why is there a perceived lack of interest in the WPS resolutions? Responses to two further questions are explored in this chapter. Why is it important for domestic CSOs to take a leadership role in using Resolution 1325 in India? And finally, what can the CSOs do in this regard?

The chapter is divided into three sections. The first section examines the muted response to Resolution 1325 in light of the apparent 'paradox' of Indian women's movements' engagement with global gender policy mechanisms wherein their contribution to the formulation of such policies appears to be disproportionately more than their use of these policies in the Indian context.[4] The second section focuses on the rationale for arguing for civil society's leadership in India, highlighting also the ways in which CSOs in other parts of the world have mobilized around the resolution and adapted it to local contexts. Third, in the concluding section, this chapter identifies the ways in which CSOs working in India could consider engaging further with WPS Security Council Resolutions, recognizing also the challenges in doing so.

I. International Policies and the Indian Context

Writing about the preparation of the seminal report, *Towards Equality: Report of the Committee on the Status of Women in India* (Guha 1974), that reframed national debates on women in Indian society, Vina Mazumdar reminisces:

> [The Union Minister of State Professor Nurul Hassan] convinced the Prime Minister that appointing me [Mazumdar] as a Member Secretary, and extending the Committee's [on Status of Women in India] term… would enable India to save face, by sending a document on the Status of Women to the United Nations at the beginning of 1975 (already declared as the International Women's Year). The Prime Minister [Indira Gandhi]–reluctant to lose face before the UN–had to agree. I can however now state confidently, that if she had any clue about our emerging conclusions, she would never have agreed. (2010, 70)

From this one statement that reflects upon a critical juncture in the Indian women's movement, it is possible to draw out the possible significance of international contexts without over-stating the same: the 'international' (here the International Women's Year declared by the UN) offered an opportunity to women's rights advocates to conduct a substantive study on the status of women in India; importantly, this was with the support of the State that would otherwise 'lose face before the UN'.[5] If the government however, had realized the radical potential of *Towards Equality*, it would have discouraged this linking of Indian and international examinations of discrimination against women. Against the backdrop of such State reluctance, this section first highlights some key elements of the relationship between international policies and the Indian women's movement before making a case for greater engagement of CSOs in India with Resolution 1325.

While the history and practices of women's movement in India has received much attention in the scholarly literature, its relationship with corresponding developments at the global level has been somewhat limited (see also Basu 2000, 76). This is certainly not the case at the level of advocacy and activism. Since the focus of this chapter is on UN mechanisms, it is worthwhile to note that Indian women's groups have been well represented at the UN World Conferences on Women–from Mexico City in 1975 to Beijing in 1995 and beyond. On the one hand, they have been part of the Third World challenge to the universalist aspirations underlying UN policy-making on women and on the other, specific elements of the Indian women's movement (itself diverse in nature) have connected with local/national movements outside the country to inform the development of international mechanisms. In at least two activist campaigns in India, one against dowry deaths (Keck and Sikkink 1998) and the other for homeworkers' rights (Prügl 1999), this advocacy has followed the 'boomerang pattern of influence' wherein domestic groups 'reach out to international allies to bring pressure on its government to change its domestic processes' (Keck and Sikkink 1998, 36). This does not preclude the development of international policies to this effect. There are a number of such instances.

First, highlighting the importance of Self Employed Women's Association (SEWA) in the adoption of the International Labour Organization (ILO) Convention on Homework, Prügl writes that

'SEWA's homeworker protection bill was stalled in the Indian parliament, and SEWA saw an international standard as a way to induce the Indian government to act' (1999, 203). Second, the issue of dowry deaths became part of the transnational campaigns on violence against women, leading up to the recognition of 'women's rights as human rights' in the 1993 Vienna Declaration. Third, while the *Towards Equality* report (mentioned earlier) drew inspiration from Ester Boserup's work on *Woman's Role in Economic Development* (1970) that also informed the Women in Development (WID) discourse at the UN, Indian feminist economists such as Gita Sen and Devaki Jain contributed substantively to the conceptualization of the subsequent discourse, especially on gender and development, with their participation in the Development Alternatives with Women for a New Era (DAWN) network that included feminist advocates from the developing world. And fourth, Peggy Antrobus has noted the significance of insights from environmental activism in India—Chipko movement, Narmada Bachao Andolan and Vandana Shiva's work on ecofeminism as well as the dangers of genetically modified varieties of seeds–as a 'source of information and inspiration for many women from the industrialized countries' (2004, 84–85) and presumably beyond. However, to what extent have these been a two-way process and, where relevant, how has the ricocheting 'boomerang' been received by women's groups in India?

While a thorough examination of all issue areas is beyond the scope of this chapter, I highlight some familiar debates here. A helpful case in point would be the engagement with the 1979 Convention on Elimination of Discrimination Against Women (CEDAW), also known as Women's Convention as well as the international bill of rights for women. In her review of implementation of CEDAW in India, Sally Engle Merry notes that it tends to be used primarily by Delhi-based groups—'those working internationally'—while most other activists and human rights advocates rely on the provisions of the Indian Constitution (2006, 165). Conversely, sociologist Dongxiao Liu (2006) suggests that Indian women's groups have largely rejected the Beijing Platform for Action (as opposed to the official support extended by the government). She distinguishes the response of 'Delhi-based national women's organizations' from that of 'autonomous and "grass roots" groups'; partly due to their access or lack of it, to the national machineries respectively, the former 'emphasiz[ed] national sovereignty and criticiz[ed] the UN for implementing hegemony of the powerful nations' while the latter 'demanded that all references to national sovereignty concerning women's human rights be removed from the PFA, and that the powers be deposited with the UN' (Liu 2006, 933–34).

A review of the 'shadow' and 'alternative' reports–separate from government reports–submitted to the Commission on Status of Women and the Beijing (1995) and Beijing+5 (2000) conferences does suggest the participation of a broader group of actors in these international processes. It appears that international gender-related policies have some traction in the Indian context though this is arguably disproportionate to the substantive contribution of Indian women's groups to international discussions on formulation of gender-related mechanisms.

At the level of implementation, evaluating the significance of the international human rights regime for addressing dowry deaths in India, Meghana Shah writes that this is aimed to 'remedy serious human rights violations when nations are unwilling or unable to do so using their sovereign powers' (2003, 211). While the 'rights' approach has been used in the campaigns against violence against women in India, it has taken place within broader concerns regarding the universalist tendencies of the global human rights regime including its privileging of political and civil rights (of interest to the Global North) over socio-economic rights (emphasized by the Global South).[6] There have also been concerns about cookie-cutter approaches to 'gender mainstreaming' that are led by donor-driven agendas and do not take account of local specificities.

Presumably, these trends–especially the focus on engaging with national and not international policies–manifest also in the WPS arena. Two factors specific to the realm of peace and security also appear to be relevant in explaining the apparent lack of interest in mobilizing Resolution 1325. First, the resolution is part of the Security Council apparatus and, as such, is seen to be reflective of its neo-imperialist tendencies. Second, the Government of India (GoI) is generally opposed to the 'internationalization' of the ongoing conflicts within the country.

With regard to the first concern, it is important to note that civil society advocacy that–as the dominant narrative of the event suggests–led to the adoption of 1325 included voices from the Global South, especially activists from African countries, which are represented now in the NGO Working Group on Women, Peace and Security in New York by Femme Africa Solidarity. Further, three countries from the Global South including Bangladesh, Namibia and Jamaica were central to the adoption of the resolution in 2000. Thus, while Resolution 1325 and its sister resolutions have Security Council as their institutional home, the primary impetus for their adoption and implementation comes from CSOs, which has also received occasional support from governments in the Global South. And indeed, Banerjee (2013) argues that Indian women's groups have been actively addressing the issues that Resolution 1325 raises; as such, Resolution 1325 becomes a useful tool that can be added to this toolbox to enhance their efforts and, thus, 'the fear that Indian women will become a voice for the northern imperialist world is moot' (2013, 51). The GoI's silence on using Resolution 1325 within the country is to be expected as it seeks to protect itself from the increasingly interventionist behaviour of the more powerful countries and international agencies. On its part then, it may well not be receptive to CSOs' employment of the Security Council Resolutions as advocacy tools. However, the relevance of the provisions of Resolution 1325 in making responses to conflicts in India gender-sensitive still stands. The following section, then, argues for the need for CSOs in India to take a leadership role in the implementation of the resolution in India.

II. Civil Society and Resolution 1325

As per Article 25 of the UN Charter, UN member States 'agree to accept and carry out the decisions of the Security Council in accordance with the present Charter' (UN 1945). In accordance with this article, presumably, Rachel Mayanja, who held the position of the UN Special Adviser on Gender Issues and the Advancement of Women, suggests that 'governments bear the primary responsibility for the implementation of the Resolution [1325]' (2008, 4). However, it is generally accepted that resolutions that are not passed under the Chapter VII mandate–with enforcement mechanisms–of the Security Council are not legally binding on member states. Thus, the GoI is not required to adopt national policies implementing the relevant provisions of Resolution 1325. As a major troop-contributing country to UN peace operations, it does make references to the WPS resolutions. However, this interest is projected outwards. Factors such as the GoI's concerns regarding internationalization of conflicts, mentioned above, as well as the low priority accorded to women's needs and interests in the peace and security arena, suggest that government initiatives towards the implementation of WPS resolutions may well be limited.

International agencies such as, most prominently, UN Women can–and have–contributed to the efforts to highlight the importance of SCR 1325, but this is bound by their institutional parameters. For instance, in February 2013, UN Women and the Centre for United Nations Peacekeeping, New Delhi, organized a summit on women's participation in peace-building. Resolution 1325 was central to the deliberations that focused on the role of female peacekeepers as well as the need to address sexual and gender-based violence (GBV) during UN peace operations. An event of this kind is to be welcomed in a country where the traditional security establishment does not generally engage in such public conversations. But here too, somewhat predictably, the possibility of using the WPS resolutions in the 'disturbed areas' within the country was not explored.

CSOs are also bound by their institutional mandates. However, for actors who highlight the gendered nature of armed conflicts and advocate for responses to the same, the provisions of the WPS resolutions would be significant for achieving their mandate. Individuals and organizations working in conflict regions also tend to have a better grasp of the situation on the ground and are best-suited to identify the relevance of these resolutions for particular local contexts. Indeed, Anuradha Chenoy lists lobbying and advocacy by civil society actors as her first point of recommendation towards implementation of Resolution 1325 in India (2012, 56).

The importance of civil society actors is also highlighted by international actors. Anne Marie Goetz, the former Chief Advisor on Peace and Security at UN Women, New York, notes that domestic women's movements can play a significant role internationally as 'strong women's movements shape what national representatives do and say in the UN,' thereby leading to changes in international policies (Hudson and Goetz 2014, 341). Thus, the work of CSOs that are part of these movements can help move forward the WPS agendas at both local and international levels. Indian actors can draw upon experiences of CSOs in places as diverse as Nepal, the Philippines, Serbia and Liberia. The remaining part of this section highlights some such insights from initiatives of CSOs outside India.

In an introductory chapter of a volume edited by Olonisakin et al. that examines the implementation of Resolution 1325 in various national and regional contexts, Barnes writes that CSOs

> play a vital role in filling the gaps [in governmental or intergovernmental efforts] and focusing attention on priority areas linked to UNSCR 1325, from those working at the grass roots level in conflict-affected contexts all the way up to those that focus their energies on the corridors of the UN headquarters. (2011, 27)

At the local and national levels, aspects of CSOs' role such as awareness-raising, advocacy and monitoring the implementation of gender policies are clearly evident. Further, in her review of the experience in Kosovo, Hall-Martin writes that 'grass roots women's organizations are the only ones consistently addressing UNSCR 1325 as an operational principle' (2011, 46). Indeed, as has been pointed out, local women's organizations–in places where Resolution 1325 has been invoked and indeed elsewhere–have engaged with issues that the WPS resolutions address for much longer periods compared to national and international efforts in this regard (Abdela 2011, 77; Barnes 2011b, 129). As such, Resolution 1325–as has been highlighted throughout this chapter–becomes another possible avenue for the achievement of CSOs' goals.

The most prominent use of SCR 1325 has been as part of UN's work in post-conflict societies, including in relation to UN peace operations. CSOs have worked with international agencies, especially UN Women and the gender offices of UN missions, to call for policies that address both participation and protection-issues relating to women. While in all cases so far success has been relatively limited, the WPS resolutions have been used by local groups to advocate for inclusion of women in peace negotiations, in calls to make post-conflict processes, such as disarmament, demobilization and re-integration, gender-sensitive (for instance, by making necessary provisions for female ex-combatants) and in efforts to promote gender equality in political institutions. In Nepal, for instance, civil society actors worked alongside international agencies to push for greater participation of women in public offices. Abdela notes that 'obvious progress has been achieved with the election of women to 33 per cent of the Constituent Assembly's seats; and with the appointment of women to several key ministries' (2011, 81).Commentators have noted that in cases where UN missions have ignored local capacities, the impact of UN missions has been limited (on Liberia, see Wamai 2011, 62–63). The role of CSOs in implementing the WPS resolutions has been recognized in the UN Secretary General's reports on WPS. There have been calls to 'establish regular and structured consultations with women's civil society groups' and to also offer funding and training to women's groups to enhance their ability to contribute to conflict resolution processes (UN 2011, 9; also see UN 2008).

CSOs have also played an important part in the formulation of NAPs (National Action Plans). As of December 2013, close to 50 member States have drafted or adopted NAPs for the implementation of Resolution 1325 at the country-level. In several cases, these documents have been the result of close engagement between governmental agencies and CSOs. In the South Asian context, Nepal has led the way. A number of CSOs were involved in the nation-wide consultations that were conducted as part of the process to formulate the NAP in Nepal. While this expanded the scope of issues covered in the document, there has been a general trend towards policymakers accepting such demands but not taking concrete steps to implement the same (Falch 2010, 34).

The Nepal case notwithstanding, CSOs can play only certain kinds of roles towards the implementation of Resolution 1325. In formal processes such as peace negotiations and gender budgeting, it is individuals holding public offices that sign on the dotted lines. And yet, it is also clear in the case of the WPS resolutions that the impetus for implementation by governmental or intergovernmental agencies comes from CSOs. This is done through the work of CSOs as advocates, monitors and experts on local needs and interests. Their leadership is necessary not only to ensure that the provisions of Resolution 1325 are addressed, but also to challenge–where necessary– the dominant interpretations of these provisions. Laura McLeod (2011), for instance, notes that the Belgrade Women in Black developed an implementation plan that is different from that of the Serbian NAP because of concerns that the latter is narrow in its scope and focuses primarily on the defence sector instead of drawing upon Resolution

1325 as a tool to reconceptualize security. As Barnes and Olonisakin also point out, there may be local interpretations of gender equality goals of Resolution 1325 that may differ from the more 'official' ones presented by their government or international actors, which may well 'offer important alternative mechanisms for achieving the same goals as those advocated by the Resolution' (2011, 8). Thus, CSOs in India can use Resolution 1325 not only as a reference to draw upon internationally-accepted standards for gender equality in the peace and security arena but also to seek support for local conflict-resolution practices. Neither–as discussions in other chapters in this volume suggest–can and would be accepted by the GoI as central to their own mandate.

III. Resolution 1325 in India: Possible Civil Society Initiatives

The final question that this chapter seeks to address relates to the specific role that CSOs in India can play towards mobilizing Resolution 1325. The nation-building project in post-independence India has had its share of failures and, as conflict has given way to armed violence in some parts of the country, CSOs have stepped into the domestic peace and security arena. Women's groups have engaged with WPS issues for some decades now. Urvashi Butalia takes note of a couple of early interventions: the Naga Mothers Association, which since its establishment in 1984, 'has been in the forefront of negotiations for peace'; and the Association of the Parents of Disappeared Persons, set up by Parveen Ahangar in 1994, which seeks to find people who have gone missing as a result of the conflict in Kashmir (2008, 258). As conflicts in these regions have become protracted and more complex, with growing vulnerabilities for women, CSOs–including those driven by women peacemakers–have sought to play a greater role in addressing gender violence, marginalization of women in peace processes and issues of conflict transformation.

As such, the puzzle that drives this chapter is not that WPS issues have not been factored into CSO advocacy. Indeed, there has been relentless critique of repressive legislation such as the Armed Forces Special Power Act that provides impunity to state-sponsored violence, including in cases of rape and sexual assaults against women (Bora 2010; also see Chapter 5 of this book). However, the employment of WPS resolutions in advocacy and monitoring has been limited. There has been some momentum in engagement with SCR 1325 since the tenth anniversary of the passage of the resolution in 2010. Organizations such as Control Arms Foundation of India (CAFI), the North East Network (NEN), Sansristi, the India chapter of Women in Governance (WinG) and Women in Security, Conflict Management and Peace (WISCOMP) have organized events, undertaken awareness-building initiatives and/or commissioned research on SCR 1325 and its relevance in the Indian context. As this volume goes into press, CAFI is in the process of preparing a draft NAP on women, peace and security for submission to the GoI. The value of NAP and the possibilities of building on existing CSO efforts–handful as these are–to engage with SCR 1325 in India are explored in the remaining part of this section.

In her recommendations for women's organizations, Banerjee suggests measures such as 'generate awareness about UNSCR 1325 within grass roots groups'; information-sharing, advocating for 'policy change', monitoring results and improving coordination; link the resolution's agenda to economic empowerment, women IDPs (internally displaced persons), trafficking, migration, peace, and care and rehabilitation of women suffering from mental health issues; identify and highlight 'positive experiences of women during conflict' as well as 'best practices on women's leadership'; ensure participation of men; 'bring dalit/low-caste women into the political mainstream'; and build linkages between women from vulnerable communities in order for them to speak together (2013, 53–54). Banerjee's recommendations primarily draw upon her intensive research on the conflict situation in Northeast India. Applying her approach to the other 'disturbed areas' in the country can offer further insights into possible strategies for CSOs in India. Indeed, the first point of Banerjee's recommendation, which is not mentioned above, is the need to commit to a 'sub-regional action plan' before considering an NAP on Resolution 1325 in India (2013, 53).

At a workshop on 'Gendered Impact of Security Policies and Legislations in India and Women's Response', held in Bhubaneshwar from 19 to 20 April 2013, that also examined the relevance of

Resolution 1325 in India, there appeared to be a general agreement about participants that in India there is a need to devise sub-national action plans tailored to the particularities of the 'disturbed areas'. The apparent reluctance to invoke Resolution 1325 by women's groups at the national level cannot be the rationale for not exploring sub-national possibilities. Part of the challenge is to increase awareness about the WPS resolutions among local women's groups and highlight the international recognition and support for their work that now exists through such resolutions. Resolution 1325, as noted in the introductory section, can be used both as a normative inspiration and for its operational value in conflict areas. And if a consensus on the formulation of NAP in India were achieved, the policy document would need to have substantive contributions from the local groups.

Even if India does adopt an NAP, its scope may well be limited due to little reflection on the domestic situation, as is the case, for instance, with the UK's NAP that does not include any reference to Northern Ireland. Since national-level plans tend to apply a narrow understanding of Resolution 1325, scholar-activists such as Asha Hans and Betty Reardon have suggested the development of a 'transnational people's action plan', including the regional level (see Chapter 1 of this book). Inspiration can be drawn from the work of the West African Women in Peacebuilding Network (WIPNET) wherein the Nigerian chapter was able to learn from the programme's operations in neighbouring countries such as Liberia and Sierra Leone (Wamai 2011, 97; also see Ikpe 2011, 96–97).

But before such concrete steps can be envisaged, there need to be efforts to create awareness about the WPS resolutions and their provisions among women's groups at national and local levels. Indeed, the most obvious contribution of CSOs will have to be towards the dissemination of information on the resolutions. Language could be an issue but the translations initiative of the PeaceWomen Project includes some Indian languages such as Urdu, Tamil, Punjabi, Marathi, Manipuri, Hindi, Gujarati and Bengali; translations are also available in South Asian languages such as Sinhala, Pashto and Nepali as well as Rakhaing, Sham, Kachin and other Burmese languages (PeaceWomen n.d.a). Additional translations could be generated with support from local groups. Such efforts to create awareness must not present Resolution 1325 in a vacuum. Instead, links have to be drawn between the 'informal' work already been done by women's groups as well as the 'formal' policies that exist at various levels including, for instance, provisions for increased participation of women at the panchayat level and national laws that are geared to protect women from sexual violence. Further, possibilities of using WPS resolutions in conjunction with international mechanisms such as the CEDAW and the Beijing Platform for Action to which the GoI has shown some commitment should also be presented. In this regard, it is notable that the 2014 NGO Alternate Report on CEDAW calls on the 'State to honor its international commitment to women in conflict transformation and peace-building under UN Security Council Resolutions 1325' (NAWO 2014, 13). It is the establishment of such linkages as well as local interpretations of the provisions of Resolution 1325 that would contribute towards the formulation of action plans (local and national) geared towards bringing about political change.

The advocacy and monitoring work of Indian women's groups should also be projected outwards, not least because that has been the arena that the GoI has focused on in its implementation of Resolution 1325. As one of the highest troop contributors to UN peace operations, including the celebrated first all-female formed police unit that was sent to Liberia in 2007, India supports the normative and policy standpoints of the UN. Of course, this has not translated into any noticeable increase in the participation of women in conflict-resolution processes at the national and sub-national levels. CSOs can play an active role both in terms of strengthening the global WPS agenda and towards highlighting the gaps between international and domestic positions adopted by the GoI. In this respect, CSOs in India lost an important opportunity for advocacy during the 2010–12 tenure of India as an elected member of the Security Council. In contrast, Australian women's groups, for instance, prepared well in advance to secure–and then monitor–the Australian government's commitment to the WPS agenda during its elected membership in the Council from 2013 to 2015 (ACFID et al. 2013). Considering that India's foreign policy would continue to focus on projecting its role as a major international player, CSOs in India should devise strategies–such as preparing report cards on India's implementation of Resolution 1325 at home and abroad–that could potentially encourage the GoI to adopt and implement policies that would improve its international image.

In conclusion, the challenge for CSOs is to be mindful of the limitations of using Resolution 1325, such as the danger of adopting universalist policies without due consideration to local contexts or letting donor agencies determine the agenda, but to use the openings for employment of the WPS resolutions that already exist: peacemaking work of their transnational and international partners; CSOs own commitment to the resolutions' provisions even if articulated differently; and the GoI's interest in being an active UN member state. Reflecting on the context of Nigeria, Ikpe writes that 'countries that are not officially recognized as being in conflict appear to be more or less excluded from the ongoing discourse regarding UNSCR 1325' (2011, 97). This certainly appears to be the case with the domestic situation in India as well. However, at a time when local opportunities for conflict resolution are shrinking with increasing militarization of the Indian society and adoption of repressive security legislation, as discussed in this volume, Resolution 1325 can be a significant tool for domestic initiatives. Towards the realization of gender equality goals through WPS resolutions, CSOs in India should build on their relationship with old partners such as regional or international women's networks, UN agencies and indeed research groups as well as develop advocacy strategies geared more directly towards governmental agencies, including the military.

Notes

1. In 2012, the open debates took place in the months of February and November. Also note that additional open debates on the theme of 'women, peace and security' and/or 'sexual violence in conflict' have taken place at the Security Council during the period 2008–13.
2. Noleen Heyzer, Executive Director of UNIFEM from 1994–2007, (2004, cited in Hill 2004–05) is one of those who refer to Resolution 1325 as having a global constituency (also see, Barnes 2011a, 27).
3. Workshops such as the one on 'Women and Peace: Moving Towards UNSCR 1325 and National Action Plan (India)', organized by Sansristi and PIPFPD (Odisha) in Bhubaneswar on 13 and 14 March 2011, that led to this volume have also been part of these debates, but the scholarly literature on this topic has been limited till date.
4. An earlier draft of this paper was presented at the first Annual International Studies Conference held at Jawaharlal Nehru University, New Delhi, from 10 to

12 December 2013. The discussions in the first part of this chapter in particular benefitted from the comments of Professor Anupama Roy who chaired the panel in which the paper was presented.

5. Referring to the Committee's report prepared for the UN International Women's Year, in her study of the Indian women's movement, Mary Katzenstein writes, 'it is true that in some senses 1975 was a beginning' (1989, 61).

6. Further, women's groups in India have actively advocated against discriminatory international policies, especially trade-related, such as those relating to pharmaceutical drugs and farming of genetically modified agricultural products (Bt cotton and Bt brinjal).

References

Abdela, Lesley. 2011. 'Nepal and the Implementation of UNSCR 1325'. In *Women, Peace and Security: Translating Policy into Practice*, edited by F. Olonisakin, K. Barnes and E. Ikpe, 66–86. London/New York, NY: Routledge.

ACFID, WILPF, ANCUNW and Gender Institute. 2013. 'Annual Civil-Society Report Card On: Australia's National Action Plan on Women, Peace & Security.' Available at: http://www.acfid.asn.au/resources-publications/files/civil-society-report-card-2013 (Accessed on 29 March 2015).

Antrobus, P. 2004. The Global Women's Movement: Issues and Strategies for the New Century. London: Zed Books.

Banerjee, P. 2013. *In the Light of UNSCR 1325*. New Delhi: WinG.

Barnes, Karen. 2011a. 'The Evolution and Implementation of UNSCR 1325: An Overview'. In *Women, Peace and Security: Translating Policy into Practice*, edited by F. Olonisakin, K. Barnes and E. Ikpe, 15–33. London/New York, NY: Routledge.

———. 2011b. 'Lost in Translation: UNAMSIL, UNSCR 1325 and Women Building Peace in Sierra Leone'. In *Women, Peace and Security: Translating Policy into Practice*, edited by F. Olonisakin, K. Barnes and E. Ikpe, 121–37. London/New York, NY: Routledge.

Barnes, Karen and Funmi Olonisakin. 2011. 'Introduction'. In *Women, Peace and Security: Translating Policy into Practice*, edited by F. Olonisakin, K. Barnes and E. Ikpe, 3–14. London/New York: Routledge.

Basu, A. 2000. 'Globalization of the Local/Localization of the Global Mapping Transnational Women's Movements'. *Meridians*, 1 (1): 68–84.

Bora, Papori. 2010. 'Between the Human, the Citizen, and the Tribal'. *International Feminist Journal of Politics*, 12 (3–4): 341–60.

Boserup, E. 1970. *Woman's Role in Economic Development*. London: Earthscan.

Butalia, U. 2008. 'Speaking Peace: An Introduction'. In *Women's Studies in India*, edited by M.E. John, 255–62. New Delhi: Penguin.

Chenoy, A.M. 2012. Countering Militarization Building Peace: The Intersectionality of SCR 1325 and the Responsibility to Protect. New Delhi: WISCOMP.

Cohn, Carol. 2004. 'Mainstreaming Gender in UN Security Policy: A Path to Political Transformation?'. Working Paper No. 204, Boston Consortium on Gender, Security and Human Rights. Available at: https://www.amherst.edu/media/view/92331/original/mainstreaming+gender+in+UN+security+policy.pdf (Accessed on 29 March 2015).

Falch, Åshild. 2010. *Women's Political Participation and Influence in Post-conflict Burundi and Nepal.* Oslo: Peace Research Institute Oslo.

Guha, Phulrenu. 1974. *Towards Equality: Report of the Committee on the Status of Women in India.* New Delhi: Department of Social Welfare, Ministry of Education & Social Welfare, Government of India.

Hall-Martin, Catherina H. 2011. 'Gendered Violence and UNSCR 1325 in Kosovo: Shifting paradigms on Women, Peace and Security'. In *Women, Peace and Security: Translating Policy into Practice*, edited by F. Olonisakin, K. Barnes and E. Ikpe, 37–51. London/New York: Routledge.

Hill, Felicity. 2004–05. *How and When has Security Council 1325 (2000) on Women, Peace and Security Impacted Negotiations Outside the Security Council.* Masters thesis: Uppsala University Programme of International Studies: Uppsala, Sweden.

Hudson, N.F. and A.M. Goetz. 2014. 'Too Much That Can't Be Said: Anne Marie Goetz in Conversation with Natalie Florea Hudson'. *International Feminist Journal of Politics*, 16 (2): 336–46.

Ikpe, Eka. 2011. 'Nigeria and the Implementation of UNSCR 1325'. In *Women, Peace and Security: Translating Policy into Practice*, edited by F. Olonisakin, K. Barnes and E. Ikpe, 87–103. London/New York: Routledge.

Katzenstein, M.F. 1989. 'Organizing Against Violence: Strategies of the Indian Women's Movement'. *Pacific Affairs*, 62 (1): 53–71.

Keck, M.E. and K. Sikkink. 1998. *Activists Beyond Borders: Advocacy Networks in International Politics.* Ithaca, NY: Cornell University Press.

Liu, D. 2006. 'When do National Movements Adopt or Reject International Agendas? A Comparative Analysis of the Chinese and Indian Women's Movements'. *American Sociological Review*, 71 (6): 921–42.

Mazumdar, V. 2010. *Memories of a Rolling Stone.* New Delhi: Zubaan.

Mayanja, R. 2008. 'Transforming Words into Action'. *Disarmament Times*, 31 (1): 4.

McLeod, L. 2011. 'Configurations of Post-conflict: Impacts of Representations of Conflict and Post-conflict upon the (Political) Translations of Gender Security Within UNSCR 1325'. *International Feminist Journal of Politics*, 13 (4): 594–611.

Merry, S.E. 2006. *Human Rights & Gender Violence: Translating International Law into Local Justice.* Chicago/London: University of Chicago Press.

NAWO (National Alliance of Women's Organisations). 2014. *Executive Summary for the IV & V NGO Alternate Report for the 58th CEDAW Committee session 2014.* Available at: http://nawoindia.org/pdf/Executive-Summary-%2012-06-2014.pdf (Accessed on 22 September 2015).

PeaceWomen. n.d.a. *Resolution Texts and Translations.* Available at: http://www.peacewomen.org/resolutions-texts-and-translations (Accessed on 29 March 2015).

Prügl, E. 1999. *The Global Construction of Gender: Home-based Work in the Political Economy of the 20th Century.* New York: Columbia University Press.

Prügl, Elisabeth and Mary K. Meyer. 1999. 'Gender Politics in Global Governance'. In *Gender Politics in Global Governance*, edited by M.K. Meyer and E. Prügl, 3–16. Oxford: Rowman & Littlefield.

Shah, M. 2003. 'Rights Under Fire: The Inadequacy of International Human Rights Instruments in Combating Dowry Murder in India'. *Conn. J. Int'l L.*, 19 (1): 209–30.

Shepherd, Laura J. 2008. *Gender, Violence and Security: Discourse as Practice.* London: Zed Books.

UN (United Nations). 1945. *Charter of the United Nations.* New York: United Nations.

———. 2000. Security Council Resolution 1325 on Women and Peace and Security. S/RES/1325. New York: United Nations.

——— 2008. Women and Peace and Security Report of the Secretary-General to the Security Council. S/2008/622. New York: United Nations.

———. 2011. Report of the Secretary-General on Women and Peace and Security to the Security Council. S/2011/598. New York: United Nations.

Wamai, Emma Njoki. 2011. 'Nigeria and the Implementation of UNSCR 1325'. In *Women, Peace and Security: Translating Policy into Practice*, edited by F. Olonisakin, K. Barnes and E. Ikpe, 52–65. London/New York: Routledge.

4

Advancing the Women, Peace and State Reconstruction Agenda: 1325 Plus

Anuradha M. Chenoy

Even as the international women's movement won victories in the Security Council by getting passed a slew of resolutions beginning from 1325 followed by others that recognized the importance of women's participation in peace-making, peace-keeping and prevention of conflict. Many countries, including those in South Asia, are yet nowhere near implementing these resolutions that now make up international law. In fact, Security Council Resolutions (SCR) following 1325 have not taken women on board when discussing issues of war, peace and intervention, even under Chapter VII of the Charter. This chapter analyses the different relationships that women, especially in South Asia, have with peace and disarmament and how we need to move ahead from SCR 1325.

The gendered nature of wars, ethnic cleansing, and genocide where rape and sexual violence has been used to humiliate women and then exclude women from peace and decision-making processes was brought into discussion by the international women's movement to the UN to discuss and pass the SCR 1325. This became a landmark resolution that makes women and gender perspectives relevant in all peace processes, addresses the urgent need for prevention of women's human rights violations during armed conflict situations, and mandates women's participation in all decision-making bodies and processes in peace and post-conflict reconstruction. Subsequently, the Security Council has passed more resolutions to strengthen 1325, which are: 1612, 1674, 1820, 1888, 1889 and 1960. We view these together as SCR 1325+.

Why Do We Need SCR 1325 and More?

It is well recognized that women have multiple roles in conflicts and are not just victims of violence but often the driving forces for building peace. Despite this, however, women's roles in peace-making are not recognized. Research established that the status and needs of women have been absent or silenced in the general discourse on war and post-war transitions and women have been systematically excluded from peace processes. Feminists relate this silence to patriarchy that is historically embedded in State and non-State institutions and actors and the militarism involved in nation/State building (Cockburn 2001; Elshtain 1987; Enloe 1983; Ruddick 1983). Tickner (1993) called the theory and practice of international relations as a 'womanless world'. Currently, even with many women leaders and the increased presence of women in public spaces in many Western countries, the continuation of imperialist and hegemonic polices reveals that 1325 is not being implemented in spirit in most countries.

Contemporary research reveals the organic link between patriarchy and various forms of masculinity that arise within societies and institutions. Patriarchal structures and ideas reinforce the unequal relations between men and women, a feature that only increases during conflict situations when binaries get sharpened, militarization increases and gender stereotypes take militant forms.

The shortcoming of 1325 in such situation arises because while it asks for an inclusion of women in decision making, it does not address the issue of militarism as ideology that underlies the international system, which is often forced to accept the idea of US's strategic stability doctrine. And neither does 1325 make an attempt to address the process of militarization that underlies both nationalist and sub-nationalist ideologies. Feminists reveal the ideological linkages between militarism, nationalism and patriarchy. Militarization is the material as well the ideological use of military values that encroaches on civilian spaces and promotes the use of force to resolve essentially civilian issues.

Military culture has been based on values, symbols and acts of male superiority and the degradation of women. It is important to note that militarization is not confined to military structures and defence economy alone. Mindsets can be militarized outside military institutions. Military culture instils into society the concept of power as force. It presumes an idea of masculinity that is supported by the complementary concept of femininity. This is because the military more than other institutions relies on male power. Gender difference is clearly demarcated with masculine privileged (Cockburn 1999, 2010; Cohn 1987; Enloe 1983). The military as an institution and militarization as an ideology are distinct phenomenon because civilians and ordinary people can have a militarized mindset. Militarism as an ideology has influenced women. Thus, as Enloe and others have shown, anything can be militarized. For example, motherhood, religion, education, and so on, can all instil military values.

The hyper nationalism–militarization link is evident in all South Asian bilateral and internal conflict situations. It is evident in virulent nationalist, fundamentalist, majoritarian, sectarian movements and State processes. For example, when India and Pakistan carried out nuclear tests in 1998, both saw this as a powerful masculine exercise. It is played out in Sri Lanka during and after the war with the Tamil Tigers, that is, the Liberation Tigers of Tamil Eelam (LTTE). Regimes use militarization to sustain themselves in power, making it a nation building and State reconstruction process, which becomes a male privileged exercise in countries of South Asia where institutions are largely controlled by patriarchal structures and individuals. Since gendered hierarchy has been associated with nation building, any reforms of the distribution of power between men and women are viewed as a threat to nationalist effort to protect or unify the community (Tickner 2002). Militarization is associated with the use of force, conflicts are resolved through force when negotiation fails. All wars in South Asia have shown that the public is mobilized to contribute to the war effort. In war mobilization, the public mindset gets militarized and it accepts the need for force to resolve conflict. This public use of force intersects with the personal use of force, and especially with the gendered use of force.

Studies show that if domestic violence increases, conflict-ridden regions and that society is more likely to rely on violent conflict resolution and to be more involved in militarism and war than in societies with lower levels of family violence (Cockburn 2001). It has also been established that State violence generally leads to higher levels of violence against women (Brownmiller 1975; Elshtain 1987). Violence demoralizes and immobilizes women and increases their isolation; it has negative impact on the family, community and society. It is clear that a real decrease in societal violence or a sustainable peace could not be possible without a decrease in gender inequality (Hunt and Posa 2001). Caprioli (2000) shows that States with higher gender equality in political, social and economic institutions are less likely to use military force to settle disputes. States with higher gender equality tend to have more sustainable peace. This kind of research and activism of the international women's movement has popularized the relevance of looking at peace with a gender lens.

In many communities, such as in all of South Asia, women are symbols of honour and their community's cultural identity. Women, thus, become easy targets. It is believed that violating women shames the entire community and, therefore, if a community cannot 'protect its women' they cannot protect their honour ('Honour killings' that are in reality brutal murders are common in all of South Asian Sates). Thus, opposing sides violate women sexually in order to humiliate and shame the enemy. On the other hand, in order to 'protect women,' instead of punishing violators women are secluded and lose their autonomy and choice to make personal decisions. Complaints by women against abuse are seen as 'dividing the community' or diverting from the 'main' issues that the community is engaged in. The consequence is that violence against women gets 'normalized' (research shows how widespread such violence is). Women's issues are put on the back burner and do not get the space or the importance they deserve. Violence against women and gender injustice continues in post-conflict and transitional societies. Further, perpetrators of such violence often get impunity because of laws that create a state of exception in disturbed areas.

In post-conflict societies, the very men who made war make the peace and build or reconstruct the State in their own image. In India, for example, the peace agreements made after the conflicts in Punjab, Mizoram, Assam and elsewhere, between the State and the leaders/political representatives of dissenting community, created a new power sharing arrangement between male elites who entrenched themselves in political power that continues decades after. Such gendered situations in post-conflict societies where political institutions are turfed by male power is the norm in South Asia. Cockburn and Zarkov have shown how the post-conflict environment is about male power systems where one set of men lose power while other men take their place. When history is written it remains silent about the different roles played by women. That is why women have to rewrite their version of history.

The exclusion of women in power structures in post-conflict political situations in South Asia arises from their absence in peace-making. Aolain argues that the institutional gaps for women can be traced to the exclusion of women from deal making by local and international institutions. She shows from reports of the International Centre for Transitional Justice (ICTJ) that 'dominant hierarchies will marginalize women's priorities, interests and participation' and once again invisibilize the gendered nature of institutions (Aolain 2009, 1055–85). She makes the argument that security sector reforms in transitional societies must have an agenda that is inclusive of women's experience and role. These steps can be taken in consonance with gender sensitive international laws. The practical experience of women from the north and east in Sri Lanka play out this dynamic.

International law is an instrument to influence and mandate States but stereotypes about women's roles and the pervasive patriarchal ideologies prevail here as well. The former UN Special Rapporteur on Violence Against Women (SRVAW), Radhika Coomaraswamy, argues: 'Women's rights are 'soft' areas of international human rights law, the area over which there is debate, discussion and sometimes frivolity' (Coomaraswamy 2002). Realist, strategic thinkers have created an entire discourse around soft power, which is relegated as the lesser aspect of power because it relates to human relations as opposed to military geo-strategic relations.

A number of feminist academics have concluded that International Humanitarian Law (IHL) 'is philosophically based on chivalric ideals of women, addresses women in terms of their relationships with others and not as individuals in their own right. Generally, women are valued in International Law (IL) in terms of sexual and reproductive aspects of their lives' (Durham 2002). International regimes have been created and maintained by primarily patriarchal concepts because States that are themselves based on male dominated institutions are the primary actors in the international system. Feminists contest and ask that these laws be changed.

Women's rights are human rights and essential for the dignity of women and society as a whole. Peace research has established that women's rights need to be especially safeguarded during conflict situations and women should be especially included in peace processes, for peace to be inclusive and sustainable. This research, experience and activism provided the foundation for 1325. However, what remains excluded in this approach is that many women cannot avail of human rights if they are relegated to their fixed roles of nurturers and carers and when they remain out of the formal economy. Again, 1325+ has been unable to address this complexity.

The Back Drop of International Conventions

Women's groups built their case for 1325+ on the shoulders of many international documents, treaties, conventions and statements, such as the Convention on the Elimination of All Forms of Discrimination Against Women (CEDAW, 1979); The Beijing Declaration and Platform for Action (1995); The Beijing + 5 declaration, The United Nations Economic and Social Council (ECOSOC) agreed conclusions on Gender Mainstreaming (1997), Windhoek Declaration and the Namibia Plan of Action (2000). Several countries such as Bangladesh, Canada and Namibia supported this as did the then Secretary General of the UN, Kofi Annan, who stated that:

> The world is starting to grasp that there is no policy more effective [in promoting development, health and education] than the empowerment of women and girls. And I would venture that no policy is more important in preventing conflict, or in achieving reconciliation after a conflict has ended. (UN 2006)

This combined effort of an international women's movement and civil and political society gradually brought awareness of women's rights on the high table of international negotiations resulting in 1325. Needless to say this was only the beginning for a gender perspective on peace and inclusion of women in any peace process.

The urgency of implementation of this resolution is clear because the use of rape in ethnic genocide and cleansing has reached 'unspeakable and pandemic proportions in some communities' according to UN Secretary General Ban Ki Moon. In order to strengthen SCR 1325 the UN Security Council passed another important Resolution 1820 in June 2008. This resolution declares that rape and other forms of sexual violence can constitute a war crime. Rape is now seen as a crime against humanity and a constitutive action of genocide. In armed conflicts rape and sexual violence has been used as a weapon of war to humiliate, terrorize, dominate and relocate civilians, ethnic groups and communities by targeting women. The Security Council passed Resolution 1960 in 2010 to strengthen laws against impunity of sexual violators during armed conflicts. However, unlike the process of consultation with the international women's movement that took place when passing SCR 1325, the same process was not taken in discussions prior to SCR 1960, much to the consternation of many international women's groups. This appears to be a trend, because after the passing of these resolutions, for example, women's groups have not been consulted on issues such as intervention in Afghanistan, Iraq, Libya or Syria. Thus, 1325 itself is conserved a 'soft' resolution.

Prevention, Participation and Protection

SCR 1325 is a political framework that sets up four guidelines for women in situations of conflict and peace: (a) Prevention of conflicts and violations of women's rights; (b) participation of women in all aspects of conflict resolution, peace-making, peace-keeping and peace-building; supporting local initiatives on peace; (c) protection of women amongst vulnerable populations, protection of survivors from attack and from other impacts of conflicts and (d) relief and recovery. If we look at the conflicts in the past decade it would be pertinent to ask if the countries that passed 1325 took into account the opinion and participation of women in the decision-making process in any of these conflicts. Further what steps were taken to prevent women and vulnerable populations in these conflicts by both the warring sides?

This resolution makes it mandatory for the UN Security Council to pursue gender equality in all its actions, whether these are mine clearing, peace-keeping, demobilization, disarmament, reintegration (DDR) and security sector reforms. The resolution, thus, addresses policy-makers at international institutions and governments as well as society at large. SCR 1325 mandates through its 18 clauses, each set in the context of the role of women during armed conflicts. We explain and contextualize these with reference to South Asia to show instances of what led to these clauses and what they mean.

Protection

Women need to be specially protected during armed conflicts and post-conflict situations from sexual assault and human rights abuse. Sexual assault has been used as a weapon of war and destruction to assert dominance over the enemy and humiliate a community by violating 'their' women. In communal riots in Muzaffarnagar, Uttar Pradesh, India, in September 2013, hundreds of complaints of rape have been reported by Muslim women. Honour killings in all of South Asia have been rampant and illustrate sexual targeting. In all armed conflicts, gender-based abuse and sexual violence remains the most sustained, underwritten and common form of violence against women. Violence against women continues in post-conflict situations and women face increased domestic violence by men brutalized by conflict. Surveys from South Asian conflicts show that the high level of domestic violence actually increases when men are brutalized and oppressed in situations of armed conflicts. The perpetrators of violence include the opposing side to the conflict, local militias and also State agencies.

During conflict and post-conflict situations, refugee camps are transitory in nature but continue for years with little infrastructure especially for women and are amongst the most neglected sites in the world. Women in camps face problems linked to health and reproductive rights, lack of basic needs and livelihoods, and problems linked with violence, both physical and structural. Refugees and internally displaced persons (IDPs) continue to be treated with disrespect as 'others' or the 'unwanted' without citizenship rights. Some examples from our region include the expelled Bhutanese refugees in Nepal, displaced Pandits from the Kashmir Valley, Tamil refugees in Sri Lanka, ethnic minority refugees of Myanmar and

Afghan refugees in Pakistan. Surveys and newspaper reports from all these camps have shown that women have faced more exploitation, less relief, and more misery and responsibility for their families in these camps. Women refugees have told the author how aid packages are gendered. For example, everyone is given packets of food and water, but women have special needs that are unavailable at times of such crises. There is a body of refugee law under the fourth Geneva Convention that focuses on the security, safety and rehabilitation of women. SCR 1325 calls on States to respect civil and humanitarian rights of refugees and take care of the special needs of women and children in these camps.

Women are increasingly involved in armed conflicts. They have different roles during these conflicts but are increasingly taking on roles as combatants. Their involvement can be strategic, circumstantial, or by choice. Female relatives of militants and security forces have little choice except to be part of conflict situations. Women in armed conflict locations get classified as 'enemies' or combatants. Some women actively support the conflicting sides out of a sense of retribution, injustice or ideological commitment. Women have been an important part of many South Asian insurgencies such as the Nepal Maoists who waged an armed struggle for 13 years (under the leadership of Hisila Yami); women have been active LTTE cadres and part of Indian Maoists—the National Socialist Council of Nagaland (NSCN) and other insurgencies. When women are charged or convicted, they often face gendered torture and inhuman treatment. In India, human rights lawyers are fighting cases of women such as Soni Sori who are victims of such torture. 1325 calls for a consideration of different needs of female and male ex-combatants as well as the needs of their dependents in DDR initiatives. SCR 1325 asks the UN Charter to consider exemptions from the use of excess force in the case of women and girls. Article 42 of the UN Charter allows for the use of force in exceptional cases when international peace and security is threatened, SCR 1325 asks that force should not be used on girls and women even when though the use of force is considered necessary in circumstances of armed conflicts.

Sexual violence is most used against women combatants, to extract information, torture, punish and humiliate. Women in need of protection or sustenance seek alliances with soldiers during conflict. Armed conflict areas increase the risk of prostitution. A UN

Department of Peacekeeping Operation study in March 2004 (UN DPKO 2004) showed that in six of the 12 countries studied, the arrival of UN peacekeepers showed an increase in prostitution, including child prostitution. In Mozambique in 1992, for example, UN Mission observers recruited girls aged 12–18 years into prostitution. There have been allegations followed by enquiries against several missions of the United Nations Peacekeeping forces (UNPK) for sexual abuse during their missions in Mozambique, Bosnia Haiti and other regions (UN New Centre, 5 November 2009). International law stipulates how States must deal with women who are in detention. Women have to be given special benefits according to their needs. However, States do not use international law standards in their domestic disputes. Human rights and gendered violations, thus, continue to occur.

The international women's movement mobilized world opinion for making rape as a war crime and for codifying it in 1993/94. This was discussed by the international community after rape was systematically used as a tool of ethnic genocide in Yugoslavia and Rwanda. SCR 1325 (clause 10) and SCR 1820, adopted in June 2008, calls rape a war crime and wants an immediate and complete halt to acts of sexual violence, saying that in some conflict zones sexual violence had become so widespread and systematic as to 'reach appalling levels of brutality'. In Bangladesh, liberation war rape was widely used by the Pakistan army against East Bengali women. In all subsequent South Asian conflicts, rape has been an instrument of punishing errant women. SCR 1820 says that rape deepens and increases conflicts. 1325+ and 1820 call for a policy of zero tolerance against rape as a weapon of war.

SCR 1325 and 1820 also emphasizes the responsibility of all States to end impunity and prosecute those responsible for crimes of genocide and sexual violence. It calls on the secretary general and all UN bodies to advocate these resolutions in order to instil the message against rape and sexual violence in all institutions dealing with conflict and post-conflict situations.

Participation

Women have remained excluded in structures engaged in the prevention, management and resolution of conflicts. Research has shown that international institutions are male dominated, have patriarchal values and are gender insensitive. Security and strategic positions remain primarily in the hands of men. Women's roles and rights have not been adequately recognized in armed conflicts or in peace negotiations. Traditional stereotypes are enforced during conflicts as women lose their autonomy and are forced to stay indoors, and men have to take up arms to protect as a measurement of a hegemonic masculinity. In many post-conflict societies, for example, in South Asia, Kosovo, Guatemala, Cambodia, Bosnia and Burundi, women's representation in the peace process as well as in elected and government bodies has been limited and disproportionate in relation to their roles. Women work as peacemakers at the grass roots, but when it comes to negotiating tables it is generally men who were engaged in war who also engage in peace. The consequence is a militarized peace. In these circumstances, the post-conflict situation brings men linked with militias into governance and politics. SCR 1325 argues for more women to be represented at all decision-making and conflict-resolution structures and asks member States to increase the representation of women at all decision-making bodies for the prevention, management and resolution of conflict and peace. SCR 1820 endorses this call for increased women's participation since it sees this as a method to empower women and end the sexual violence against women.

Resolution 1325 asks the secretary general to appoint more women as special representatives and envoys on his behalf and asks to include more women in all UN institutions and especially those dealing with peace-building and in field operations that have been historically considered men's domains. The UN Secretary General has the mandate to appoint special representatives, envoys and rapporteurs to report on issues of human rights' violations. This resolution is in keeping with earlier resolutions of the UN such as the Beijing Declaration, the Platform for Action and subsequently the 23rd special session of the UN General Assembly. All these meetings and resolutions have been a consequence of successful lobbying by women's groups. They pay special attention to issues of gender and development, and are particularly concerned with women and armed conflict. There is a need to bring women's experience into reportage and policy-making at all levels. The media plays an important role in war, peace and development. Many South Asian women have been appointed as representatives of the UN Secretary General on different commissions, for example, Ms Asma Jahangir from Pakistan and Ms Radhika

Coomaraswamy from Sri Lanka, (both peace women) who were the UN Special Rapporteurs.

The creation of an all women civil police unit by India to engage in the UN Mission in Liberia (UNMIL) is recognized as a possible model that other countries should follow. Liberia's civil war had seen some of the most extreme cases of sexual violence and crime. The peace-keeping in Liberia and end of civil disturbance and elections resulted in a woman president. SCR 1325 advocates that peacekeeping operations have a gender perspective. Since UN peacekeepers are men from regular armies, they lack a gender perspective. This resolution asks for more women to be engaged in the field. In keeping with this, the DPKO has issues guidelines for integrating gender in peacekeeping operations in November 2009.

The International Security Assistant Forces (ISAF) in Afghanistan has used gender mainstreaming within its structure. They have women working within the force in peacekeeping and security operations and all officers are given gender sensitive training. ISAF review committees show that the use of more women in peace-keeping has given them increased access to women, children and society as a whole in Afghanistan.

Women remain excluded from national and international assemblies and decision-making institutions. Most national-level institutions have only 10–12 per cent of women's representation. South Asian governments have attempted to change this by some steps of affirmative action. Women form one third of the Nepal Constituent Assembly. Pakistan and India have reservation for women at the local self-government levels; Indian women are struggling for 33 per cent reservation in parliament. Since parliaments take the decision to make war and peace and discuss international treaties, women remain excluded from such processes.

Women's movements, organizations and activists support peace processes in different ways during and after conflicts. They do this from their homes and communities, through interaction and as active negotiators. In hundreds of conflicts, women's groups, 'mothers' organizations' and individual women have tried to keep the channels of communication between opposing sides open and have found creative ways of diffusing tensions and paving the way for reconciliation. The Sri Lanka Mothers' Fronts, the Naga Women's Association, the Meira Paibis of Manipur and hundreds of different women's groups in South Asia and beyond have used their agency to intervene for peace in many creative ways. Yet, despite their role, they are excluded and not consulted for confidence building, decision-making and peace processes. For example, the talks between the Nagas and the Government of India (GoI), or the Kashmir round tables of civil society by the Indian government had no women representatives. The Indian government appointed one woman as part of the three interlocutors to make a report on the Kashmir issue. Women are excluded from the traditional village councils. Women, thus, do not form part of 'official' negotiations but work in unofficial and powerless spaces.

States and militias use the symbols and idea of motherhood to muster emotions for the construction of nationalism and nationhood. They construct the image of mothers that hold together the community or the nation in pain. The 'power' of the mother is seen as different and gendered in relation to male power. Yet, mothers or women get left out when power is actually being negotiated or transferred as one set of male elite pass on power to a new group of male ruling elite. This deal making excludes women. SCR1325 asks that gender and rights of women be part of all consultations. SCR 1820 calls for a special rehabilitation of women who have been victims of sexual crimes. It calls for all regional bodies to implement policy and advocacy to benefit women victims of rape.

Prevention

For the past several decades, 90 per cent of wars have been within states. These conflicts have claimed over 5 million lives, damaged livelihoods of millions and turned millions into refugees, of whom, 70 per cent are women. It is well known that in areas of armed conflicts, local militaries and militias have indulged in wide human rights abuse and sexual crimes. UNPK missions have been on the rise since the end of the Cold War (1991). For example, troop deployment has been on an increase, for example the numbers of UNPK has increased from 10,000 to 62,000; UNPK have been present in conflicts in Iraq-Kuwait, Yugoslavia, Uganda, Rwanda, Somalia, Tajikistan, Haiti, Guatemala, Sierra Leone, Afghanistan, Congo, Liberia, Sudan and so on. Haiti, Rwanda, Angola and Yugoslavia have experienced many failures.

In circumstances where States send troops as UN peacekeepers and deploy police and military in areas of local armed conflict, it is of utmost importance that the police, paramilitary and military get trained on gender sensitivity, and the rights and particular needs of women. SCR 1325 asks that all personnel engaged in security exercises must be trained in universal standards of human rights (especially women's rights) on the CEDAW 1979 and so on.

India, Pakistan and Bangladesh provide large numbers of soldiers as peacekeepers. These troops need to be trained as peacekeepers, as we have shown in the earlier sections. UNPK training centres have been established in places such as New Delhi, India, where officers are trained before they leave for operations. Gender sensitization and peace-building is an integral part of the training program. However, gender training constitutes a one hour session, sandwiched between de-mining activities and how to conduct elections. This provides a basic toolkit for the officers but, clearly, more conversation on the issue is necessary. Many such centres are needed, with more innovative methods of gender training for all levels of security forces. Gender and human rights training should be a serious and sustained effort. This can be done, as the SCR 1325 says, with the cooperation of member states. It is critical that States and all officials must receive training guidelines and material on protection, rights and particular needs of women. SCR 1325 asks member States to incorporate this into its national training programme for military and civilian police forces in preparation for deployment and to increase their financial, technical and logistical support for gender-sensitive training efforts. Training of all armed forces should include training and an awareness of resolutions 1325 and 1820.

SCR 1325 has become part of international laws. These laws are to guide State practice in dealing with other States and with citizens as well as non-state actors. International law remains a difficult terrain because implementing international law is dependent on the autonomous will of each State as we see below.

1325 as International Law

The Geneva Conventions mandate how States must behave and protect human rights during wars. These laws apply to international conflicts and wars between states. Additional Protocol II to the Geneva

Conventions (1977) relates to armed conflicts of non-international nature and is binding to both State and non-state actors. This protocol has not been signed by many States with internal armed conflicts, for example, India, Malaysia, Iraq and Israel, to name a few. In all South Asian countries, anti-insurgency measures and national security laws have been adopted. These security laws hand over considerable powers and give impunity to the security forces that allow for civil and political rights' violations. Several South Asian States do not want to sign Additional Protocol II of the Geneva Conventions because, in the war against insurgency and terror, they do not want to be circumvented and held accountable by any international laws.

Similarly, many countries have not signed the Rome Statute and not accepted the International Criminal Court (ICC), including the USA, India, China, and so on. SCR 1325 and 1820 calls on parties to respect international law, especially the Geneva Conventions, Additional Protocols 1977, CEDAW 1979, Rome Statute, ICC and so on (Para 9) and, thus, endorses these important legislations of international law while urging due respect to these. Since many States have accepted the idea of responsibility to protect (R2P) which can be used to protect citizens from humanitarian crimes.

During armed conflict, gendered crimes and violations are committed by opposing sides. Insurgents commit acts of terror and often target civilians as well as representatives of the state. States respond and to regain control and annihilate insurgents, they use the National Security Acts that allow the army/paramilitary to function in civilian areas with considerable power that gives them exception from the constitution. 1325 states that no impunity should be given to those who commit sexual crimes. SCR 1325, thus, covers major issues that impact women. The focus of the international women's movement now needs to be on strategies of its implementation.

Research is Needed

Studies on the impact of armed conflict on women have been subject of recent research, in an area where war was largely chronicled by men. Feminist research on armed conflict situations and its impact has changed the prism of looking at conflicts. Enloe (2000) has theorized how power is linked to masculinity and how militarization intersects with certain ideas of manliness and certain ideas of motherhood. This kind of power-wielding is most effective when people believe that these ideas are part of a shared culture. We would support Enloe's argument that feminists' analytical skills can reveal these linkages.

The UN Secretary General has commissioned many studies to analyse how gender impacts social processes. Yet, mainstream theories on armed conflict, security and peace treat these as 'soft areas' and marginalize them. It will be up to feminist scholars to do further research on aspects of gender, violence, war, masculinity and patriarchy, and so on and popularize these studies and build pressure that women be included in peace-building and peace processes. It is in this context that this resolution asks the secretary general to study the impact of armed conflict on women and girls, and the role of peace-building in peace processes and give his report to Security Council. This report is to be based on gender mainstreaming through peacekeeping missions and monitoring how countries and institutions implement 1325+ (SCR 1325, para 16, 17, 18) There is concern in the Security Council about the treatment of women in war and peace. However, given the lack of implementation, the Security Council needs to put more pressure on States to accept all the clauses of SCR 1325. It is in in this context that a set of indicators has been evolved for the purpose of monitoring that we explain below.

Indicators for Monitoring the Implementation of UNSCR 1325

To judge the progress of SCR 1325, the UN Secretary General has accepted a list of indicators that are designed as 'signposts of change along the path to development'. These are meant to indicate trends and allow tracking of progresses towards implementation and to check out for effective monitoring and evaluation. It is believed that a monitoring checklist will (in UN language)

> improve decision making for ongoing program and project management; measure progress and achievements as understood by the different stakeholders; clarify consistency between activities, outputs, outcomes and impacts; ensure accountability to all

stakeholders by demonstrating progress; assess program, project and staff performance, and identify the need for corrective or remedial action. (UN 2010)

The indicators are based on the norms of 1325. The first set of indicators is meant to monitor prevention and requires that data be collected using surveys of sexual violence and where violence occurs. They record how UNPK offices include violation of women's human rights in their reporting and how these are assessed and responded to. The effort here is to develop a code of conduct that is informed by the gender dimension of missions for peacekeepers and all personnel deployed on peace operations (Keating and Knight 2004).

The indicators assess if violations of women's rights are referred and investigated by human rights bodies, and to what extent is there women's inclusion in civil society groups. Other indicators record the percentage of reported sexual exploitation and abuse cases, allegedly perpetrated by uniformed, civilian peacekeepers and humanitarian workers that are referred, investigated and acted upon.

The role of military/peacekeepers to primarily provide a safe haven for advancing peace is measured by the indicators to make sure that once the protocols in place they will be of value to the personnel for pre-deployment training. Other indicators (Paras 5 and 6) assess the actions taken around addressing human rights violations of women and girls in conflict situations. This is done to make a concerted effort towards the implementation of 1325 and not compartmentalize it as another 'reference point' to 'engender peace and security'.

The next set of indicators is on women's participation in security apparatuses, in decision-making, in prevention of conflict, in peace-building bodies and conflict resolution. Indicators ask for quantifying the number and proportion of women in decision-making roles in relevant regional organizations involved in preventing conflict to show the levels of the women's involvement. The number of women in senior UN positions and their level of participation in formal peace negotiations are to be noted and quantified through the indicators. This shows the importance of mapping a gender analysis of international and regional institutions and practices. The idea is that women's participation should be evident since any legitimate transformation of conflict and building peace should be an inclusive and participatory process. Women bring a different perspective to the negotiating table based on their experiences as single heads of households, as community leaders, as humanitarian and social workers, and as peace activists. When it comes to mainstreaming gender, there has been some successes but at the same time there is a gap between pronouncing policy, generating mandates/protocols and taking actions on the ground. This is where the roles and responsibilities of women's organizations come in. They can push and prod the UN and other international missions to abide by the commitments made in favour of women and girls.

Another set of indicators is on the protection of women and girls security and safety. This is to be done through responsible and ethical surveys. The idea is that the physical and psychological integrity of women and girls must be respected. Laws governing protection of women and girls must be emphasized upon during times of conflict. Data gathering further helps in mapping and providing timely relief and assistance to vulnerable women and girls. The attempt to get national laws in tune with international standards in order to protect the life, physical and mental integrity of women and girls, is evident in the indicators (Paras 14 and 15) that tracks gender sensitive laws. Further levels of women's participation in the justice and security sector in conflict-affected countries are also tracked by the courts. Since women have been excluded from political power and from governance structures, they have had little space in policies related to mitigating violence from public affairs. Women, thus, need to be equal participants in creating a culture of peace.

Women are victims of proliferation of small arms and light weapons (SALW) and the indicators include one on the national mechanisms in place for control of these. This is in keeping with the projected DDR that is designed for post-conflict societies and the attempt to make these gendered, since women are disproportionately affected by these.

Research and assessment has established that development projects that leave out women are less likely to succeed. When women are included in development and recovery projects, faster development is evident (Boserup 1970; Ghosh 2009). Indicator 18 gauges women as a percentage of the adults employed in early economic recovery programmes.

Women do not report sexual crimes to the judiciary because of stigmatization and retaliation. In many conflicts, perpetrators of rape have got impunity. It is, therefore, important for mechanisms and laws to exist for protecting women and girls. Indicators (Paras 19 and 20) assess the number and percentage of cases of sexual violence against women and girls that are referred, investigated and sentenced, and the number and percentage of courts equipped to try cases of violations of women's and girl's human rights, with due attention to the victim's security—the level of investigation and prosecution of cases of sexual and gender based violence remains low in many contexts. These indicators refer to the access of justice systems to the victims of sexual violence.

Relief and recovery are the fourth pillar of 1325 and the next set of indicators measure the gender component of these. This includes reporting on maternal mortality and primary and secondary education enrolment rates. The attempt is to reaching the vulnerable population who have less access to basic education is a major challenge. This requires targeted programmes and interventions that should also seek to eliminate gender disparities and is based on the Millennium Development Goals (UN 2008).

Research suggests that funding tends to focus on specific issues such as health, education and social infrastructure. However, very little attention has been paid to gender considerations in other areas, including economic infrastructure and private sector development. These areas have traditionally been considered gender neutral, which has been shown to be incorrect. For example, Unifem research has shown that factors such as discrimination, illiteracy, the threat of sexual and gender-based violence, and uneven household responsibilities can mean that the private sector is not equally accessible to men and women. The need for incorporating gender analysis in strategic planning frameworks in conflict-affected countries, and in targets, indicators and budgets, and proportion of the allocated and disbursed funding to civil society organizations (CSOs), emerges in the form of indicators (22–24).

It has been revealed by the ICTJ that despite some ad-hoc efforts, recent examples of truth commission mandates judicial opinions, reparations programs and policy-reform proposals that have shown little regard for the distinct and complex nature of gender-based violations. It is also established that recommendations made by truth commissions and reparations programs can challenge discriminatory practices that contribute to women's vulnerability during conflict, as well as the long-term consequences of gender-based violations. This is also incorporated into the indicators (Para 25) to measure the gender mainstreaming into transitional justice, reparations and other programmes.

Security sector reforms advocate that DDR programmes address the special needs of women and girls and indicator 26 measures this to ensure that the gender-blind processes in DDR programs undergo a change. DDR programs often promote a traditional sexual division of labour by offering training for female combatants in 'female' skills, such as cooking, tailoring and mat weaving that support the 'return' of women into the 'domestic and private sphere'. A third set of obstacles for women in DDR processes, as shown by the ICTJ is related to the breakup of chains of command and the disintegration of collective group identity in favour of individual identity.

R2P also is being monitored by special offices designated for preventing genocide and other crimes against humanity. Secretary General Ban Ki Moon asked for fact-finding missions in cases of rape committed during wars. He stated that the international community needs to be vigilant in preventing crimes against women during conflicts.

Clearly, the aim of these indicators is to push for implementation of 1325 and R2P and make all international processes and institutions working in conflict areas more gender just and accountable. The indicators also have the aim of working as a model for other agencies and national governments to be more inclusive of gender needs and justice.

Implementation Issues

The ideals that underlie 1325 are tested by their implementation. International organizations and international women's movements are evaluating the implementation of 1325. For example, PeaceWomen celebrated the 10th anniversary of 1325 in Berlin in October 2010 and demanded that all States bring out national action plans (NAP) as the next steps for implementation.

UN and Security Council Resolutions are often viewed with some level of cynicism because States have so often ignored them. The recent peoples' upsurges in all of West Asia that were put down by force, once again raised the question of R2P and re-opened the debate on the role of the international community in such a situation. Evidence shows that gender issues have received more salience in the last decade. Some researchers argue that Security Council deliberations have given legitimacy and authority to gender norms. But clearly, women's and civil society activism that has accompanied the resolution at every stage is now pushing for its implementation (Keck and Sikkink 1998). Thus, if implementation is weak at its very source then diffusion of a norm would be weak. But it is also evident that gender norms have been enhanced through the legitimacy and authority bestowed by Security Council deliberations and the follow up by several national governments, institutions and civil society organizations (CSOs).

There are valid concerns on getting the governments of South Asia to implement 1325 and to relate it to the South Asian experience.

Furthering 1325 for South Asia

In South Asia, militarization is not restricted to militaries or military regimes. Ethnic, communal, economic and gender relations have a militarized component. Militarization as a process has been shaped by the specific history of this subcontinent. Its roots lie in its colonized past and the construction of the nation, particularly the partition experience and State making. Militarization has been aggravated through the particular choices regarding development and it is the women who consistently lose. The reasons for militarization lies with both, the way dissent movement resort to arms and the State responses to dissent movements with the use of force. This becomes a spiral where opposing sides resist engagement or negotiations.

The South Asian Region (SAR—India, Nepal, Pakistan, Bangladesh, Sri Lanka, Bhutan and Afghanistan), all face multiple armed conflicts and security threats. Two of the countries of SAR—India and Pakistan—have a long-standing inter-state dispute over boundaries and Kashmir. They both possess nuclear weapons, have very high military expenditure and have threatened to use nuclear weapons against each other. This is of concern for regional as well as global peace.

Afghanistan faces internal conflict where the Taliban militia and war lords attempt to take over control from the elected Afghan government of President Karzai that is supported by the North Atlantic Treaty Organization (NATO) and the ISAF. This war is being fought on the borders of Afghanistan and Pakistan and it severely impacts both countries and has regional impact.

All South Asian countries face different types of internal conflicts or insurgencies and several of these are rebuilding their States after prolonged armed conflicts. Each of these conflicts is deeply gendered where masculinities and femininities are stereotyped and defined, as shown with examples in the previous sections. Linkages between economic marginality, exclusion of women and use of violence and militarization are evident in these conflicts. The tactics used by almost all the struggles have been based on extremist, terrorist and political violence.

Women in South Asia represent the honour of their communities and gender roles are strictly laid down in South Asian cultures and norms. Community rights take precedence over individual rights in most of South Asia and, thus, patriarchal customary and family laws bind women in roles that make them less equal in almost all spheres of life and activity. In all South Asian conflicts, women have been victims of gendered crimes and targeting and have been unequally treated during peace and rehabilitation. Women have been part of almost all insurgent groups and militia, for example in the LTTE in Sri Lanka and the Maoist insurgencies in India's North East, but in combat too their gendered and unequal roles follow. Women have mobilized and worked for peace in all South Asian conflict zones, but when peace negotiations take place, they are part of the background and not on the high tables. They have different roles in South Asian conflicts and peace-building but remain largely out of leadership roles and institutional processes, as power in South Asia is largely a male domain. Though there have been many powerful women in leadership and have achieved positions of power largely because of their relation with powerful men. The inequality between men and women in the system of power remains skewed in favour of men.

While there are many similarities in the impacts and role of women during armed conflicts and post-conflict reconstruction, there are several cultural and social specificities in the way women have been impacted and the way they have responded.

Strengths of South Asia for 1325

South Asian States have many strengths that can enable the use of 1325. The greatest strength of the SAR is that it is increasingly democratized, even though there is much scope for increasing and deepening democracy. Gender awareness has increased in the SAR though women's empowerment is still at a nascent stage. Civil societies of all South Asian States apply pressure on these States for conforming to human rights and women's rights principles, with uneven and varying success. The democratic movement and the presence of women in the human rights commissions are testimony to this.

Some illustrations of the impact of 1325 in South Asia include: In September 2010, the Nepal Ministry for Peace and Reconstruction prepared and presented a national plan for the implementation of 1325 and 1820. This plan was based on wide and democratic consultations. It has had an impact on the making of Nepal Constitution, which is comparatively a more gender-sensitive document.

In Sri Lanka some 80,000 war widows in the north and east needed support and the government has been seeking international assistance for them in the context of 1325. Meanwhile, in the Lessons Learnt and Reconciliation Commission, Tamil women complained that in the context of 1325, only some select women were listened to, while the rest were turned away as they looked for their missing relatives and closures. One woman was appointed an interlocutor to look at confidence building measures on the Kashmir issue in India. Thus, while there are challenges for South Asia in moving towards gender equality, there are also these strengths that can be built upon. We look at the major hurdles and the strengths around which 1325 can build in South Asia.

Hurdles in Implementing 1325 in South Asia

Governments in South Asia face violent insurgencies, identity struggles and terrorist activities, as we have shown previously, and use force and draconian laws to fight these. They do not want to invite any international censure on the violation of human rights that occur with regularity. They see international laws, resolutions and conventions as an intervention in their sovereignty. Further, their prime concern is the State's and not the people's security. This results in militarization that is manifest in both increased defence expenditures that receive priority over social spending and the militarization of political responses on all issues of security. India is now the biggest purchaser of arms in the world, Pakistan is second biggest and Bangladesh that signed a billion dollar deal with Russia in 2013, is 24th on the list of arms purchasers. Clearly, the global military industrial complex is shifting its interest to this region as wars in Europe have declined with the establishment of the European Union.

All the South Asian governments deal with insurgency with militarist methods and State nationalism. The priority of both the governments and insurgents is to establish control and power based on patriarchal discourses that are part of militarization.

Another major problem amongst South Asian States is of compliance and implementation. There is a disconnect between their position in international forums, policymaking and its implementation. This gap is even wider as far as international laws and conventions are concerned. States sign and accept many UN and Security Council Resolutions only to disregard them in practice. For example, most South Asian States have signed the International Convention of Civil and Political Rights (ICCPR). However, the national security laws of these States provide clear exceptions to the implementation of human rights.

The South Asian States resist the UN and international civil societies from probing, monitoring and make judgments on the security situations and internal conflicts. They see this as an intervention in their internal affairs and sovereignty. Thus, while they are all party to the R2P and 1325, the national implementation can at best be regarded as far from satisfactory, falling far short of what is expected from them. (e.g., post-conflict Sri Lanka resisted UN and other international pressure on IDPs and other post-conflict peace rebuilding.)

A major hurdle is in the manner in which governments in South Asia implement policies and resolutions such as 1325 and others. For example, there is token presence of women in select security bodies, but most institutions dealing with national security, peace-keeping and confidence building between warring groups, have few women in their leadership. India, Nepal and Afghanistan can show official records of women's participation and inclusion and, at the same time, independent reports from CSOs show the exclusion and marginalization of women. Thus, throughout South Asia, the number of women participating in institutions dealing with conflict and peace is low. There is a low level of financing of women programmes in post-conflict situations and an absence of mechanisms of either monitoring or taking actions on violations of 1325.

A weakness in South Asia is that the ideas of 1325 have not been diffused into civil society. There is an information deficit on SCR 1325+ since many grass roots organizations, social movements, civil society groups and women's groups have not sufficiently engaged with SCR 1325 even though they are aware that women should be included and have a role in political and economic processes. Political parties' women's groups have not directly taken up issues around SCR 1325, specifically, and their major focus is challenging national patriarchal structures. Civil society groups in India and South Asia have been taking up issues of peace, national security and foreign policy in specific.

Women's groups working on the grass roots level are often left out of the formal/State-organized peace processes. This grievance is expressed by, for example, the women's groups in India—in Manipur, Naga and Kashmiri women—and other women's groups in all of South Asia. For example, the Afghan Peace Jirga held in May 2010 did not give women the kind of space that was necessary. Women were only briefly engaged in the Sub-Committee on Gender in Sri Lanka during the ceasefire agreement in 2002 that ended soon after (Samuel 2010). The belief that issues concerned with security, peace, foreign policy and regional inter-state issues are purely the business of the State and exclusive clubs made up mostly of men and a token presence of women who are acceptable is being challenged by women's and civil society groups. South Asia has had several women who have represented their States as ambassadors and foreign secretaries, which is laudable, but women's movements have also shown that there is patriarchal and patronage politics in this selection.

The heavy presence of women in most of the South Asian conflicts (LTTE, Nepal Maoists, Indian Maoists and so on) and their roles are changing perceptions, which can be further changed. There is a critique from feminists that, often women in positions of government bureaucracy reflect their government/state/party and thus, extra-nationalist position on the peace process. Thus, for example, Lily Thapa from Nepal stated that during peace negotiations women were excluded from all peace committees (Canadian High Commission 2007). Similarly, Sri Lankan women have shown their exclusion from peace and post-conflict reconstruction. In India, there is an occasional, token representation, but the business of security and peace is seen as essentially that of the State and its 'boys'.

The crux is that, in South Asia, women are comparatively more visible in public spaces and institutions currently than ever before. Gender awareness is increasing as rhetoric about women's empowerment has gained currency. However, women are still very far from holding equal power in economic and social structures and political power is still male domain. At the same time the SAR also has strengths that provide the basis for a better implementation of 1325. We list these in the section below.

Some Positive Influences in South Asia

1. Women and peoples movements have a history of collective action. They have mobilized and participated in all actions of national liberation in all South Asia. There is a fairly strong and vibrant women's movement and women activists inside as well as outside political parties. CSOs and NGOs abound. All these can be used to make a peace coalition. There is also some level of peace movements, unions and others who are potential allies.

2. Women's roles in representative structures have increased in the last few years in many of the South Asian countries. This representation is from the highest bodies in parliaments to grass root local governance bodies. In India, Bangladesh, Pakistan, Nepal and Sri Lanka, women have been given representation through affirmative action at grass root level institutions; in India the 33 per cent reservation has now been raised to 50 per cent. Other countries have also increased the number of women. In Nepal 33 per cent women are part of the Constituent Assembly, though the Cabinet is dominated by men. In India, the Bill

for 33 per cent reservation for women in parliament has been resisted by the male dominated lower house–Lok Sabha.

3. Women are being appointed by governments in South Asia at higher levels of policymaking on issues of peace and security. Thus, India has a woman foreign secretary and other South Asian countries have women in important commissions.

4. Some level of gender sensitization has been introduced to security officers and peacekeepers, but it remains insufficient.

5. Rape as weapon of humiliation during conflict has decreased in comparison to earlier. A mixture of reasons can be attributed to this including: the participation of women in militancies in Nepal, Sri Lanka and Maoist insurgency areas in India. Other variables are a greater popular mobilization against rape, stricter rules in armed forces, and the impact of 1325 and other international law that make rape a war crime.

6. International institutions from those of the UN, UNIFEM and other multilateral institutions function well, have legitimacy and are engaged in the processes of peace and security.

7. Regional institutions such as those of South Asian Association for Regional Cooperation (SAARC) have been set up and are expanding, despite problems.

Strategies

Civil society actors have used the strategy termed as 'rhetorical entrapment', which translates to be a strategy of holding governments accountable to their own rhetoric, constitutional and civil rights commitments that shows up the contradictions between their statements, speeches in international forum and their practice of not making these into legally binding practices. Rhetorical entrapment pressurizes governments to put their words into actions (Risse 2000; Schimmelfenning 2001). This strategy can work if civil society becomes more aware of how SCR and UN Resolutions work.

Noeleen Heyzer rightly stated of 1325, that 'it has captured attention like few other Security Council Resolutions' and some even claim that it is the only Council resolution with an active global constituency monitoring implementation. Several governments have developed NAPs for implementation of resolution 1325, 21 and a handful of governments have altered their training modules for military personnel, especially those sent to peacekeeping missions. Some governments have altered their development aid packages to post-conflict countries, in keeping with 1325 (UN Women's Watch monitors this). We make some recommendations as part of the strategies that can make 1325 work.

It would be pertinent for South Asia to develop a civil society/grass roots/women's groups-based plan of making specific indicators for monitoring 1325 as suited to South Asian conditions. This would mean developing further from 1325+ to include indicators for militarization, the militarized political economy and gendered local conflicts. South Asian States are likely to take little or no interest in such indicators. It is women's groups that must take this initiative.

Experience has shown that civil society advocacy has been instrumental in the adoption, change and implementation of policies and practices. Lobbying by women's and social movements have led to changes in laws and practices to be more inclusive of women and deprived groups.

There should be a people's plan of action to implement the ideas and framework behind 1325. The pressure for gender equality and gendered human security as well as the responsibility of regimes to protect their citizens can only come through peoples/women's pressure and movements. People's plan can come by linking research, education and advocacy, with movements and policymakers.

This plan should be based on a methodology of demilitarization by transforming the dominant ideas of the militarized–patriarchy nexus and replace it with gendered human security paradigm. We have to have a notion of daily security practice and experience of the most excluded and effected women who struggle to sustain the family and their environment.

The role of research that deconstructs gender and masculinity norms and connects violence against women with power relations has been recognized, but needs to further increase. There is a need to deconstruct and reduce the negative aspects of masculinity and to include boys and men into programs aimed at reducing violence against women (Aolain 2009). The patriarchy inherent in international, regional and national institutions, needs to be uncovered and the masculinities in the structures, institutions and the actors need to be analysed and given a gender perspective. It would be worthwhile for feminist research to enquire into the meaning of masculinities and femininities and track the relation that power has to these at all these levels and what the consequences are of the intersections of masculinity, militarization and power.

The indicators suggested by the secretary general should be used for making a shadow public report. Women should be present in tribunals. South Asia is (in)famous for the impunity given to security personnel, even though there are complaints of torture, disappearances, sexual crimes and harassment, as the hundreds of reports from civil society and human rights groups show. Civil society, women's groups, human rights groups and others have been making a case for more accountability (for details, see the collection of Refworld—The Leader in Refugee Decision Support).[1] The proposals that there should be more women in judicial structures and civil institutions and bodies that deal with insurgencies should be implemented.

Research and advocacy must show the full nature of the order that produces armed conflict in South Asia. It must reveal how we meet the daily security needs of women. Women's groups must show how a gendered human security discourse and practice replace a militarist patriarchal one. For this, the questions raised by the women's movement provide a framework. These questions are: Who sets and defines the goals and objectives for policies and practices? Who implements these goals and objectives? Who monitors the progress and how often? Is there a participatory process that can change policies and implementation? Is there a social audit that measures policy and accounts for funding in programmes?

There has been much reference in international policy on security sector reforms, which conceptualizes a linkage between security personnel, professionalization and issues of development and governance. Security sector reforms are important in all of South Asia that is prone to violent resolution of conflict. The focus of SSR would be on democratizing it; having it under civilian control; increasing the number of women at all levels; and women being part of decision-making. 1325 mandate should be an integral part of security sector and police reforms, which are being proposed in several South Asian countries, such as India. Through training, accountability and reforms, we must make the police, military and paramilitary sensitive to the needs of women and their rights.

Similarly, politicians, bureaucracies and academic institutions need to be made aware 1325 since they are the ones that make policies and lead society.

Case studies of DDR show that these are integral aspects of peace processes in multiple conflict situations. Compromises are generally made by influential men. The women's movement should ensure that both SSR and DDR are done in keeping with 1325.

Women's groups should demand that women be part of daily security practices, work and policy in all State and formal institutions dealing with security and peace in disturbed areas and zones of conflicts, so that women are protected and are able to participate in peacekeeping and peace-building efforts. While closing the gender gap is important, it cannot in itself be expected to be a solution to conflict issues. Better gender balance among decision-making personnel, unless accompanied by a change in policy perspective/sociological/ ideological changes, might only displace the pacific characteristics of women by militarist ones, especially if militarism and nationalism are dominant ideologies.

In South Asia, women understand the need for peace, even as they have supported nationalist and sub-nationalist aspirations that form the basis of South Asian conflicts as we saw previously. For example, women in Sri Lanka have spoken out against the use of military force against the Tamil minority caught in the LTTE conflict, just as much as women have supported State military action. But women have been against gendered violence against women during conflict. Thus, women's opposition to sexual crimes and other aspects of 1325 and a call for protection from atrocities can become a common demand that women's groups work for and monitor their implementation.

In India, NGOs and CSOs working with women have been successful in bringing forth the impact of conflict on women in the Eleventh Plan document. This was also a result of extensive consultations and seminars with various groups over issues faced by women all around the country. However small this outcome (only a couple of passages were added but ultimately no steps were taken towards ensuring safety of women in conflict zones), it is clear that governments are not likely to follow up, so women's groups will have to make their alternate plans. Currently there are reversals and contestations where the GoI refers to these regions as 'disturbed situations' and does not see the relevance of 1325 in internal security.

Conclusion

Women's agency is essential to end conflict, victimhood and to bring gender equality and development, which has been the goal of the women's movement for decades. New concepts of security that challenge the narrow paradigms can come only when women and the excluded participate in the security discourse.

UNSCR 1325+ are major steps towards demilitarization and for safeguarding the rights of women and civilians in the face of gross atrocities wherein the former is based on explicit gender dimension and the later has some explicit reference, but addresses crimes against humanity. But this is not enough and there is need to move forward. 1325 calls for the agency of women and seeks to end the blindness about women in security discourses and practices, in conflict resolution and peace-building processes and calls an end to the gender imbalance in decision-making in all security related issues. This indicates that military expenditures be cut and public issues of health, education and justice be prioritized,

Women's groups have, thus, cautioned that the 1325 framework is the one that must be followed and focused on the protection of women and their inclusion in peace and security. It takes forward the human rights, human development and human security agenda that has been promoted by the UN and is backed by normative principles and supported by research grounded in women's and human rights philosophies. Feminists and human security and human development analysts, have joined with activists to push for policy changes. They can claim a moral victory for furthering normative theory and practice in international relations. Security Council Resolution 1325 on women, war and peace adds to the broadening and gendering of security. It is time to take this exercise further.

The key to 1325 lies in its implementation. It is clear that States will implement international laws better under the watch of women's and civil society groups. It is for this effective and peaceful resolution that creative strategies are necessary. The importance, necessities and outcomes of such strategies cannot be underestimated. They would in the least lead to the proper implementation of the two. This will give the necessary attention to women in armed conflict and post-conflict situations, from where they have historically been most excluded even though they are the most vulnerable central actors and victims. It will bring women and women's perspective into peace building, conflict mediation, resolution and management and will provide for a more lasting, just and inclusive peace.

Note

1. http://www.unhcr.org/refworld/country/4562d8cf2/IND.html (Accessed on 1 January 2015).

References

Annan, Kofi. 2000. 'We the Peoples: The Role of the United Nations in the 21st Century, Report of UN Secretary General. Available at: http://unpan1.un.org/intradoc/groups/public/documents/un/unpan000923.pdf (Accessed on 25 November 2010).

Aolain, Fionnula Ni. 2009. 'Women, Security, and Patriarchy of International Transitional Justice'. *Human Rights Quarterly*, 31 (4): 1055–75.

Boserup, Esther. 1970. *Women's Role in Economic Development*. London: Allen and Unwin.

Brownmiller, Susan. 1975. Against Our Will: Men, Women and Rape. New York: Simon & Schuster.

Canadian High Commission. 2007. "Report on Involving Men in the Implementation of UN Security Council Resolution 1325 on Women, Peace and Security," A Report based on a GAPS event of 13th March 2007, hosted by the Canadian High Commission at Canada House, UK. Available at: http://www.international-alert.org/pdf/GAPS_Men1325_report.pdf (Accessed on 28 November 2010).

Caprioli, Mary. 2000. 'Gendered Conflict'. *Journal of Peace Research*, 37 (1, January): 51–68.

Chandler, David. 2008a. 'Human Security: The Dog that Didn't Bark' (Review of Tadjbhaksh and Anuradha Chenoy, *Human Security: Concept and Implications*). *Security Dialogue*, 39 (4): 427–38.

———. 2008b. 'Human Security 11: Waiting for the Tail to Wag the Dog—A Rejoinder to Ambrosetti, Owen and Wibben'. *Security Dialogue*, 39 (4): 463–69.

Chenoy, Anuradha M. 1999. 'Militarization, Conflict and Women in South Asia'. In *Women and War Reader*, edited by Lois Ann Lorentzen and Jennifer E. Turpin, 101. New York, NY: New York University Press.

———. 2001. *Militarism and Women in South Asia*. New Delhi: Kali for Women.

———. 2008. *Women, War and Peace: Security Council Resolution 1325*. Available at: http://www.1000peacewomen.org/media/Broschueren/Booklet_Teil_1bis4.pdf (Accessed on 12 October 2010).

———. 2011. *Countering Militarization, Building Peace: The Intersectionality of SCR 1325 and the Responsibility to Protect*. New Delhi: WISCOMP.

Chodorow, Nancy. 1994. *Feminities Masculinities, Sexualities: Freud and Beyond.* The Lexington: University Press of Kentucky.

Cockburn, Cynthia. 1999. 'Gender, Armed Conflict and Political Violence'. Paper presented in The World Bank, Washington, DC, on 10–11 June 1999. Available at: http://www.genderandpeacekeeping.com/resources/3_Gender_Armed_Conflict_and_Political_Violence.pdf (Accessed on 25 November 2010).

———. 2001. 'The Gendered Dynamics of Armed Conflict and Political Violence'. In *Victims, Perpetrators, or Actors? Gender Armed Conflict, and Political Violence,* edited by Caroline O.N. Moser and Fiona C. Clarke, 13–29. New York: Zed Books.

———. 2010. 'Gender Relation as Causal in Militarization and War'. *International Feminist Journal of Politics,* 12 (2): 139–57.

Cohn, Carol. 1987. "Sex and Death in the Rational World of Defense Intellectuals," *Signs,* 12 (4): 687–718.

———. 2004. 'Feminist Peacemaking'. *The Women's Review of Books,* 21 (5): 8–9.

Connell, R.W. 1987. *Gender and Power: Society, the Person and Sexual Politics.* Stanford, CA: Stanford University Press.

Coomaraswamy, Radhika. 2002. 'Are Women's Rights Universal? Re-engaging the Local'. *Meridians,* 3 (1): 6.

Durham, Helen. 2002. 'Women, Armed Conflict and International Law'. *International Review of the Red Cross,* 847: 655–59. Available at: http://www.cicr.org/eng/assets/files/other/irrc_847_durham.pdf (Accessed on 20 October 2010).

Elshtain, Jean Bethke. 1987. *Women and War.* New York, NY: Basic Books.

Enloe, Cynthia. 1983. *Does Khaki Become You? The Militarization of Women's Life.* London: Pluto Press Ltd, 9–10.

———. 1989. *Bananas Beaches and Bases: Making Feminist Sense of International Politics.* Berkeley: University of California Press.

———. 2000. *Maneuvres: The International Politics of Militarizing Women's Lives.* Berkeley: University of California Press.

Galtung, Johan. 1990, August. 'Cultural Violence'. *Journal of Peace Research,* 27 (3): 291–305.

GAPS (Gender Action for Peace and Security). 2007. 'Report on Involving Men in the Implementation of UN Security Council Resolution 1325 on Women, Peace and Security'. A Report based on a GAPS event of 13 March 2007, hosted by Canadian High Commission at Canada House, UK. Available at: http://www.international-alert.org/pdf/GAPS_Men1325_report.pdf (Accessed on 28 November 2010).

Ghosh, Jayati. 2009. *Never Done and Poorly Paid.* New Delhi: Women Unlimited.

Heyzer, Noeleen. 2004. 'Women, War and Peace: Mobilizing for Peace and Security in the 21st Century', Dag Hammarskjöld Lecture presented at Dag Hammarskjöld Foundation, Uppsala, Sweden, 22 September 2004. Available at: http://www.unifem.org/news_events/story_detail.php?StoryID=173 (Accessed on 26 November 2010).

Hill, Felicity. 2005. 'How and When Has Security Council Resolution 1325 (2000) on Women, Peace and Security Impacted Negotiations Outside the Security Council?'. Master Thesis: Uppsala University Program of International Studies, 2004–05. Available at: http://www.un1325.de/data/felicity-hill-thesis.pdf (Accessed on 24 November 2010).

Hudson, Valerie M., Mary Caprioli, Bonnie Ballif-Spanvill, et al. 2008/09. 'The Heart of the Matter: The Security of Women and the Security of States'. *International Security*, 33 (3, Winter): 7–45.

Hunt, Swanee and Cristina Posa. 2001. 'Women Waging Peace'. *Foreign Policy*, No. 124 (May–June): 38–47. Available at: http://www.huntalternatives.org/ download/170_fparticle_women_wagin_peace_inclusive_security.pdf (Accessed on 24 October 2010).

ICTJ (International Center for Transitional Justice). *Gender Justice*. Available at: http://www.ictj.org/en/tj/786.html (Accessed on 27 November 2010).

————. 2010. *Transitional Justice and Female Ex-Combatants: Lessons Learned from International Experience*. Available at: http://www.ictj.org/en/research/projects/ ddr/thematic-studies/3501.html (Accessed on 28 April 2011).

Keating, Tom and W. Andy Knight, eds. 2004. *Building Sustainable Peace*. Tokyo: United Nations University Press, 119.

Keck, Margaret E. and Kathryn Sikkink. 1998. *Activists Beyond Borders*. Ithaca, NY/ London: Cornell University Press.

Lindsey, Charlotte. 2001. *Women Facing War*. Geneva: International Committee of the Red Cross.

MacKinnon, Catherine. 1989. *Towards a Feminist Theory of the State*. Cambridge, MA: Harvard University Press.

Nussbaum, Martha C. and Johnathan Glover, (eds.) 1995. *Women, Culture and Development: A Study of Human Capabilities*. Oxford: Clarendon.

Owen, Taylor. 2008. 'The Critique That Doesn't Bite: A Response to David Chandler's The Dog that Didn't Bark' (Review of Tadjbhaksh and Anuradha Chenoy, *Human Security: Concept and Implications*). *Security Dialogue*, 39 (4): 445–53.

Pateman, Carol. 1998. *The Sexual Contract*. Oxford: Basil Blackwell.

Peterson, Spike V. 1999. 'Gendered Nationalism: Reproducing "Us" versus "Them"'. In *Women and War Reader*, edited by Lois Ann Lorentzen and Jennifer E. Turpin, 41–49. New York: New York University Press.

Reardon, Betty A. 1985. *Sexism and the War System*. New York: Teachers College Press.

Risse, Thomas. 2000. 'Let's Argue!: Communicative Action in World Politics'. *International Organization*, 54 (1): 1–39.

Rothschild, Emma. 1995. 'What is Security?'. *Daedalus*, 124 (3, Summer): 53–98.

Ruddick, Sara. 1983. 'Pacifying the Forces: Drafting Women in the Interests of Peace'. *Signs*, 8 (3, Spring): 471–89.

Samuel, Kumudini. 2010. *The Centrality of Gender in Securing Peace: The Case of Sri Lanka*. WISCOMP Monograph. New Delhi: Rupa and Company.

Schimmelfenning, Frank. 2001. 'The Community Trap: Liberal Norms, Rhetorical Action, and the Eastern Enlargement of the European Union'. *International Organization*, 55 (1): 48.

Steans, Jill. 1998. *Gender and International Relations: An Introduction*. Piscataway, NJ: Rutgers University Press.

Sylvester, Christine. 1994. *Feminist Theory and International Relations in a Postmodern Era*. New York: Cambridge University Press.

Tadjbhaksh, Shahrbanou and Anuradha M. Chenoy. 2007. *Human Security, Concept and Principle*. London: Routledge.

Tickner, Ann. 2002. 'Feminist Theory and Gender Studies: Reflections for the Millennium'. In *Critical Perspectives in International Studies: Millennial Reflections on International Studies*, edited by Frank P. Harvey and Michael Brecher, 193. Ann Arbor, MI: University of Michigan Press.

Tickner, Anne. 1993. *Gender in International Relations: Feminist Perspectives on Achieving Global Security*. New York: Columbia University Press.

———. 2005, March. 'What is our Research Programme? Some Feminist Answers to International Relations Methodological Questions'. *International Studies Quarterly*, 49 (1): 1–21.

United Nations. 2006. 'No Policy for Progress More Effective than Empowerment of women, Secretary-General says in Remarks to Women's Day Observance'. Document Secretary-General Nos. SG/SM/10370 OBV/543 WOM/1549. Available at: http://www.un.org/News/Press/docs/2006/sgsm10370.doc.htm (Accessed on 22 March 2010).

———. 2008. Available at: http://www.peacewomen.org/themes_theme. php?id=18&subtheme=true (Accessed on 5 July 2016).

UNDP (United Nations Development Programme). 2010. *Human Development Report*. Palgrave Macmillan: New York.

UNDPKO (United Nations Department of Peacekeeping Operations). 2004. 'Human Trafficking and United Nations Peacekeeping'. DPKO Policy Paper. Available at: http://www.un.org/womenwatch/news/documents/ DPKOHumanTraffickingPolicy03-2004.pdf (Accessed on 20 November 2010).

UNDPKO/DFS (United Nations, Department of Peacekeeping Operations and Department of Field Support). 2010. *Integrating a Gender Perspective into the Work of the United Nations Military in Peacekeeping Operations*. Available at: http://www.un.org/en/peacekeeping/documents/dpko_dfs_gender_military_ perspective.pdf (Accessed on 26 November 2010).

United Nations Department of Public Information, News and Media Division. 2006, 8 March. 'UN Secretary-General Kofi Annan says in Remarks to Women's Day Observance, "No Policy for Progress More Effective Than Empowerment of Women'. Document Secretary-General Nos. SG/SM/10370, OBV/543, WOM/1549. Available at: http://www.un.org/News/Press/docs/2006/sgsm10370. doc.htm (Accessed on 26 November 2010).

UNIFEM (United Nations Development Fund for Women). *Funding and Budgeting*. Available at: http://www.unifem.org/gender_issues/women_war_peace/funding_ budgeting.php (Accessed on 26 November 2010).

United Nations Security Council. 2010, 28 September. *Women and Peace and Security*. Report of the Secretary-General, Document No. S/2010/498. Available at: http://www.securitycouncilreport.org/atf/cf/%7B65BFCF9B-6D27-4E9C-8CD3-CF6E4FF96FF9%7D/WPS%20S%202010%20498.pdf (Accessed on 28 November 2010).

Valasek, Kristin. 2006. 'Securing Equality, Engendering Peace: A Guide to Policy and Planning on Women, Peace and Security (UNSCR 1325)'. United Nations

International Research and Training Institute for the Advancement of Women (INSTRAW), 1. Available at: http://www.iknowpolitics.org/files/GPS-1325Guide_UN%20INSTRAW.pdf (Accessed on 21 November 2010).

Whitworth, Sandra. 2006. *Men, Militarism and UN Peacekeeping: A Gendered Analysis*. New Delhi: VIVA Books Pvt. Limited.

Wibben, Annick T.R. 2008. 'Human Security: Towards an Opening'. *Security Dialogue*, 39 (4): 455–62.

Zarkov, Dubravka and Cynthia Cockburn, eds. 2002. *The Postwar Moment: Militaries, Masculinities, and International Peacekeeping*. London: Lawrence & Wishart.

Web Resources

For a comprehensive list of all UN documents, treaties and resolutions that contain references to women, peace and security from the UN Charter onwards see, http://www.peacewomen.org/themes_theme.php?id=18&subtheme=true, accessed on 21 November 2010.

For member States' responses on the implementation of Security Council resolution 1325, see Division for the Advancement of Women, Department of Economic and Social Affairs website - http://www.un.org/womenwatch/osagi/responses1325.htm, accessed on 25 November 2010.

For online training course on 'Gender and Peacekeeping', jointly developed by Canada and the UK, see, http://www.genderandpeacekeeping.org/, accessed on 24 November 2010.

The NGO Working Group on Women, Peace and Security has issued these reports which can be found at: http://www.peacewomen.org./, accessed on 20 November 2010.

Thematic News of peacewomen.org on Disarmament, 'Small Arms and Light Weapons', available at: http://www.peacewomen.org/themes_theme.php?id=34&subtheme=true, accessed on 24 November 2010.

5

Security Laws in India with Special Reference to AFSPA: A Gendered Perspective

Amrita Patel

Conflict and Gender

A peaceful world can only be built with equal involvement of women along with men in all aspects of society. However, while conflict is recognized as an inevitable political process in a modern complex social structure, women have been found to be both agents and victims in conflict. Thus, it becomes important to problematize their role and to see how they are recruited and deployed as either the agents of the State or its rebels and become harbingers of violence and/or peace. Additionally, it is also essential to investigate the root causes of vulnerabilities confronted by these women caught up in conflict and try to privilege their own voices. Unless women's security issues are addressed, the political agenda for peace cannot be sustainable.

With this understanding, it is important to analyse and recognize the issues of conflict prevention, resolution and peace building from a gender perspective. It is also pertinent to understand and assess various perspectives existing in the field of security studies and the feminist stand on the role of modern state as an important institution in projecting women's cause in society. Women's security, their participation in peace processes, promotion of their human rights and their protection in war and peace are the broad issues.

Conflict, Security and Peace-building Process: A Gendered Perspective

The role of the State in moments of conflict is at the centre of the conventional agenda of security studies. However, a conscious attempt has been made here to remove that centre and bring discourses on women's role in conflict situations to replace it in this discussion. This paradigm shift gives this discourse the status of non-traditional security studies which argue that the security agenda should also include hunger, disease, threat to people's empowerment and natural disasters and, in retrospect, gives security a human face (*Women, Peace and Security* 2010, 34). This non-traditional theory also is based on the assertion made by Asha Hans and Betty Reardon, which suggests that human security derives from the experience and expectation of wellbeing of persons, communities and the planet which sustains those (Hans and Reardon 2010, p. 2). Human wellbeing is dependent on four major conditions for the maintenance and continuation of human life: 'a life sustaining environment; the meeting of essential physical needs; respect for the identity and dignity of persons and groups; and protection from avoidable harm and expectation of remedy for unavoidable harm'. In other words, the discourse aims to move beyond a narrow military or State-centric preoccupation and articulates the concerns of women whose voices are marginalized in the mega narratives of conflict analysis and peace-building.

Situating this theoretical stand in the Indian context, it may be pointed out that the militarization of Indian border lands has taken up security issues in a strictly traditional sense by grossly confusing military security with human security. Despite being the largest democracy of the world, the subcontinent is guilty of dehumanizing security issues in the name of protecting the borders and its adverse impact is severely felt by the women of the land.

Contradicting the view that 'democracies are inherently peaceful,' made by political philosopher Kant, Paula Banerjee remarks that the Indian experiment in democratic State formations has neither led to social justice for all nor has it facilitated conditions of peace (Banerjee 2010, 137). In fact, it has shown that in a multi-ethnic and multi-cultural State, democracy may lead to the reinforcement of traditional cleavages based on religion, language, ethnicity, caste and gender and transform them into newer inequities. In such a situation, there is a continuous effort to create a homogenized identity of citizenship that supports the central role of the ruling elite. Such an identity is forged through the State's privileging of majoritarian, male and monolithic cultural values.

Within this framework, the role of the democratic state in representing women's concern, especially during armed conflict, may legitimately be questioned. Women form nearly half the world's population and have achieved political citizenship in most of the societies. Yet, their status and position have remained marginal within the social, economic and political spheres. As State has been understood to be integral in providing security in a modern complex structure, it becomes important to analyse its role in reflecting women's concerns in this context. Using the lens of gender and drawing on experiences of women, feminist scholars have uncovered the patriarchal underpinnings of the security discourses that dominate international politics (Basu 2010, 290). Women's insecurities in armed conflict emerge primarily from the duel forces of patriarchy and militarization, and the violence against women and human relations that they respectively denote. Sexual violence in conflict situations is a historical experience across cultural and geographical specifications.

In India, the arbitrary application of security laws in the disturbed political areas (which includes Jammu and Kashmir, the North Eastern Region and Naxal-affected tribal belts of India) have been observed by the development activists and intellectuals as strongly biased against the human rights issues. Heavily loaded with state-centric and patriarchal ideologies, these laws have been seen to be adversely impacting the lives of the vulnerable. Women's rights violation may be picked up as a grave social concern in this regard and despite sporadic activism shown by the brave women, the movement has to go a long way to achieve its destination.

Security Laws

Security laws can be broadly categorized into three (Basu n.d., 3): First, special national laws that apply in non-emergency situations; second, area-specific central laws in select areas to deal with insurgencies and militancy and third, special laws enacted by State governments to deal with public order and organized crime.

Examples of the first category are preventive detention laws aimed towards preventing an individual from acting in a manner prejudicial to the defence or security of the country such as the Unlawful Activities (Prevention) Act.

Armed Forces Special Powers Act (AFSPA), 1958 is an example of the second type.

Some examples of the special laws enacted by state governments to deal with public order and organized crime are the Chhattisgarh Special Public Security Act, 2005, the Jammu and Kashmir Public Safety Act, 1978 or the Maharashtra Control of Organized Crimes Act, 1999.

Thus, during the period of evolution of India as an independent country as well as a democracy, there have been security laws enacted, implemented and enforced at different points in time for the whole country or for specific geographical area by the Central or the state government.

Pre-independence Period

1. **Government of India Act 1935:** This empowered the State to detain a person preventively for reasons of defence, external affairs or in the discharge of functions of the Crown in its relations with the Indian states.

2. **Defence of India Bill 1939:** This Bill was for maintenance of order, control of meetings and control over press. This Bill was primarily to control the swadeshi[1] movement. The Bill had special measures to ensure the public safety and interest and the defence of British India. It continued beyond its original tenure of six months. The Bill could control space and people's mobility to maintain order.

3. **Armed Forces (Special Powers) Ordinance 1942:** Armed Forces (Special Powers) Ordinance appeared at a crucial phase in India's freedom struggle in the year 1942. Viceroy Lord Linlithgow declared emergency all over British India and promulgated the Armed Forces (Special Powers) Ordinance, 1942 on 15 August 1942 conferring vaguely defined special

powers to the armed forces to arrest and use force (even kill) civilians on mere suspicion. The act was applied to the whole country.

Post-independence Period

The newly independent India too saw many security laws. After attaining independence, the violence witnessed during partition forced the Government of India (GoI) to pass the Punjab Disturbed Areas Act, Bihar Maintenance of Public Order Act, Bombay Public Safety Act and Madras Suppression of Disturbance Act, aimed at curbing forces that were using religion to incite violence. The rise of the Naxalites (left-wing extremist) movement prompted the West Bengal government to pass the West Bengal (Prevention of Violent Activities) Act of 1970.

Subsequently, there have been a number of legislations enacted to tackle various specific contingencies related to an area such as Jammu and Kashmir, Punjab or in general national security.[2]

The history of post-Independent India is replete with ordinances and acts which have seriously affected the civil and democratic rights of the Indian people. While most of these legislations were enacted with a view to deal with specific issues, their actual implementation has directly affected the rights of trade unionists, voluntary activists and dissidents as well as the poor and the landless, the dalits[3] and the tribals struggling for their basic rights (PUCL 1985, 3).

The Indian Constitution vide its Article 355 envisages the methodology on how to control internal and external disturbances. Specifically, Article 355 stipulates that the duty of the Union is to protect the states against external aggression and internal disturbance and to ensure that the government of every state is carried on in accordance with the provisions of this Constitution. This article has, however, never been used and the Sarkaria Commission[4] did not suggest any change in it. The Commission's recommendation on its use was that it is entirely for the Union to decide, *suo motu*, whether the situation in a State calls for deployment of the Central forces, though 'it is desirable to consult the State concerned, whenever feasible, before deploying its armed forces, otherwise than at the request of the State' (*Hindu* 2002).

Whether it be the security laws and the right to deploy forces to control internal disturbances, the situation is paradoxical. Paula Banerjee argues that an interesting situation arose where the Indian Constitution while giving extensive rights to the people also made provisions to constitutionally abrogate these same rights. Democracy not only coexists with violence but also legitimizes it (Banerjee 2010, 200).

Thus, on a look at the whole gamut of the security laws that are in place in the country today, it is observed that while on one hand there has been redundancy of many of the laws, on the other hand, there has been wide spread misuse and human rights violations, particularly with regard to women. The details of some of the laws since independence will validate the above.

1. **Madras Suppression of Disturbances Act (1948):** One of the first acts of independent India was the Madras Suppression of Disturbances Act (1948) that authorized the use of military violence against the peasants in Telengana. The peasant struggle in Telengana which began in 1946 was against forced labour, illegal exactions, evictions by feudal landlords and oppression by village Patels, among other things, and later developed into an agrarian liberation struggle to get rid of feudal landlordism and the Nizam's dynastic rule in the state.[5]

2. **Preventive Detention Act (PDA) 1950:** This was brought into force within weeks of adopting the Constitution. PDA authorized detention up to 12 months to prevent a person from acting in a manner prejudicial to the defence or security of India, India's relation with foreign powers, state security or maintenance of public order, or maintenance of essential supplies and services. This law lapsed in 1969 but the later years saw many such laws with similar objectives.

3. **Unlawful Activities (Prevention) Act (UAPA) 1967:** Applicable for the whole of the country, this law accords the Central government the power to declare 'any association that engages in activities that support any secession claims' or 'disclaims, questions, disrupts' the sovereignty and territorial integrity of India or causes disaffection against India. Once an association is declared unlawful, the Central government has broad powers to restrict its activities and criminalize individual involvement with such associations. This law was amended twice—in 2004 and

2008—to include counterterrorism provisions, some of which were contained in previous anti-terror laws, namely, the Terrorist and Disruptive Activities Act (TADA), 1987 and the Prevention of Terrorism Act (POTA), 2002.

Supporting claims of secession, questioning territorial integrity and causing or intending to cause disaffection against India fall within the ambit of 'unlawful activity' (Section 2(o) UAPA).[6] Section 13[7] punishes unlawful activity with imprisonment extending to seven years and a fine.[8]

Closely following the repeal of the POTA, the UAPA was amended in 2004 to bring back a number of provisions from the POTA. The UAPA was further amended in 2008 in the aftermath of the 26/11 terror attacks in Mumbai. Some of the salient features of the UAPA post-2008 are that the Central government has power to designate 'terrorist organizations' and criminalize membership or any form of association with such organizations.

4. **Maintenance of Internal Security Act (MISA):** This was a controversial law passed by the Indian parliament in 1973 giving the administration of Prime Minister Indira Gandhi and Indian law enforcement agencies super powers—indefinite 'preventive' detention of individuals, search and seizure of property without warrants, wiretapping and so on in the quelling of civil and political disorder in India, as well as countering foreign inspired sabotage, terrorism, subterfuge and threats to national security. The legislation gained infamy for its disregard of legal and constitutional safeguards of civil rights, during the period of national emergency (1975–77) as thousands of innocent people were believed to have been arbitrarily arrested, tortured and in some cases, forcibly sterilized. MISA was subsequently repealed in 1977.

5. **National Security Act 1980:** This continues to be in force today, retains some of the PDA and MISA provisions and allows preventive detention for a maximum period of one year. Similar to the PDA, this law empowers the Central or the state government to detain a person to prevent him from acting in any manner that is prejudicial, inter alia, to the defence of India or its relation with foreign powers, to the security of the state, or

to maintenance of public order or the maintenance of supplies and services essential to the community. At the time of its enactment it was stated that 'these powers were needed to deal with black marketeers and smugglers and that the question of its use to curb political action did not arise,' however, practice revealed otherwise. In its very first year 'who's who of political activists and trade unionists', while not a single big smuggler or black marketer was caught (PUCL 1980).

Terrorist Laws

Terrorist and Disruptive Activities Prevention Act (TADA) 1987

Enacted shortly after the then Prime Minister Indira Gandhi's assassination in 1985, the TADA was specifically aimed at penalizing 'terrorist acts'. This law granted broad ranging powers to law enforcement agencies that went well beyond those prescribed under the Code of Criminal Procedure (CrPC) and the Indian Evidence Act (IEA). For example, confessions of detainees in police custody was made admissible as evidence in legal proceedings—a practice that is expressly prohibited under the IEA.

Another harmful feature of the bill is that the definition of 'disruptive activity' is so wide as to include a mere expression of opinion, not accompanied by any violence or incitement to violence. Any Sikh who says that he agrees with the Anandpur Saheb Resolution, any Muslim who says that there should be a plebiscite in Jammu and Kashmir, any Naga or Mizo or Manipuri who says that the people of his or her state should have the right to self-determination, is guilty of 'disruptive activity' and can be punished by a sentence which may extend to imprisonment for life and shall not be less than imprisonment for a term of three years (PUCL 1985, 7).

By the end of 1992, 67,000 had been arrested under the TADA, of which 8,000 were put on trial and only 275 were convicted. Also, religious minorities were selectively targeted under the TADA. For instance, in Rajasthan, of the 115 TADA detainees, 112 were Muslim and three were Sikhs. The misuse of TADA was reported from states that did not have a history of terrorism, for instance, 19,000 persons were arrested in Gujarat by 1993—a state that had no history of terrorism. These figures demonstrate that TADA was used more as a preventive detention law and tool of misuse by the police rather than an effective counterterrorism strategy.

Although the Supreme Court upheld the validity of TADA, it was allowed to lapse in 1995 pursuant to political pressure.

Prevention of Terrorism Act (POTA) 2002

Following an attack on the Indian parliament in December 2001, the POTA was brought into force in 2002. Critiqued by some as being more draconian than the TADA, the POTA included provisions on criminal liability for mere association with suspected terrorists without possession of criminal intent. Similar to the TADA, the POTA allowed for pre-trial police detention (for up to 180 days) and the setting up of special courts for trials. The enforcement outcomes of this law were also strikingly similar to that of TADA, hence, many of the arrests under the POTA were conducted in states that had had no prior history of terrorism. It was applied discriminatorily against religious minorities, dalit and tribal groups and used as a tool to harass political opponents. Again, as with the TADA, although the Supreme Court upheld its constitutionality in People's Union for Civil Liberties (PUCL) versus Union of India, it was repealed in 2004 following public and political pressure.

Even though these have been repealed, both the TADA and POTA continue to apply to individuals. Cases already instituted under the TADA continue despite its repeal and the state and the Central governments retain the power to institute new cases under the TADA on allegations based in periods that the law was still in effect.[9]

Jammu and Kashmir Public Safety Act (JKPSA) 1978

The JKSPA empowers the state to restrict movement to certain areas by declaring it to be a 'prohibited place' or a 'protected area' and to maintain communal and regional harmony by prohibiting the circulation of documents considered prejudicial and detaining persons to prevent them from acting in a manner that is prejudicial to the 'security of the state' or 'the maintenance of public order'. Under these broad powers, a person may be detained without trial for up to two years.

A 2011 Amnesty International report has found that state officials often implement this law in an arbitrary and abusive manner and even if detainees approach the High Court to quash detention orders 'J&K authorities consistently thwart the High Court's orders for release by re-detaining individuals under criminal charges and/or issuing further detention orders, thereby securing their continued incarceration'. As a result, the scale of detentions remain indisputably high estimated at 8,000 to 20,000 over the past two decades (Basu n.d., 16).

Chhattisgarh Special Public Safety Act (CSPSA) 2006

The CSPSA was enacted to counter Naxal violence in the state.[10] This law defines 'unlawful activities' to include acts that pose or have a tendency to pose danger to public order, peace or to the administration of law. Encouragement to disobedience of established law is also included in the definition of 'unlawful activities'. Any organization or person who commits or abets or tries to commit or even plans to commit an 'unlawful activity' may be imprisoned for up to seven years.

This law also empowers the state government to declare an organization as being unlawful, criminalize membership thereof and notify a place as being used for the purpose of unlawful activities. There is limited scope for review and appeal against notification of places under this law.

Overall, it is felt that the plethora of security laws and its enactment has caused more harm than good. The situations and circumstances when these laws are adopted and enacted are elaborated in the concept of extraordinary laws. The characteristics of the extraordinary laws are as follows (Mohanty et al. 2011, 61):

1. These laws are brought to address specific problems of extraordinary nature (as claimed).

2. Thus, these laws are expected to be temporary and their lives to be *co terminus* with the extraordinary events that they intend to overturn.
3. The laws consist of extraordinary provisions. Make exceptions to provisions pertaining to arrest, detention, bail, investigation, evidence and punishment.
4. These extraordinary laws bring in a parallel system of investigation, trial and given enhanced punishment for offences (to make them as deterrent). These give extraordinary powers to the executive, the police, the special cell and the army and a parallel system of courts.

One such extraordinary law is the AFSPA which provides total legal immunity to officers of the armed forces in the disturbed area. The conditions as to where and why an area is to be declared as disturbed rests with the administration.

Armed Force Special Powers Act (AFSPA)

Genesis

The present AFSPA has its origin in the Armed Forces (Special Powers) Ordinance of 1942. The Act was introduced in the monsoon session of the parliament in 1958 to replace the ordinance[11] by Govind Ballabh Pant, the then Union Home Minister who remarked:

> This is a very simple measure. It only seeks to protect the steps the armed forces might have to take in the disturbed areas.... It will be applied only to such parts as have been declared by the administrations concerned as being disturbed.... After such a declaration has been made, then alone the provisions of this Bill will be applicable to that particular area.

Some members of parliament (MPs) opposed it on the ground that blanket powers being conferred on the army by this act would lead to the violation of the fundamental rights of the people. Two MPs from Manipur—R. Suisa and Laishram Achaw Singh—vehemently opposed it. Laishram Achaw Singh, while objecting to the Armed Force Special Powers Bill, had remarked,

How can we imagine that these military officers should be allowed to shoot to kill and without warrant arrest and search? This is a lawless law. There are various provisions in the Indian Penal Code and in the Criminal Procedure Code and they can easily deal with the law and order situation in these parts.

MP Surendra Mohanty from Dhenkanal, Orissa, had said that the provisions of the Act came under emergency conditions which could only be given by the President of India and that if states were to be given that power it would be unconstitutional. He, in fact, also said that 'this Parliament is giving approval to a legal monstrosity to quell another kind of monstrosity' (Haksar and Hongray 2011, p. 269).

Unfortunately, these remained largely unheard and the Act was passed (Hashmi n.d.). It was known as the Armed Forces (Assam, Manipur) Special Powers Act, 1958.

Purview

AFSPA was meant for only the Naga hills and parts of Manipur and was to be in force for one year.[12] Specifically, the Act was amended in 1972 to cover the states of Assam, Manipur, Meghalaya, Nagaland and Tripura[13] and the two Union Territories (UTs) of Arunachal Pradesh and Mizoram.[14] Section 3 was amended to give power to declare any area as disturbed to the Central government. Thus, the picture presented was that the disturbances was no longer confined to Nagaland and Manipur but had spread to the whole of North East (NE).

Originally the Act was a short-term measure to allow deployment of the army to counter an armed separatist movement in the Naga hills. But the reality is that it has been in place for the last five decades and has been extended to all the states of NE.

The states of Punjab (in 1983)[15] and Jammu and Kashmir (in 1990 under a notification of the Kashmir Criminal Procedure Code) are also covered under the Act (Haksar and Hongray 2011, 91).

This is one of the first instances wherein the Indian army has been deployed to contain and control, and manage an internal conflict.[16]

Today the AFSPA is in full force in the states of NE and the state of Jammu and Kashmir.

Provisions

The AFSPA allows the government to define, at its discretion (the Act's language is deliberately vague) and without judicial review, an area as 'disturbed' and empowers the armed forces to shoot to kill, conduct warrantless searches and arrests, arbitrarily detain people and demolish structures in order to 'maintain...public order'.

Under this Act, all security forces are given unrestricted and unaccounted power to carry out their operations once an area is declared disturbed. AFSPA gives the armed forces wide power to shoot, arrest and search, all in the name of 'aiding civil power'.

Armed forces enjoy de jure and de facto impunity under the AFSPA. Section 7 of the AFSPA provides that no prosecution, suit or other legal proceedings shall be instituted against a member of the security forces except with the previous sanction of the Central government. This *de jure* impunity to the armed forces has allowed most to escape any legal accountability. The extraordinary powers given to the armed forces allows even a non-commissioned officer to fire upon or otherwise use force, even leading to death of any person who is acting in contravention of any law, or is in possession of deadly weapons or against an assembly of five persons or more; arrest without a warrant and with the use of necessary force arrest anyone who has committed certain offences or is suspected of having committed offences; or enter and search any premises in order to make such arrests (CSCOHRM 2012, 3).

The power that the state has in declaring a particular area as disturbed is amply exhibited in the case of Mizoram when in March 1966 the Government of Assam declared the Mizo area as disturbed. The activities of the Mizo National Front were considered to be prejudicial to the security of the Mizo district in Assam and the adjoining areas (Nag 2012, 2). Earlier the Nagaland Security Regulation 1962 was also passed, in addition to the AFSPA. However, it is to be noted that this Act which is imposed on 'disturbed areas' are largely the border states.

The expenditure towards policing, anti-insurgency activities consumes the state and national exchequer. For example, the state of Manipur spends 70 paisa per rupee on administrative expenses out of which 70 per cent is towards police sector. The Ministry of Home Affairs (MHA) sponsors schemes for modernization of police forces in the NE. All counter-insurgency expenses incurred by the NE states in the last 20 years are reimbursed by the Centre. The chief minister of Manipur had given a requisition of ₹1,040 million as reimbursement for counter insurgency activities (Gangte 2011, 29).

Violations Including Sexual Abuse

AFSPA has become a subject of wide debate by many human rights organizations including Amnesty International, Human Rights Watch and even the UN to review the constitutional validity of this Act, which is termed by them as a dated and colonial era law that breaches contemporary international human rights standards.

The Act is only a symptom of a larger malaise—that of alienation, militarization (Hayes 2012, 10)[17] and a flawed counter-insurgency strategy practiced in the region (Goswami 2010, 1). The fallout has not merely been a brutalization of the security forces, but a legitimization of violence. This has resulted in the internalization throughout the NE of what Capt. (retired) Ashok K. Tipnis, in his memorandum submitted to the Committee to Review the Armed Forces (Special Powers) Act, 1958 (2005) has termed as the 'Freedom (to) Assume Special Powers (with) Arms (FASPA)'.

The act is a classic example of how the democratic system (elected representatives) legitimize violence on the people that it considers as errant.

Evidence of militarization of a society is manifested in Manipur, the smallest and most militarized state in NE which has more than 60,000 military and security personnel and more than 300 security checkpoints (Hayes 2012, 10). Dozens of rebel groups control small different areas. State-sponsored Village Defence Forces (VDFs) are being established and more and more households own a weapon.

Thousands of people are estimated to have been killed in the last three decades by the armed forces and other law enforcement officials. In Manipur nearly 400 people are shot dead each year, leaving behind old mothers, young widows and children, with no means of survival (Nepram 2009). With the inception of the Act, 'state terrorism' has been unleashed on the people of NE (*Morung Express* 2008, 1).

In conflict situations and due to the use of draconian laws, women suffer the most. They are assaulted, humiliated, raped and murdered during conflicts, which are not of their making (PTI 2010).

The violence faced by women takes the form of sexual, mental or physical abuse, killings and clashes. Although all the members of communities are affected by the armed conflict, the impact on women and girls is far greater because of their status in society and their sex.

Thus, in the NE the armed forces have frequently been accused of using sexual violence as a tactic for fighting their wars, accusations they have often blatantly brushed aside. Women have faced violence by the security forces, including rape, death in custody and disappearances (Making Woman Count for Peace 2012).

The mass rape at Kolashib (Mizoram) in 1966 has been well documented. It has been recorded how the Assam police would come and commit rapes and even the mentally ill women would not be spared (Nag 2012, 11). During Operation Bluebird in Manipur, the details of the atrocities committed on women and girls by the armed forces had been a part of the writ petition of Naga People's Movement for Human Rights (NPMHR) in 1987. The petitions had specific prayers on compensation besides other prayers. It was perhaps the first time that compensation would be given to so many victims and their families. The first medical study on torture in India was the report titled 'Post Torture State of Mental Health: A Report of a Medical Study on the Delayed Effects of Torture on Nagas in Manipur' which was based on findings of 104 victims of torture in a health camp organized in 1989 in Purul. The report brought to the fore the effects of torture and the post-traumatic stress disorder (Haksar and Hongray 2011, 291).

In the Naga area, the atrocities committed by the security forces and army are documented by the Naga Women's Union Manipur (NWUM).[18] In remote villages, the Indian security forces have perpetuated sexual violence. The Naga women negotiate with local commanding officers to secure the release of family members. They advocate the removal of army posts as these generate terror in the community. There are evidences of Naga women physically preventing the security personnel from arresting and torturing, and, in extreme cases, executing the locals (Manchanda 2005, 15).

According to the memorandum of Civil Society Coalition on Human Rights in Manipur (CSCOHRM) submitted, a total of 1,528 cases of extrajudicial executions have occurred in Manipur since 1979 till May 2012, out of which 31 are women victims directly, 1,399 are men (thus, making 1399 women widows) and 98 are children. Of these, 419 were killed by Assam Rifle while 481 were killed by the combined teams of Manipur police and Central security forces.

The sexual violence that women face in conflict situations is well evident in the NE of India and more so due to the presence of huge numbers of security personnel and the impunity under AFSPA.

The region, under the shadow of conflict, has witnessed a resurgence of patriarchal values and norms, which have brought with them new restrictions on the movement of women, the dress they wear and more overtly physical violence such as rape, which is systematically used as a tactic against a particular community. All this is compounded by the long social, economic and psychological trauma of armed conflict. This violence is different from the violence experienced by them in .normal times, for here even the state, which is supposed to be a guardian of their lives and rights, poses a threat to them (NCW 2004, 2).

The experiences of the women of Kashmir are in tandem with that of the women of NE states in the context of the AFSPA. The government legisled the AFSPA in 1990, after which violence escalated in the valley of Jammu and Kashmir.

> A savage thirst for blood seemed to have gripped the Central Reserve Police Force(CRPF) as evident from the calculated manner in which they went about pumping bullets into bodies of injured people...blot on the country's defence forces who are required to be highly disciplined cadre dedicated to the task of protecting our people. (Khan 2011, 91–92)

Kashmiri women are exploited sexually both by separatists and the security forces. Often, women endure sexual abuse in return for life of their families. Women in villages of the border districts of Rajouri or Poonch in Jammu and Kupwara and Uri in Kashmir are known to submit to sexual exploitation by militants from across the border, besides giving them food and shelter, in return for the safety of their families. More often, cases of sexual crimes go unreported either due to remoteness of the location or victims choosing to stay silent out of fear or social stigma attached to such exploitation. The disappearance of men and the struggle that women face have been documented in Kashmir. It is not only individuals and families that are subjected to 'authority,' but the whole community. The disappearance of young sons has added to the woes of mothers. Judicial redressal seems impossible as National Human Rights Commission (NHRC) and State

Human Rights Commission do not have powers of jurisdiction over the army. The recommendations of these human rights bodies are non-binding. There are 60,000 habeas corpus petitions filed by individuals since 1990 in Kashmir (Kazi 2009, 106).

There are 20,000 widows and at least 100 half-widows (those whose husbands have disappeared) due to the continuous conflict and the heavy presence of army. The impact on children is severe as 25,000 children have been orphaned (Nayeem 2011, 129). Muslim Khawateen-e-Markaz (MKM), an all women group in Kashmir, claim that there are hundreds of cases of rape or sexual abuse by the military and, in 2004, the organization was working on 75 cases (Kazi 2009, 144–46). The brutality of the army is horrific, The aim is to sexually exploit the young adolescent girls and there seems to be a deliberate attempt to make women the primary target (Committee for Initiative on Kashmir 2002[1990], 79).

The impact of the AFSPA and army's behaviour is well documented. One of the resultant indicators is that more women in Kashmir are driven to suicide as compared to men (Kazi 2009, 119). Also, hospitals in Srinagar claim that the number of neurological disorders among women is on the rise (Walikhanna 2004, 111). The widows and the half-widows face harassments and torture from the security forces. The scale of the gendered fall out of the state's attempts to impose law and order in Kashmir is known if one considers that there are about 8,000 pending applications for widow compensation in one district as of 2002 (Kazi 2009, 151). The report of 2005 on 'Impact of Conflict on Children and Women in Kashmir' states that there can be no two opinions that the women of Kashmir have been fighting battles against all kinds of injustices and crimes against humanity committed by the state (Khan 2011, 105). A survey done in 2008 by Médicines Sans Frontièrs (MSF), more women respondents were found to have symptoms of psychological distress and more so as they are dependent on others for their daily living as they (women) could not go out of their homes for work due to the presence of the armed forces. The fields outside where the women traditionally worked were no longer safe and in rural areas daughters were often not allowed to attend educational institutions (Dasgupta 2011, 99–101).

Thus, in a conflict zone, targeting women's honour becomes a contest between the warring parties. And the reported cases of rape by army or the paramilitary forces in Manipur and in Kashmir are just the tip of the iceberg. There are many more rape cases but most go unreported.[19] Even if the victim reports the crime, most of these cases remain unsolved and justice remains elusive.

The first time a fact finding team went to study the human rights violation by the Indian armed forces, they visited the Naga area of Manipur. It was an all-women team (Pramila Dandavate from Janata Party, MP Premila Loomba of the National Federation for Indian Women affiliated to CPI, Urmila Phadnis of PUCL, Kirti Singh of Janwadi Mahila Sangh affiliated to CPI(M), Subhadra Joshi from Congress and Nandita Haksar from People's Union for Democratic Rights (PUDR) and in August 1982 they visited the area (Haksar and Hongray 2011, 87).[20] Much later, in June 1990, an investigative report was brought out by the women's team visit to Kashmir. The team consisted of Premila Lewis, Nandita Haksar, Suhasini Mulay and Sakina Hasan.

The impact of the continued presence of the AFSPA is felt more on the women due to the gender differences. Whether it is due to fake encounters or otherwise, the large number of widows or half-widows in a conflict affected state is a situation which cannot be wished away. The bitter experiences of women with the security forces are omnipresent and the undemocratic environment strengthens it.

Overall, the AFSPA has created a milieu of uncertainty, fear and violence within states and the spectre of violence has pervaded over the mode of governance, and women are the greatest victim of this.

It has been documented that state police are powerless with regard to complaints as they have to first submit a case file to the state home secretary who then forwards it to the Central home ministry and this too causes long delays. Even if cases are filed, the complaints are forced to be changed to unidentified gunmen rather than security forces as the perpetrator.

The powers to armed forces under AFSPA are slowly entering the state police administration. In fact, in the state of Manipur, the state police also enjoys de facto impunity under the policy of the State Government as per the CSCOHRM. The impunity has, thus, filtered down from the army to the state security forces.[21] Many encounter killings are attributable to the Manipur police commandos who do not have a de jure existence but are accepted de facto. The political impunity is also enjoyed by the police as it is seen that till date not a single police personnel involved in extrajudicial execution is prosecuted.

The broad range of powers that are granted to the armed personnel and the lack of accountability of armed personnel pose a serious challenge to human rights norms.[22] Sexual crimes in armed conflicts are always treated with a 'forget and forgive' policy.[23]

The AFSPA, by its form and in its application, violates the Universal Declaration of Human Rights (UDHR), the International Covenant on Civil and Political Rights (ICCPR), the Convention Against Torture, the UN Code of Conduct for Law Enforcement Officials, the UN Body of Principles for Protection of All Persons Under any form of Detention and the UN Principles on Effective Prevention and Investigation of Extra-legal and Summary Executions.

The UDHR articles, which the AFSPA violates, are the following: 1: Free and Equal Dignity and Rights; 2: Non-discrimination; 3: Life, liberty, security of person; 5: no torture, 7: equality before the law; 8: effective remedy; 9: no arbitrary arrest; and 17: property.

AFSPA violates the following principles of the Indian Constitution. The right to life is violated by Section 4(a) of the AFSPA, which grants the armed forces power to shoot to kill in law enforcement situations. Lethal force is broadly permitted under the AFSPA if the target is part of an assembly of five or more persons holding weapons or 'carrying things capable of being used as weapons'. The terms 'assembly' and 'weapon' are not defined. The right to liberty and security of person is violated by Section 4(c) of the AFSPA, which fails to protect against arbitrary arrest by allowing soldiers to arrest anyone merely on suspicion that a 'cognizable offence' has already taken place or is likely to take place in the future. Further, the AFSPA provides no specific time limit for handing arrested persons to the nearest police station. Section 5 vaguely advises that those arrested be transferred to police custody 'with the least possible delay'. This use of vague language has allowed the security forces to hold people for days and months at a time. The right to remedy is violated by Section 6 of the AFSPA, which provides officers who abuse their powers under the AFSPA with immunity from legal accountability. This section of the AFSPA prohibits even state governments from initiating legal proceedings against the armed forces on behalf of their population without Central government approval. Since such a sanction is seldom granted, it has in effect provided a shield of immunity for armed forces personnel implicated in serious abuses. Non-application of due process of law makes the armed forces be their own judge and jury. In practice the AFSPA also facilitates violation of the right to be free from torture and from cruel or degrading treatment. Since the AFSPA provides powers to arrest without warrant and then detain arrested persons for unspecified amounts of time, the armed forces routinely engage in torture and other ill-treatment during interrogation in army barracks. Thus, the said Act contravenes Articles 14, 21, 22 and 32 (A) of the Indian Constitution.[24]

The Act violates the established CrPC also, which has laid out the procedures that the police officers are to follow for arrests, searches and seizures. The CrPC clearly delineates the ranks which can disperse assembly of persons, whereas the Act grants the power to use maximum force to even to non-commissioned officers. The CrPC has a section on the maintenance of public order but the Act grants the power otherwise. CrPC sets out the arrest procedure the police are to follow but the AFSPA is even more excessive with Section 4(a) letting the armed forces kill a person who is not suspected of an offence punishable by death or life imprisonment.

Regarding the tenure of the notification of an area being declared as disturbed as given in the Act, there has been much debate and violations. The disturbed area notification cannot be for an indefinite period but the evidence is that the notifications, for example, in Manipur, is without any time limit. Further the restrictions that are placed on people due to an area being declared a disturbed area is contravening the right to personal liberty.

Protests and Resistance of Women

Over the years the AFSPA has become a symbol of oppression, an object of hate and an instrument of discrimination and high handedness.

Women from all ethnic groups of the NE have taken part in the resistance movements and one of the common points of state oppression shared is the AFSPA which they demand to be repealed (*Women, Peace and Security* 2010, 251).The nude protests by the women in front of the Kangla Fort in Imphal in 2004[25] was the testimony against the atrocities and the blatant misuse of the Act by the security forces. It questioned the legitimacy of the security forces, local administration and the GoI, and the rule of law. The Manipur valley in particular has turned into a field of overt social and political struggle where women often have to invent different ways of speaking for themselves. In speaking for themselves and protesting they have used their body, their phanek.[26] The more-than-a-decade-long fast of Irom Sharmila[27] against the AFSPA is another manifestation of the deep threat that she presents to the state. The people of Manipur have been agitating for the repeal of AFPSA. But it seems that the issue of sexual violence committed against women in Manipur has been marginalized by the people's movement for the repeal of AFSPA, which takes the repeal of the act to be the 'larger' political issue (Making Women Count for Peace 2012, 7).

In Kashmir too, there have been wide spread public protests against the rape of Shabnam Rashid and her mother in November 2004 by the Major of 30 Rashtriya Rifles. In fact, Shabnam was portrayed as the Manorama of Kashmir. Association of Parents of Disappeared Persons and Daughters of the Nation are some of the organized mobilization of women to tackle custodial disappearances, custodial deaths and sexual violence in Kashmir by the armed forces.

Reviews, Repeal Campaigns and Legal Cases

Armed conflict is a law and order problem, but the solution sought centres around militarization. Containing insurgency through AFSPA seems to be the only road map used. Rather than using the ordinary processes of law, special powers continue to be in place. The prolonged application of the Act has institutionalized militarization and strengthened violations against the citizens, particularly the women (CSCOHRM 2012, 17). The fundamental principle is that whole of NE is an area under threat (both external and internal) and is a special case due to its geo-political location.

In numerous instances, even the government officials, including political leaders, have acknowledged that the presence of the Act is redundant and that the Indian armed forces were indulging in an orgy of murder and rape of women, for example, in Mizoram, as stated by Dr Ram Manohar Lohia in the Lok Sabha (Nag 2012, 8).

Jeevan Reddy Committee was appointed on 19 November 2004 in the wake of an intense agitation[28] launched by various civil society groups in Manipur following the death of Thangjam Manorama Devi on 10 July 2004 while in custody of the Assam Rifles.[29] The Committee has not exactly recommended the repeal of AFSPA but rather suggested that the appropriate provisions be put in the UA(P)A.[30] This Committee had no women representatives and there were no special hearing for women's groups or for the women where they could share their grievances (*Women, Peace and Security* 2010, 263).

The legal tangles which the cases of violations have landed in have obviously led to more anger and protests at the grass roots. When the state government in Manipur appointed a single member commission of inquiry—the Upendra Commission[31]—under the Commission of Inquiries Act to enquire into the facts and circumstances of the case of the death of Manorama, the Central government filed a case to prevent the state government from taking action on the recommendations made in the report submitted by it, on the ground that it was beyond the state government's ambit of jurisdiction as proceedings against armed personnel can be initiated only after obtaining Central government permission and that inquiries had already been instituted by the armed forces. The state Government argued that the Upendra Commission had been constituted to avert a public order situation and that the armed personnel did not share information with the state government. The court accepted the state government's argument and allowed for action to be taken on the Upendra Commission Report.[32] In 2011, the Guwahati High Court issued notice to Assam Rifles as to why Manorama was not handed over to civil custody. Subsequently, in July 2011, Assam Rifles filed a Special Leave Petition (SLP) in the Supreme Court.[33] This case indicates the issues that are raised and never resolved when central forces operate in a state, even if it is towards ensuring accountability of armed personnel.

The Prime Minister of India met with a delegation of Anunpa Lup in 2007[34] and admitted that the AFSPA is a draconian law and assured the delegation that the Act will be replaced by a more humane one. The Administrative Reforms Committee headed by Veerappan Moily (2007) recommended that the Act should be scrapped. The Working Group on Confidence-Building Measures in Jammu and Kashmir headed by Mohammad Hamid Ansari constituted in 2007 has also recommended its repeal.

On the other hand, the judiciary (specifically the Supreme Court) has time and again endorsed the AFSPA and gone back and forth on the Act's safeguards which the Supreme Court itself had set. For example, in 1997, in the Naga People's Movement for Human Rights (NPMHR) versus Union Of India case, the Supreme Court of India upheld the constitutionality of the AFSPA which was challenged in the case, but placed various checks on the force's exercise of power.[35] Earlier, in February 1983, the Supreme Court in the NPMHR case had also given some directions for the Indian army to follow such as not to use churches and educational institutions as detention centres (Haksar and Hongray 2011, 98). But there is total lack of credible information on the decisions of the home ministry to grant or withhold sanction to prosecution requests under the AFPSA. The complainant has to have information on the status of the request for prosecution. However, later on 2 May 2007, in the Masooda Parveen versus Union of India and Ors case,[36] the Supreme Court ruled that the action of army in the concerned case was very much within its authority, that is, the army's lack of cooperation with local police forces.

States like Nagaland have passed four resolutions against the extension of AFSPA (Hayes 2012, 10). The Congress-led Secular Progressive Front (SPF) government has lifted AFSPA from Imphal municipal areas of Manipur covering seven assembly constituencies in 2004 in the aftermath of the massive public protest against the rape and killing of Thangjam Manorama.[37]

In fact, the first person to challenge the Act was Inderjit Baruah, an Assamese engineer. He filed a case in the Guwahati High Court during 1983. The case was transferred to the Delhi High Court which upheld the constitutionality of the Act. The next petition was filed by Manipur Human Rights Forum. In 1983, the NPMHR and PUDR filed petitions which were sent to the constitutional bench (Haksar and Hongray 2011, 82). NPMHR was probably the first in the region to voice its protest against the Act (Das 2008, 68).

Recently, in 2013, the then Chief Minister of Jammu and Kashmir, Omar Abdullah, too had asked all stake holders concerned to support lifting of the AFSPA in Jammu and Kashmir. He advocates the lifting of it partially and not from areas close to the Line of Control (LoC), specifically from Srinagar and Jammu cities.[38] But this stand does not find approval of the Bharatiya Janata Party (BJP) leaders such as L.K. Advani as reported in media.[39]

The latest in the series of recommendations for the repeal of the Act is the report of the Varma Commission[40] which stated that women in conflict areas are entitled to all the security and dignity and that impunity for systematic and isolated sexual violence in the process of internal security duties is being legitimized by the AFSPA. The report recommended that sexual violence against women by members of the armed forces or uniformed personnel must be brought under the purview of ordinary criminal law along with a review of the continuance of the AFSPA. Specifically, it recommended the amendment to Section 6 of AFSPA, that is, no sanction shall be required if the person has been accused of committing an offence under Section 354, 354A, 354B, 354C, Section 376(1), 376(2), 376(3), and Sections 376A, 376B, 376C, 376D, 376E of the Indian Penal Code (IPC) 1860.

In 2014, the absolute majority that the BJP got in the national general elections in the country, with the new government in place since 26 May, put the spot light back on the subject. Across political ideology, it now understood that the AFSPA is doing more good than harm. The Union Home Minister, Rajnath Singh, is of the opinion that the time is not right to withdraw AFSPA (as of March 2015). The defence minister of India (during 2015) is also of the opinion that the AFSPA should continue. The Chief Minister of Jammu and Kashmir, Mufti Mohammad Sayeed's, remark that the government would work towards a phased withdrawal of the AFSPA from areas in the state that are free from militancy for some time has generated a lot of political heat. The interesting development is that the state government of Tripura in its Assembly in May 2015 recommended to the national government for non-extension of the tenure of the AFSPA. Considering that the Community Party of India (Marxist) chief minister has spear headed this with the BJP government at the centre, it is a political dance worth watching. The logical end of this recommendation, of the state of Tripura towards the ending of the AFSPA, will be reached only after a long drawn political process.

The activist Irom Sharmila's fast enters the 15th year even though she was released and then rearrested in August 2014.

So in the long drawn out struggles and resistance and protests both at the formal level of judiciary or political parties or mass mobilization or individual, women have been at the central of this process. Be it due to the adverse impact of the regressive law on women who have victims of it or because women are the peace-movers, the role that women play in the movement of repealing the Act is significant.

International

The international agencies have also done their bit in not only assessing the impact of the Act on women but also strongly recommending its repeal.

Margaret Sekaggya, UN Special Rapporteur, in January 2011 had expressed concern about the arbitrary application of security laws at the national and state levels (in Jammu and Kashmir and in the NE of India), most notably the Public Security Act and the AFSPA, the JKPSA and the UAPA.[41]

The Committee on Convention on Elimination of All Forms of Discrimination Against Women (CEDAW) had observed in its 2000 session that the AFSPA be reviewed so that special powers given to the security forces do not prevent the investigation and prosecution of acts of violence against women in conflict areas and during detention and arrest. Subsequently, in 2007, it also observed that the steps taken to abolish or reform the Act have not been informed to the Committee. The 4th and 5th NGO alternative report to CEDAW documented by National Alliance of Women's Organisations (NAWO), India, in July 2014 has further elaborated the need for the repeal of the AFSPA. It, in fact, reiterated the recommendations of Justice Varma Committee.

In the context of the UN Security Council Resolution 1325 which prioritizes the issue of the women in armed conflict and puts women's rights and gender equality squarely on the agenda for societal reconstruction and underlines the relevance of determining women's needs in a post-conflict settlement, an instrument like UNSCR 1325 becomes very important to articulate the voices of resistance of the women in conflict areas and who are particularly affected due to oppressive laws such as the AFSPA in the conflict zones. The transformative message of the resolution is that it recognizes the vulnerabilities of women in conflict zones and that linkage is well established in the areas where in AFSPA is in place. If effectively used, it could address issues of prevention, protection, participation and promotion against violence against women.

Concluding Remarks

In India, which remains a democratic state with regular and reasonably fair elections, the record of democratic governance is not as impressive. The range of rebellions against the state whether in NE or Kashmir or Punjab have been controlled using entire infantry brigades and battalions of the army. The state has time and again showcased its might in controlling and crushing regional voices of dissent and the powerful state has justified its authority. The power to declare laws and enforce it ruthlessly (ignoring resistance voices) rests with the state. The use of military as a proxy for civil governance reflects the state's failure in resolving the political challenges. The politicization of the armed forces is evident in the enactment and enforcement of acts and laws which stifle the human rights. The wide range of security laws in place in the country today may have had its genesis due to some important and significant need, but the misuse is now widely accepted. The violations of rights of the women who are used as pawns are well documented and in place.

Specifically, the AFSPA was enacted to deal with the Naga insurgency but in due course of time it has expanded its coverage (geographically) and also the tenure. As a result of the powers and liberties that the armed forces enjoy under the said Act, women have been raped, children orphaned and men tortured. The AFSPA has created and maintained an environment of fear and violence. The women who have suffered and still continue to suffer due to the presence of armed forces have raised their voices time and again but it has not been any heed to. Campaigns, protests and legal cases against the Act have dominated the NE and Jammu and Kashmir. The failure of the legal cases in many instances and the continuation of the Act and its atrocities show the limitations of democracy and the failure of the Indian democracy. Though the political apparatus at the state level may have initiated action towards the repeal of the Act, as of today, the Act is entrenched in the governance system of the conflict areas.

International forum such as CEDAW committee has played a proactive role in advocating for the removal of the AFSPA. The gender impact of the Act has received the attention of the civil society organizations, activists and academics but the legislature which has to take cognizance of the evidence seems to be either taking time for accepting or turning a blind eye. The UNSCR 1325 has the opportunity to take the agenda forward and in the context of the civil society initiative on developing the National Action Plan (NAP) of India in the light of the UNSCR 1325 has yet to be materialized, the struggle on not only the resistance by women against the security laws such as AFSPA continues, but also the journey towards a secure world continues to be arduous.

Notes

1. Swadeshi movement was a part of the Indian independence movement and developing Indian nationalism aimed at removing the British Empire. Swadeshi (self-sufficiency) movement involved the boycotting of British products and the revival of domestic products and production processes.
2. Some of these acts include Jammu and Kashmir Public Safety Act (1978); Assam Preventive Detention Act (1980); National Security Act (1980, amended 1984 and 1987); Anti-Hijacking Act (1982); Armed Forces (Punjab and Chandigarh) Special Powers Act (1983); Punjab Disturbed Areas Act (1983); Chandigarh Disturbed Areas Act (1983); Suppression of Unlawful Acts Against Safety of Civil Aviation Act (1982); Terrorist Affected Areas (Special Courts) Act (1984); National Security (Second Amendment) Ordinance (1984); Terrorist and Disruptive Activities (Prevention) Act (1985, amended 1987); National Security Guard Act (1986); Criminal Courts and Security Guard Courts Rules (1987) and the Special Protection Group Act (1988).
3. Dalits are the traditional untouchable in the Indian caste system.
4. Sarkaria Commission was set up in June 1983 by the Government of India to examine the relationship and balance of power between state and Central governments in the country and suggest changes within the framework of the Constitution of India. The Commission was headed by Justice Rajinder Singh Sarkaria, a retired judge of the Supreme Court of India.
5. http://www.binayaksen.net/wp-content/uploads/indian_repressive_laws.pdf (Background information on repressive laws in India, accessed on 10 August 2015).
6. Section 2(o) reads: '"unlawful activity", in relation to an individual or association, means any action taken by such individual or association (whether by committing an act or by words, either spoken or written, or by signs or by visible representations or otherwise), (i) which is intended, or supports any claim, to bring about, on any ground whatsoever, the cession of a part of the territory of India or the secession of a part of the territory of India from the Union, or which incites any individual or group of individuals to bring about such cession or secession; or (ii) which disclaims, questions, disrupts or is intended to disrupt the sovereignty and territorial integrity of India; or (iii) which causes or is intended to cause disaffection against India'.

7. Section 13 reads: 'Punishment for unlawful activities: (1) Whoever—(a) takes part in or commits, or (b) advocates, abets, advises or incites the commission of, any unlawful activity, shall be punishable with imprisonment for a term which may extend to seven years, and shall also be liable to fine.'
8. http://www.nls.ac.in/resources/csseip/Files/SeditionLaws_cover_Final.pdf (Sedition laws and death of free speech in India, accessed on 10 August 2015).
9. A 2001 news report from Kashmir mentions a 1987 TADA case against 52 people including former Chief Minister (who passed away in 2009), in which—even after the lapse of 23 years in 2000—charges had not been framed.
10. The bill received the assent of the president of India and notification issued on 12 April 2006. Six organizations were banned. Dr. Binayak Sen, General Secretary, Chhattisgarh PUCL, and Vice President, National PUCL was detained under this act on 14 May 2007 allegedly for his linkages with the Communist Party of India (Maoist). There has been resistance against this.
11. It took only three hours for the Indian Parliament to enact the Act in the Lok Sabha and four hours in the Rajya Sabha.
12. Initially to the entire state of Assam and UT Manipur. In 1965, Mizoram (then the Lushai district of Assam) came under AFPSA. In 1970, the AFPSA was extended to Tripura. In any case the Armed Forces Special Powers Ordinance was in force in Manipur and Tripura area since 1950.
13. At the time of writing the paper, the state government of Tripura has recommended to the Union home ministry to withdraw the notification regarding AFSPA, that is, not give any further extension.
14. The entire state of Manipur (except Imphal municipal area), Nagaland and Assam, Tirap and Changlang districts of Arunachal Pradesh and a 20 km belt in the states of Arunachal Pradesh and Meghalaya having a common border with Assam have been declared 'disturbed areas' under the AFSPA, 1958, as amended in 1972. The Government of Tripura has declared the areas under 34 police stations in full and part of the areas under six police stations as a 'disturbed area'. The states of Manipur, Meghalaya and Tripura were created in 1972.
15. The Act was in force from June 1984 to July 1985 and then again from Nov 1991 till the end of 1993 in Punjab.
16. Assam Rifles has been deployed for counter-insurgency and border guarding role on the Indo–Myanmar border. Out of sanctioned strength of 46 battalions, 31 battalions are for counter-insurgency and 15 are for a border guarding role (MHA Annual Report, 2010–11).
17. Total military and paramilitary including border guards and police commandos are as high as 450,000 in NE (Hayes 2012).
18. NWUM comprises of all the women of the Naga tribe of Manipur. It was registered in 1994.
19. http://timesofindia.indiatimes.com/india/Women-suffer-big-in-Indias-state-vs-rebels-war/articleshow/17802432.cms (accessed on 16 August 2015).
20. The report of this visit was, however, not signed by two members who felt that it would be anti-national (Haksar and Hongary 2011).
21. http://infochangeindia.org/governance/books-a-reports/manipur-a-history-of-strife.html (accessed on 16 August 2015).

22. However, recently in February 2012, two Supreme Court judges said AFSPA's immunity ought not to cover cases in which crimes such as murder or rape were committed. 'You go to a place in exercise of AFSPA, you commit rape, you commit murder, then where is the question of sanction?' asked the Judges 'Home Ministry shoots down pleas to prosecute killer soldiers', (*Hindu* 2012).

23. http://timesofindia.indiatimes.com/india/Women-suffer-big-in-Indias-state-vs-rebels-war/articleshow/17802432.cms (accessed on 20 August 2015).

24. Under Section 4(a) of the AFSPA, which grants armed forces personnel the power to shoot to kill, the constitutional right to life (Article 21) is violated. This law is not fair, just or reasonable because it allows the armed forces to use an excessive amount of force. The AFSPA is in place in limited parts of India. Since the people residing in areas declared 'disturbed' are denied the protection of the right to life, denied the protections of the criminal procedure code and prohibited from seeking judicial redress, they are also denied equality before the law. Residents of non-disturbed areas enjoy the protections guaranteed under the Constitution, whereas the residents of the NE live under virtual army rule. This directly contradicts Article 14 of the Indian Constitution which guarantees equality before the law. Under Section 4(c) of the AFSPA a person can be arrested by the armed forces without a warrant and on the mere suspicion that they are going to commit an offence. The armed forces are not obliged to communicate the grounds for the arrest. There is also no advisory board in place to review arrests made under the AFSPA. Since the arrest is without a warrant it violates the preventive detention sections of Article 22. Section 32(1) of the Constitution states that 'the right to move the Supreme Court by appropriate proceedings for the enforcement of the rights conferred by this part is guaranteed but Section 6 of the AFSPA takes it away, abrogates, pinches, frustrates the right to constitutional remedy which has been given in article 32(1) of the Constitution'.

25. Women protestors of All Manipur Social Reformation and Development Samaj barred themselves in front of the Kangla Fort, the headquarters of Assam Rifle on 15 July after the Manorama case.

26. Phanek is the traditional attire (skirt or sarong) worn by the women of Manipur.

27. Sharmila started her fast from 2 Nov 2000 subsequent to the gunning down of 10 civilians waiting at a bus stand in Malom near Imphal.

28. The agitation against Manorama's rape and murder was sustained and subsequently became an integral part of the struggle against the AFSPA. The protests were led by the Meira Paibis (torch bearers) and Nupi Marups (women's organizations).

29. Thangjam Manorama alias Henthoi was picked up by the *jawans* of the 17 Assam Rifles from her home at Baman Kampu Mayai Leikei village outside Imphal, the capital of Manipur. Her arrest describes her as a suspect of People's Liberation Army and her bullet-ridden and mutilated body was found the next day. This was not an ordinary event.

30. Some legal analysts have criticized the Reddy Committee Report for expanding rather than restricting State powers under the guise of recommending a repeal of the Act after incorporating the into the Unlawful Activities (Prevention) Act (Combat Law; Justice Jeevan Reddy Report on AFSPA; Evil is Intact; February 21, 2010 http://www.combatlaw.org/?p=74).

31. The Commission was headed by District and Sessions Court Judge C. Upendra.

32. No recommendations of the Report have been implemented.

33. http://articles.timesofindia.indiatimes.com/2011-07-11/guwahati/29760275_1_ manorama-devi-c-upendra-singh-thangjam (accessed on 21 August 2015).

34. The umbrella grouping of 32 organizations spearheading the campaign against the AFSPA in Manipur.

35. In the NPMHR case, the Supreme Court rejected the petitioners' argument that the AFSPA was unconstitutional because it transferred to the armed forces full power to maintain public order in a disturbed area whereas the Constitution only permits Parliament to enact laws relating to the 'use of the Armed Forces in aid of civil power'. But in rejecting this argument, the SC held that the 'in aid of civil power' clause mandated the continued existence and relevance of the authority to be aided. Under the AFSPA, therefore, the armed forces cannot 'supplant or act as a substitute' for a State's civilian authorities in the maintenance of public order, but are strictly required to act in cooperation with them. Accordingly, the Court understood the armed forces' power under AFSPA Section 4(c) to arrest any person without a warrant for suspected commission of a cognisable offence in light of Section 5, which requires handing over the arrested person to the nearest police station with the 'least possible delay'. The Court further stressed that the 'least possible delay' language of the AFSPA reflected the requirements of the Criminal Procedure Code (CrPC) and the Constitution, which mandate production of a detainee before the nearest Magistrate within 24 hours of arrest. (http://www. hrdc.net/sahrdc/hrfeatures/HRF168.htm, accessed on 15 September 2015).

36. Masooda involved a writ petition filed by the widow of a practising advocate, Ghulam Mohi-ud-din Regoo, who had been arrested, tortured and killed by security forces in Jammu and Kashmir as a suspected militant. First arrested by the army in 1994 and held in custody for three months based on allegations of being a Pakistani-trained Militant (PTM), he was released. Later in 1998, an army unit along with surrendered militants searched his house and took him to the local army headquarters. According to his widow, Regoo was 'tortured mercilessly leading to his death whereafter explosives were placed on his dead body and then detonated to camouflage the murder.' She petitioned several State authorities and the Chief Justice of India seeking compensation. She argued that at no point did the members of the army involve the police during either the search or arrest operations. Accordingly, the petition was that while the Army had exercised its powers of search and arrest under the AFSPA, its failure to inform the State police of either operation until after the arrestee's death 'completely excluded the participation of the local administration and the police', thereby violating the AFSPA. (http://www.hrdc.net/sahrdc/hrfeatures/ HRF168.htm).

37. http://articles.timesofindia.indiatimes.com/2012-10-29/india/34796970_1_irom-sharmila-chanu-malom-village-memngou (accessed on 22 August 2015).

38. http://www.rediff.com/news/report/cm-to-seek-phased-withdrawal-of-afspa-in-kashmir/20130107.htm (news dated 7 January 2013).

39. http://in.news.yahoo.com/afpsa-not-withdrawn-kashmir-says-advani-111908102. html (accessed on 27 August 2015).

40. The Varma Commission was set up in Dec 2012 in the wake of tremendous public protest on violence against women.
41. http://e-pao.net/GP.asp?src=17..220111.Jan11 (accessed on 27 August 2015).

References

Banerjee, Paula. 2010. *Border, Histories, Existences: Gender and Beyond.* New Delhi: SAGE Publications.

——— ed. 2008. *Women in Peace Politics, South Asian Peace Studies Vol. 3.* New Delhi: SAGE Publications.

Basu, Asmita. n.d. *Routinization of the Extraordinary: A Mapping of Security Laws in India.* Available at: http://www.southasianrights.org/wp-content/uploads/2009/10/IND-Security-Laws-Report.pdf (Accessed on 1 August 2015).

Basu, Soumita. 2010. *Security Council Resolution 1325: Towards Gender Equality in Peace and Security Policy Making.* In *Human Security vs. State Security—The Gender Imperative,* edited by Asha Hans and Betty Reardon. New Delhi: Routledge Taylor and Francis Group.

Committee for Initiative on Kashmir. 2002[1990]. 'Kashmir Imprisoned'. In *Speaking Peace: Women's Voices from Kashmir,* edited by Urvashi Butalia. New Delhi: Kali for Women.

CSCOHRM. 2012. *Manipur: A Memorandum on Extra Judicial, Arbitrary or Summary Executions.* Imphal, Manipur.

Das, Samir. 2008. 'Ethnicity and Democracy Meet When Mothers Protest'. In *Women in Peace Politics,* edited by Paula Banerjee. New Delhi: SAGE.

Dasgupta, Sumona. 2011. 'Renegotiating Internal Boundaries by Women of Jammu And Kashmir'. In *Women in Indian Borderlands,* edited by Paula Banerjee and A. Basu Ray Choudhury. New Delhi: SAGE Publications.

Gangte, Priyadarshini M. 2011. *Women of North East in Present Context.* New Delhi: Maxford Books.

Hans, Asha and Betty Reardon. 2010. *Human Security vs State Security: The Gender Imperative.* New Delhi: Routledge Taylor & Francis Group.

Hashmi, Syed Junaid. n.d. AFSPA In Jammu And Kashmir. Available at: http://www.countercurrents.org/hashmi180607.htm (Accessed on 3 September 2015).

Haksar, Nandita and S.M. Hongray. 2011. *The Judgment That Never Came: Army Rule in North East India.* New Delhi: Chicken Neck.

Hayes, Ben. 2012. *The Other Burma: Conflict, Counter Insurgency and Human Rights in North East India.* Amsterdam: Trans National Institute.

Hindu. 2002. 'Use of Article 355.' *The Hindu.* Available at: http://hindu.com/2002/05/04/stories/2002050401351200.htm (Accessed on 5 September 2011).

———. 2012. *The Hindu.* "Home Ministry Shoots Down Pleas to Prosecute Killer Soldiers." Available at: http://www.thehindu com/news/national/article2866609.ece?homepage=true (Accessed on 20 August 2015).

Kazi, Seema. 2009. *Between Democracy and Nation: Gender And Militarization In Kashmir.* New Delhi: Women Unlimited.

Khan, Nyla Ali. 2011. *Islam Women and Violence in Kashmir Between India and Pakistan*. Kashmir: Gulshan Books.

Manchanda, Rita, 2005. *Naga Women Making a Difference: Peace Building in NE*. New Delhi: Women Waging Peace Policy Commission.

Ministry of Home Affairs (MHA). *Annual Report 2010–2011*. New Delhi: Government of India.

Mohanty, Manoranjan, K.B. Saxena, Sebastian Gilbert and Prashant Trivedi. 2011. *Weapon of the Oppressed: An Inventory of People's Rights in India*. New Delhi: Council for Social Development.

Morung Express. 2008. 'Impact of Conflict on Women.' *Morung Express*, 22 May.

Nag, Sajal. 2012. *A Gigantic Panopticon Counter Insurgency and Modes of Disciplining and Punishment in NE*. Kolkata: MCRG.

Nayeem, Hameeda. 2011. *Demystifying Ideology: Identity, Gender and Politics in Kashmir*. Kashmir: Gulshan Books.

NCW (National Commission for Women). 2004. *Violence Against Women In North East India: An Enquiry*. Report by The North East Network. Available at: http://ncw. nic.in/pdfreports/Violence%20against%20women%20in%20North%20East%20 India%20-%20An%20Inquiry.pdf (Accessed on 20 June 2016).

Nepram, Binalakshmi. 2009, 17 June. *Northeast India Women Initiative for Peace*. Manipur Women Gun Survivor Network. Available at: http://cafi-online.org/ articles.php?event=det&id=39 (Accessed on 20 August 2015).

Ningthoujam, Irina. 2008. 'Solidarity as Social Capital: Gender, Roles and Potentials'. *Eastern Quarterly*, 5 (II–III).

PTI (Press Trust of India). 2010. *Northeast's Women Take Initiative or Peace*. Guwahati.

PUCL (People's Union for Civil Liberties). 1980. *NSA, A Weapon of Repression*. Available at: http://www.pucl.org/from-archives/may81/nsa.html (Accessed on 1 September 2015).

———. 1985. *Black Laws 1984–85*. New Delhi: PUCL.

2003, 27–28 December. *Regional Conference on Non-traditional Security Discourse: Gender and South Asia—A Report*. New Delhi: WISCOMP.

Walikhanna, Charu. 2004. *Women, Silent Victims in Armed Conflict: An Area Study of Jammu & Kashmir, India*. New Delhi: Serials Publications.

Women, Peace and Security. 2010. Available at: http://www.peacewomen.org/assets/ file/Resources/Government/1325_implementation1325finnishdevelopment-kenyanepalneindia_banerjeeetal_jan312010.pdf (Accessed on 1 September 2015). Finnish Development Policy, Ministry for Foreign Affairs.

6

Rights of the People Versus Rights of the State: Jammu and Kashmir

Ritu Dewan

The Armed Forces (Special Powers) Act (AFSPA) is probably the single most direct instrument impacting the democratic rights of the Indian people. Passed in 1958, when the Naga movement had just begun, the Act is implemented when an area is declared 'disturbed' by either the Central or the state government, under the Disturbed Areas Act, and when the army is 'summoned' to help civil authorities control 'armed insurrection'.

The Act is under much debate today on several grounds, not only in Jammu and Kashmir and the North East, but in the entire nation. First, it enables security forces to 'fire upon or otherwise use force even to the causing of death'. Second, according to Section 6, no criminal prosecution can be initiated against any person who has taken action under this Act. Third, till now, not a single army or paramilitary officer or soldier has been prosecuted for destruction of property, or murder or rape. Fourth, the Verma Committee has recommended drastic changes in AFSPA especially in relation to trying military personnel for sexual assault under normal law. Fifth, the Planning Commission in the Twelfth Five-year Plan document passed by the National Development Council (NDC) has for the first time ever asked for not only a gendered review of the Act, but also of gendered violence in 'disturbed areas'.

This short chapter is being written in the context of rising violence, of the increasing culturalization of especially gender and sexual violence, and of the institutionalization of State violence. The focus is not on AFSPA, per se, on which much has been written and much more will be written, but on how AFSPA is being used as a base for other anti-people legislations, in a conflict as well as in a 'non-political and non-conflict' scenario. It is hoped that highlighting and debating these issues will strengthen the process of opposition to the negation of the rights of people and enhance the democratization of our people and our nation.

Agricultural Biosecurity Bill, 11 March 2013, Ministry of Agriculture

The Agricultural Biosecurity Bill, introduced in the Lok Sabha with the purpose 'to prevent bio-terrorism, trans-boundary genetic diseases and pests', seeks to bring together plant, animal and marine protection, and quarantine setups under a high powered body—the Agricultural Biosecurity Authority of India (ABAI)—which would have adequate powers to cover four sectors—plant health, animal health, living aquatic resources and agriculturally important micro-organisms. This Bill states—in a straight lift from AFSPA (see Armed Forces [Jammu & Kashmir] Special Powers Act, 1990 Number 21 of 1990, 10 September, Section 7, p. 3)—that

> [N]o prosecution or legal proceedings shall lie against the Government or any member of proposed authority or officer or other employees of the Central Government for anything which is done in good faith or intended to be done by any official engaged in any experimentation of introducing Genetically Modified seeds, resulting in crop destruction, swarming of pests, etc.

This Bill, therefore, extends impunity to areas beyond those defined as 'conflict areas' to regions where the majority of Indian citizens reside and eke a livelihood, thus, bringing vast multitudes of people as well as areas under State-appointed agricultural authorities who are granted exemption from punishment. This is a blatant attempt to not only control people's struggles, but to extend the concept of 'conflict' beyond the 'political' definition to the economic one of the on-going contradictions between the people and the prevailing dominant growth paradigm and development strategies. India, in fact, has witnessed the hitherto unprecedented articulation of especially rural contradictions via peasant suicides.

Jammu and Kashmir Police Bill, 14 February 2013, State Government

Introduced in an utterly insensitive manner through posting on the state home department's website on 15 February, in the immediate aftermath of the hanging of Afzal Guru when Kashmir was under curfew, this Bill permits the state government to replicate AFSPA even if this AFSPA is ever withdrawn. The Bill states that the state government would have the right to declare any area as 'disturbed', and that a police officer would be considered as being 'always on duty', even when dressed in mufti. Also incorporated is a confidentiality clause that can override the Right to Information Act (RTI), a Central law that has been legislated after years of people's struggles for transparency in governance. Also guaranteed for the 'protectors of the state' is a six-month deadline for complaints against a police official from 'occurrence of the incident'. And, of course, also guaranteed is the ubiquitous legal immunity regarding decisions taken 'in good faith or intended to be done'.

What is indeed quite shocking—given the fact of several judicial judgements and also evidence to the contrary even in the region itself—is the attempt to 'democratize' conflict-control in the name of people by introducing what is termed as 'community policing' via setting up of civil society committees. Para 62 of the Draft Bill states that

> 1) Subject to the approval of the government, the Director General of Police may constitute as many Village Defence Committees as he may deem necessary and District Superintendent of Police engage members thereof on voluntary basis for the protection of life and property of the inhabitants of that particular Village.

And

> 2) The members of such Village Defence Committees may also be issued suitable arms and ammunition of prescribed specifications.

This arming of civilians is not restricted to rural areas, but, in recognition of the process of increasing urbanization, extended to non-rural areas. Additionally, given the horrifying experience of Salwa Judum as a civilian militia mobilized and deployed as part of India's State-created anti-insurgency strategy, as well as the huge upsurge in communal enmity in the Jammu region in the 1990's following the formation of Village Defence Committees, one wonders what levels regional satraps would stoop to in order to maintain control, all the while swearing their commitment to a 'peaceful' resolution via 'peaceful' means. The recruitment of 'special police officers' outside the existing police structure in the past had resulted in the appointment of informers and *ikhwanis*, as pro-government militia who are 'reformed' militants are called in Jammu and Kashmir. Reports of the violence perpetrated by this regularized militia are well-documented.

The Jammu and Kashmir Police Bill gives the right to prohibit the free entry of people into any public/private space that can be deemed as reserved at any time. The attack on physical mobility covers all spaces. A police officer can direct people in whole or part of the district to keep order on public roads, streets and so on or any public place, to prevent obstruction, injury, annoyance to passersby, and can also temporarily reserve for any public purpose, any street or other public place, and prohibit public from entry. Barriers or any other necessary structures can be erected on public road and streets to check vehicles or occupants. Linked to this is, of course, one of the longest lasting denials of democratic dissent in Jammu and Kashmir—the right to take out a procession or even to assemble.

The police will also have the power to—hold your breath—impose a six-month jail sentence for the following activities. It is a list, with my reasoning—or lack of it—in brackets.

a. *'Cleaning a furniture or vehicle in public'* (no, try as I might, I cannot trace any logical basis of terming this as a crime).

b. *'Slaughtering an animal, cleaning a carcass or grooming an animal in public'* (numerous possible explanations for this definition of crime: environmental issues; vegetarianism; clean drainage systems; waste management; anti public celebration of Bakri-Eid; ethical treatment to animals by not keeping them as pets; the right of pets to remain un-groomed; opposition to using horse-carriages as is the tradition in many parts of the state, while not opposing hand-rickshaws, thus, the rights of animals overpowering the rights of people to a dignified life and livelihood).

c. '*Defecating or urinating in public*' (no logical explanation at least in my reasoning, although I cannot resist pointing out that people would not commit this crime if there was more investment in the creation of public toilets for both men and women, ensuring not only availability but also accessibility and affordability. Maybe this is actually a crime perpetrated by the State against the people by denying them a dignified health status).

d. '*Breaking any queue*' (again I would rationalize in an opposite manner by punishing the State for this crime. People break bus queues because there is not enough public transport provided and also because they have to get home before curfews; queues are broken as the public distribution system is woefully inadequate; queues are broken because new State-sponsored unconstitutional cards such as *Aadhar* have to be applied for as identity proof; queues are broken in order to apply for school and college admissions and even pay the fees as State expenditure on education has declined—the list is indeed long. My question, therefore, is, who commits the crime and who is punished?).

e. 'Driving, dragging or pushing any non-motorised vehicle at any time between half an hour after sunset & one hour before sunrise' (I truly believe that this activity has been identified as a crime at the behest of manufacturers of cars, jeeps, scooters, and motorcycles, in order to expand their market and enhance their sales. No other explanation can provide a rational for banning carts, rickshaws, horse-drawn carriages such as tongas, bullock-carts, cycles, and other non-motorized means of transport).

What is indeed rather creatively draconian is the power of the police to prohibit or control in any manner

a. exhibition of living persons or corpses.
b. preparation, exhibition, representation, distribution or dissemination of pictures, symbols, placards, printed matter, pamphlets, books, audio-video recordings, digital records,

posters which may inflame communal or religious passions or offend general standards of public morality or seriously affect public peace or endanger security of the nation.

This is a clear attack on the prevalent cultural practices of taking out processions (*janaza*) of those deceased, especially of those revered as '*shahid*' [Muslim martyr]—a practice that has gained prominence in the last few decades and is perceived as a 'permissible' form of protest.

Part (b) is truly inexplicable and smacks of utter paranoia and a deep-seated fear on the part of the State of any manifestation whatsoever of people's expression. Books, articles, exhibitions, posters, banners, hoardings, films, music, and so on are now considered as worth prohibiting and to be punishable in case they not only inflame religious feelings but also morality.

The questions here are obvious: Whose religion? Which religion? Will religious sentiments be hurt when different communities seek solace at Baba Rishi's, when they tie *mannats* [special prayers] at Shankaracharya Temple, when they visit Vaishnodevi Mandir, or when they meditate at Thikse Monastery? What is morality? Who defines morality? Is wearing jeans a crime? Is using makeup to be made punishable? Can the use of kohl be viewed as being immoral? Is not wearing a veil a crime? Is singing to be made punishable, especially in a state that has been historically steeped in the culture of Sufism where singing and chanting are the cornerstones, and where Lal Ded's verses are sung even today by all communities in all regions?

Special Security Zones (SSZs)

The creation of SSZ's seems to have been inspired by the ubiquitous special economic zones, special manufacturing zones, special tourist zones—most of which have been spectacular failures. The Bill states that any inflow of funds as well as 'production, sale, storage, possession or entry of any devices or equipment' into SSZs can be banned if these are 'reasonably considered a threat to internal security or public order in any manner'. These devices and equipment could well include kerosene, gas cylinders, stoves, batteries, torches, electrical equipment, wires, axes, spades, hoes, ploughs, cutters, scissors, kitchen knives,

screw drivers, garden snippers, scalpels, lancets, surgical instruments—
the possibilities are endless.

Possibly the most innovative and most dangerous clause of the
Bill is that in these SSZs 'administrative & development measures'
are integrated with police response for 'problems of public
order and security'. The denial of the application of the current
rights-based approach to the people in these SSZ's disaffirms the
application and implementation of all governmental schemes and
flagship programmes such as Mahatma Gandhi National Rural
Employment Guarantee Act (MGNREGA), Prime Minister's Rural
Road Connectivity Programme, that is, the Pradhan Mantri Gram
Sadak Yojna (PMGSY), Total Sanitation Campaign, Rajiv Gandhi
Urban Housing Scheme or Rajiv Awas Yojana (RAY), Indra Rural
Housing Scheme or Indira Awaas Yojana (IAY), Public Distribution
System, Rehabilitation of Victims of Violence, the plethora of women's
schemes and so on. The denial of the recently passed National Food
Security Act (NFSA) to the residents of Jammu and Kashmir in the
name of security is not only a travesty and lampoonery, but is, in
fact, clearly subversive of the rights of people who it is claimed are
an 'integral' part of India.

7

Women, Peace and Security: The Context of North East India

Paula Banerjee

Thangjam Manorama was arrested from her house in the middle of the night and the next day her dead body was found in a hillside. Even if she was involved in insurgency under which law is it legitimate that a woman can be arbitrarily arrested, raped and murdered brutally. Her body and private parts were ridden with bullets. It was the high point of our discontent. Eventually I was one of the 12 mothers who protested nude in front of Kangla Fort, at that time occupied by the Assam rifles. I shouted 'rape us kill us, we are all Manorama's mothers.' I shouted in English because I want this message to be heard through the world.[1]

This was how Lourembam Nganbi, a leader of the Meira Paibis considered her role in the movement against violence in Manipur. The history of violence has shown the various ways in which conflict impacts the security of women and men in North East India. A review of the impact of violence reveals a deep understanding of how 'security; in conflict societies is connected to peace. In this connection we must remember that 'the relationship between women, peace and security is not automatic question—peace must be made to work for women' as suggested in the review of the UN Security Council Resolution 1325 (hereinafter Resolution 1325) by the NGO Working Group on Women, Peace And Security in its report 'From Local to Global: Making Peace Work for Women' (October 2005). Through the 'three P's' of participation, protection and prevention, Resolution 1325 endeavours to ensure the engagement of women from bottom to top, through encouraging grass root level, feminist activism in prevention, management and resolution of conflict situations. These three stages are important, as most societies oscillate between these three stages particularly in the areas affected by protracted 'conflict', such as is the case in Manipur and Nagaland, two states in North East India. The P's of promotion and protection further call for the active participation of both state and non-state actors to ensure gender-just approaches during times of conflict. The three P's taken together can be read as effective tools for transforming victims of gender-based violence into agents of political engagement, through providing them with legal safeguards. The implementation of Resolution 1325 needs to be contextualized within the changing nature of political and democratic engagement by women's groups in Manipur and Nagaland. The three common issues that women's groups in Manipur and Nagaland have been working on are: (a) repel of Armed Forces Special Powers Act (AFSPA); (b) protest against gender-based violence (GBV); and (c) anti-militarization.

Women are often portrayed as passive victims in conflict situations but that is certainly not the only role they play. Stereotypical of women as the victims and men as the perpetrators of violence denies each their agency and associated voice as actors in the process. In previous studies we have seen that women play multiple roles in conflict. They can be both the aggressor and the peace maker. Women are part of the people killed and belong to the thousands displaced by ensuing violence. They witness their children killed and maimed by the conflict. During conflict they live, laugh, cry, sometimes miscarry or give birth to their children in the bush, and always try to survive. Some lose their livelihoods, others lose their crops. Conflict leads to impoverishment of many women and so their protection needs are heightened. Governance in the post-conflict period is also a matter of serious implications. It is often the cause for re-emergence of conflict.

Sometimes, however, conflict governance produces some other phenomena. As has been stated earlier, women play multiple roles in conflict. They can be both the aggressor and the victim. But in both capacities they are always unequal to men and this inequality can bring forth unusual alliances. In different parts of the world women often ally with their own men during conflict and their actions can range from encouraging their men folk to wage war, cooking for the warriors and secretly transporting weapons. For example, among the Kisii tribe, women scream to declare the start of war between the Kisii and the Maasai. Women who refuse to scream are divorced by their husbands because it is the women who are supposed to scream to announce the beginning of a conflict. Kisii women collect stones for men to fight. The women also sharpen arrows and poison them in preparation for war. In some cultures, women taunt men for cowardice if they do not seem ready to participate in a conflict between their community and other communities. In India we were brought up with the story of the women from Rajputana who refused to recognize their husbands who fled from the battle field. Amongst pastoralist women, they give blessings to young men to go to war. They transport arms and food for warriors and pass on important information. It is futile to think that women will stay away from supporting their communities when the said community is embroiled in violent actions. However, appeals can be made and are made to these women so that they favour political and non-military solutions. In this process they can enter other creative alliances that can have the potential of changing the nature of conflict. That is what seems to have happened in the northeastern states of Nagaland and Manipur in India.

Most of the women's groups' in North East India have adopted non-traditional security approaches as ways to contain and prevent conflict. Such approaches encourage women to participate in a dialogic process and explore possible ways to engage with the state without precipitating further violence. In the case of Manipur and Nagaland, various women's organizations have played a key role in translating their 'traditional' roles as 'mothers' into being social and political agents; they have successfully used the social sanction of being a 'protector' that 'motherhood' has traditionally offered in Indian culture and history. 'Motherhood' has been time and again evoked to challenge the masculinist discourse of nationhood. The two organizations that have played a key role in Manipur and Naga society are Meira Paibis and the Naga Mothers Association (NMA). Both share a unique history and both have worked in anti-militarization movements, and for peace, reconciliation, and the mobilization of women in their respective societies. While the NMA has played an important role in the ceasefire negotiation between the Government of India (GoI) and the National Socialist Council of Nagaland-Isak Muivah (NSCN-IM), the Meira Paibis are considered to be in a liminal zone between the state and non-governmental organizations (NGOs), although they have launched and are known for leading some of the largest and most publicized protests and rallies. The liminal space these movements occupy in societal structures arises from its non-engagement with other forms of gender violence such as domestic violence and the inheritance rights of women. These movements have been successful in the spaces between public and political discussion, since they conform to the patriarchal division of private and public space without invading either. In other words, women in North East India have resorted to traditional spaces of 'motherhood' to transform themselves into political agents of peace among their communities through reconstituting themselves on ethnic lines. They have emerged as the women's voices of their respective communities and have tried to contain the violence from within and from the outside. However, in the 1996 parliamentary elections in India, there were only two women candidates out of a total of 28 from Manipur. Only recently have women's groups raised their voices to speak loudly about women's participation in representational politics.

To understand the politicization of women in Nagaland and Manipur, one has to look at the history of conflict in these two regions.

Nagaland and Manipur: The History of Conflict

Since childhood, I have great affection for my community and for the older people and weaker sections of the society. I got this bent of mind from my grandmother Lamabam Amubi who participated in Second Women's Agitation in Manipur in 1939. I participated in the 27 August, 1965 movement against the price rise of food grains. I also participated in the students' movement. In the movement for the demand of the statehood of Manipur as a student I took part. After I got married I was confined to my home raising five kids and because of this I could not devote myself to the social causes. By late 1990s as my children grew up I could get time to be involved in the social causes. We took over the movement of nisa bandi which was once led by our mother and elders and started working with Meira Paibis of other localities for various social issues.[2]

North East India shares borders with Bangladesh, Bhutan, China and Myanmar and so the eight states can be called 'border states'. The British began administering the area through a series of acts such as the *Schedules District Act of 1874* and the *Frontier Tracts Regulations of 1880.* In 1873, the British passed the inner line regulation. According to one analyst, the logic behind this regulation was that the, 'unrestricted movements which existed between the British subjects in Assam and the wild tribes living across the frontiers frequently led to quarrels and sometimes to serious disturbances' (Hazarika 1996, 74). The British administration also wanted to control the rubber trade that was still in the hands of the hill people and that caused frequent skirmishes between the groups. The inner lines regulation was a means to separate the *civilized* plains people and the *wild* hill people. The inner line did not in any way give the sovereignty to the hill people rather it was a means by which administrative zones of the hills and the plains were separated ostensibly because the civilized faced problems with cohabiting with the wild. The Government of India Bill of 1935 classified the hill areas of Assam into excluded and partially excluded areas. This was done mainly to exclude the hill areas of Assam from the jurisdiction of the reformed provincial government that included the plain lands of Brahmaputra and Barak Valleys. This policy resulted in the separate political evolution of the hill and the plain lands. The excluded areas were not demarcated to protect regional autonomy. Rather, it was meant to keep recalcitrant groups at bay. It also meant that the hill areas remained excluded from all constitutional experiments that were embarked upon within the jurisdiction of British India. To justify such demarcations, there was a process of demonization of certain groups of people, at least in the official discourses that were considered recalcitrant.

During the constituent assembly debates, the process continued. During the debate on the provisions of the Sixth Schedule, such a mentality was apparent particularly among members of the dominant groups. When there were discussions of making the Naga Hills an autonomous council some of the responses of the members of the Assembly reflected the attitude of the architects of the Constitution towards these people. Kuladhar Chaliha from Assam was particularly vocal. He said:

> The Nagas are a very primitive and simple people and they have not forgotten their old ways of doing summary justice when they have a grievance against anyone. If you allow them to rule us or run the administration it will be a negation of justice or administration and it will be something like anarchy. (Chaliha 1949)

Although not as vociferous as Kuladhar Chaliha, there were many more who made it obvious that the Nagas did not belong. Brajeshwar Prasad from Bihar during the same debate stated that

> responsibilities of parliamentary life can be shouldered by those who are competent, wise, just and literate. To vest wide political powers into the hands of the tribals; is the surest method of inviting chaos, anarchy and disorder throughout the length and breadth of this country. (Prasad 1949)

Even Gopinath Bordoloi who drafted the Sixth Schedule commented that currently hardly any of the tribes can be called self-governing but 'the time may come when they may become fit to govern themselves' (Bordoloi 1946).

Discussions on the Sixth Schedule were a precursor of things to come in the future. The members of constituent assembly who were deliberating on the creation of a democratic constitution for India were not merely obsessed with the idea of maintaining order as Paul Brass has suggested. That was just one of the things that they concerned themselves with. They were also in the business of constructing a citizenship that would be loyal to the order that they were seeking to maintain. On the basis of such criteria, they constructed notions and discourse of who belonged and who did not. They created a hierarchy of citizenship and in that hierarchy, many North Eastern tribal groups were at the bottom rung. Their avowed difference was considered deviance and they were at best patronized and at worst vilified. At the back of everyone's mind was the fact that these people were not *us* and so unworthy of any autonomy or self-rule. Even as early as in the constituent assembly, the nation's leaders were using the language of their colonizers to deal with all those they considered as *other*/deviant. This was decisive in shaping state attitude towards the region. An analysis of later laws such as the AFSPA, the National Security Act and so on will also portray how groups were marked recalcitrant by evolving border laws and then they were treated as criminals.

The region that North East India borders is one of endemic poverty, social imbalance and political violence particularly against vulnerable groups of whom women form a large part. It is the region between India, Bangladesh, Nepal, Bhutan and Myanmar among others. This region is undergoing certain social and political turmoil where more and more women are getting marginalized. There are increasing numbers of cases of human rights abuse against women in this region who are considered by the majoritarian state as belonging to alien groups. Rapes, torture and the ultimate abuse of women through trafficking and flesh trade have multiplied over the years. Therefore, notwithstanding state discourse, it is not just women from Bangladesh, Burma and Nepal who are victims of multiple injustices but also those of North East India. Women here habitually fall prey to army bullets and traffickers alike. In newspaper reports, this predicament that women face in the region is often highlighted. In one such coverage it was stated: 'Of late, there have been reports in the media that trafficking in women is taking place from Assam and other states of the North East, and a well-established conduit is functioning to dispatch the hapless women to the metros of the country' (*Meghalaya Guardian* 2004). In another such report it was stated that

> Human trafficking is not a new problem in our country. What is of concern is that, of late, the north-east has become a supply zone for trafficking women and children of not only in the flesh trade but for forced labour, child labour, organ transplantation, camel jockey and others. (*Imphal Free Press* 2005)

The protracted state versus community and community versus community conflict has not helped matters at all. It has increased the level of violence in the entire region leading to marginalization of women.

Nagaland and Manipur: History from Inside

The historiography of North East India from the other side, that is, from the side of Manipur and Nagaland, looks very different. It is vivid with 'treacherous' accounts of accession by the 'Indian state' post the declaration of independence of the Indian dominion by the British Crown on 15 August 1947. Most of the armed resistance groups are said to be fighting for autonomy under the leadership of those who believe in the right to self-rule. In Manipur some of the armed resistance groups are the Manipur People's Army (the armed wing of

United Nations Liberation Front), People's Liberation Army (PLA) and the People's Revolutionary Party of Kangleipak (PREPAK). The list is endless. With time the number of armed resistance is on a rise and the only way of coping with the conflict that the Indian state has resorted to is through militarization of Manipur. The massive militarization that Manipur has witnessed over more than six decades is further legitimized by the existing AFSPA, where the army officials of any rank and order could resort to violence to maintain law and order. Present day Manipur is flagged with multi-layered problems with the parallel existence of democratic functionaries and institutions like the panchayats, municipality and state legislative assembly on one hand and the day to day challenges posed by militarization by the state and the increasing number of armed resistance groups on the other. The presence of military forces has created frictions between ethnic groups and a clear divide between the valley people (areas dominated by Meiteis) and the hill people (areas dominated by Naga and Kuki Tribes).

The Naga struggle is embedded in a much deeper history of ethnic identity and territoriality, which could be traced back to the Treaty of Yandabo 1826, which brought the British to the North Eastern part of India. According to Achumbemo Kikon, for administrative convenience, the British established the Naga Hills district in 1866, which later on merged with Assam in 1874 (Kikon 2003). With the formation of Naga club in 1918, the Naga voices became consolidated to assert the sentiments and voices of the people. A memorandum submitted to the Simon Commission in 1929 made it quite clear that 'Naga areas be left out of the proposed reform scheme'. In 1946, under the leadership of Angami Zapu Phizo, the so-called 'father of the Naga Nation', Naga National Council (NNC) was formed. Under the banner of NNC, the Nagas declared their independence on 14 August 1947, a day prior to the 'Indian' independence. The sentiments of the Naga people went unheard and the nascent Indian state in order to safeguard the 'integrity' of the Indian nation 'adopted repressive policies and suppressed the Nagas with its military strength'.

From 1948 onwards, the Naga problem escalated. In 1947, the Naga Hills were divided between Assam and Manipur and the next year many Nagas, including Daiho Mao, were arrested following their efforts to blockade an entry point to the Naga Hills. Within the mainland it was widely held that Burmese communists infiltrating into Assam were aiding the Nagas. By early 1951, the Nagas asked for a plebiscite and predictably were refused. Under the auspices of NNC the Nagas themselves called a plebiscite where, overwhelmingly, almost everyone voted in favour of independence. On 16 May 1951 that plebiscite was held where 99.9% voted to reassert Naga position of an independent homeland devoid of domination and political control of any sort. Following the plebiscite, the Nagas boycotted the two Indian general elections in 1952 and 1957. In 1963, Nagaland was created on the basis of what is known as the 'sixteen point agreement' which has been the subject of critique as some like Achumbemo believe that this agreement was offered to 'Naga People's Convention' (NPC), a group handpicked by the Indian Intelligence to mediate between the Naga resistance groups and the Indian government. Nagaland state was created based on this memorandum which never incorporated the views of the Naga people or resistance groups. Thus, post-independence Nagas were distributed in four states, Manipur, Assam, Arunachal Pradesh, with a majority in Nagaland. In the 1950s, the GoI placed restrictions on NNC. The movement for Nagalim spearheaded by NNC was divided into two factions in 1980. Under the leadership of General Secretary Th. Muviah, NNC Vice President Issak Swu and President of Eastern NNC, SS Khaplang, broke away to form National Socialist Council of Nagaland (NSCN). In 1988, there were further factions and the two groups are now known by the name of the leaders, Isak Muivah faction and Khaplang faction.

The Indian State chose to cope with the crisis of sovereignty and autonomy movements through militarization of Manipur and Nagaland. A paternalistic top-down securitization approach through militarization and enforcement of AFSPA in Nagaland and Manipur has been the reason behind many a bloodshed and atrocities. The ceasefire agreement between the GoI and the NSCN has been in place for more than 15 years. The contradictory nature of ceasefire lies in the very existence of AFSPA in Nagaland, presence of Indian Army and the way women continue to become victims of community honour in this transitional phase of political instability. The violence generated by state and non-state actors have been responsible for loss of human dignity and gross violation of human rights that completely engulfed the lives of people. Before getting into any other discussion, it is essential to explore the nature of violence.

The Disturbed Areas Act

One of the preferred modes of governance in Nagaland and Manipur for the GoI in the last century was through extraordinary powers. Assam Disturbed Areas Act 1955 was one of the first of such extraordinary legislations. This declared most of the Naga areas in Assam as disturbed areas. As has been repeatedly explained, the Act in question

> was enacted with a view to make better provision for the suppression of disorder and for restoration and maintenance of public order in the disturbed areas in Assam. Section 2 of the State Act also defines disturbed area to mean an area which is for the time being declared by notification under Section 3 to be a disturbed area. Section 3 lays down that the State Government may, by notification in the official gazette of Assam, declare the whole or any part of any district of Assam, as may be specified in the notification, to be a disturbed area.[3]

The Act, however, could not bring peace. In fact it led to more disturbances. Although the Act was meant to suppress disorder, it actually added to it. Probably, the most problematic section of the Act of this genre is the following:

> In a 'disturbed area', any Magistrate or Police Officer not below the rank of Sub-Inspector or Head Constable in case of the Armed Branch of the Police may, if he is of opinion that it is necessary so to do for the maintenance of public order, after giving such due warning, as he may consider necessary, fire upon, or otherwise use force, even to the causing of death, against any person who is indulging in any act which may result in serious breach of public order or is acting in contravention of any law or order for the time being in force, prohibiting the assembly of five or more persons or the carrying of weapons or of things capable of being used as weapons or of fire arms, ammunition or explosive substances.[4]

Provisions of this kind made the Disturbed Areas Acts so notorious. Once in place, it became almost impossible to repeal them. The Acts of this had a penchant of multiplying areas within its jurisdiction in leaps and bounds. Although the Assam Disturbed Areas Act started as a state legislation, it almost inevitably led to the Disturbed Areas (Special Courts) Act, 1976 (No. 77 of 1976) passed by the central government and then finally the Jammu and Kashmir Disturbed Areas

Act of 1992. Even in the last one year (2012), Tripura and Manipur both asked for an extension of this Act. But among the Acts of this genre the most notorious is the AFSPA.

The AFSPA was a take off, with certain modifications, from the Armed Forces (Special Powers) Ordinance 1942 of British India. Only it is much harsher than the previous Ordinance. In the previous Ordinance, power to take action was authorized on an officer of the rank of captain but in this Act power rested even with non-commissioned officers. Also, the previous Ordinance was meant for the whole of India unlike the present one. Protests escalated in the Naga Hills when reprisals came in the form of the Assam Maintenance of Public Order (Autonomous District) Regulation Act in 1953. It was operative in the Naga Hills and Tuensang districts. The Act empowered the governor to impose collective fines, prohibit public meetings and detain anybody without a warrant.[5] While protests continued, those portions of Naga Hill districts that formed parts of Assam were placed under military rule in 1955 on the basis of the recently formulated Assam Disturbed Areas Act. The same year, the NNC set up the 'Federal Government of Nagaland', which had a military wing. Before the year ended, it was said that there were 'nearly one security troop for every adult male Naga in the Naga Hills' (B.N. Mullick, the head of Indian Intelligence Service, quoted in Luithui and Welman 2002). The 1958, AFSPA was meant for only the Naga Hills and parts of Manipur. But like the Ordinance, the AFSPA is meant to suppress civil society, curb dissent and legitimize state violence. As one observer has maintained, 'logic demanded that an India that fought against such powers would, when independent, get rid of such legislation. Events, however, have proved the contrary' (Khala 2003).

G.B. Pant, the Home Minister, introduced the bill stating that it was intended to quell 'arson, murder, loot, dacoity etc. by certain misguided sections of the Nagas'. It was because of such violent actions of the Nagas that 'it has become necessary to adopt effective measures for the protection of the people in those areas'. So it was in the name of the people that this bill was introduced, which gave the armed forces almost unlimited power over the life and death of these same people. There were some members who cautioned against such blanket powers to the army but their voices were generally disregarded. The deputy speaker of the Lok Sabha criticized the government by stating,

[I]t pains me that we have an occasion in this House to give our assent to martial law which was forced on us by an Ordinance.... Why have they (the Congress Government) smuggled this legislation in this way? It is really a challenge to the concept of democracy and freedom that we have.[6]

Among the other critiques there were some that felt the 'Parliament is giving its seal of approval to a legal monstrosity to quell another kind of monstrosity'.[7] Even the speaker asked the home minister:

Does the Honourable Minister feel that this is the procedure, he can shoot if it is a disturbed area, that is the procedure established by law? He can shoot [italics added]. Anybody can be killed or shot at, but is this procedure established by law, does it go to that extent? Article 21 says that no person can be deprived of his life. Here any person can be deprived of life by any commissioned officer, he can shoot [italics added].[8]

When the bill was being debated, both the members of parliament (MP) from Manipur vehemently objected to it. Laishram Achaw Singh, MP from Inner Manipur parliamentary constituency argued:

In my humble opinion, this measure is unnecessary and also unwarranted. This Bill is sure to bring about complications and difficulties in those areas, especially those which are going to be declared as disturbed areas. I fail to understand why the military authorities are to be invested with special powers. I have found that these military authorities have always committed excesses in many cases, especially in the sub-divisions of Kohima and Mokokchung. In such a situation, I do not like that the officers should be invested with special powers .... This piece of legislation is an anti-democratic measure and also a reactionary one. Instead of helping to keep the law and order position in these areas, if they declare some areas as disturbed areas, it would cause more repression, more misunderstanding and more of unnecessary persecutions in the tribal areas. This is a black law. This is also an act of provocation on the part of the Government. How can we imagine that these military officers should be allowed to shoot to kill and without warrant, arrest and search. This is a lawless law.[9]

Even after such ringing protest from MPs of the region the AFSPA of 1958 was enacted after mere three hours of debate in Lok Sabha and four hours of debate in Rajya Sabha. The Act was meant to be in the statute books for only one year but it is operative even today. The AFSPA of 1958 gave the state government the power to define any area as disturbed. The home minister argued, when faced with the criticism, that he is wresting power away from the state governments, that he was actually increasing the powers of the state as by this Act they had the power to summon the military whenever they wanted to do so. That this was hardly the case would become apparent when in 1972 this provision was changed. For now the state government had the power to declare any area as disturbed. The AFSPA is a prime example of how democracy legitimizes violence on the people that it considers errant/deviant. The evolving history of this Act will portray how a state by institutionalizing violence securitizes a certain area and how that leads to the securitization of the whole region.

Among its many articles in AFSPA, there is one that says that anyone can be shot dead even on suspicion of being a terrorist by a commissioned member of the armed forces. A decade back, a young woman named Irom Sharmila started her protest against this Act by fasting unto death. Today, she is kept alive by forced feeding through the nose as the state can little afford another martyr with a history of non-violent protest that is the specialty of many women protestors in the region be they Naga, Kuki or Meitei. The operation and history of the Act portrays how women have suffered under this Act and in the hands of the two patriarchies—the rebel and the armed forces (Banerjee 2001). The Act militarized the entire region of North East India, particularly Manipur and Nagaland. A result of this Act is that it has caused an inflow of men working with security structures of the government. Hence, in many parts of North East India, infrastructure work such as road building for safe movements of troops necessitated the presence of skilled labour and technical hand and so it attracted largely men. Also the inflow of security personnel in the region increased the share of male migrants. Such a situation affected the sex ratio negatively. It coincided with the growing violence against the women in the region. Another aspect of AFSPA is that it requires a mandatory sanction from the central government for any legal proceeding against the armed forces. Section 6 of the Act says that no prosecution, suit or other legal proceeding shall be instituted without the previous sanction of the central government against any person for anything done in exercise of powers conferred by this Act. Undermining of the civil space, that is a direct consequence of immunity extended to the army, this has eroded the available space for democratic and peaceful dissent. The requirement of 'prior sanction' has resulted into virtual immunity to armed forces.

After almost half a century, the AFSPA continues to occupy the centre-stage of a bitter debate over its existence. Vociferous calls for its repeal from civil rights activists have been acknowledged by the Second Administrative Reforms Commission, which has recently recommended its repeal. As with previous recommendations of repeal, such as the Reddy Committee's in 2005, government officials reacted with immediate and emphatic disapproval. They concede possibilities of improvement in the law but categorically reject its repeal.

One of the biggest debates on AFSPA was generated in 1997. Discussing the Supreme Court rulings on AFSPA in the NPMHR versus Union of India in 1997, the Human Rights Features stated the following:

> In the 1997 case Naga People's Movement of Human Rights v. Union of India the Supreme Court upheld the constitutionality of the AFSPA but placed various checks on the armed forces' exercise of power thereunder. Specifically, the Court rejected the petitioners' argument that the AFSPA was unconstitutional because it transferred to the armed forces full power to maintain public order in a disturbed area whereas the Constitution only permits Parliament to enact laws relating to the 'use of the Armed Forces in aid of civil power'.
>
> But in rejecting this argument, the apex Court also held that the 'in aid of civil power' clause mandated the continued existence and relevance of the authority to be aided. Under the AFSPA, therefore, the armed forces cannot 'supplant or act as a substitute' for a State's civilian authorities in the maintenance of public order, but are strictly required to act in cooperation with them.
>
> Accordingly, the Court understood the armed forces' power under AFSPA Section 4(c) to arrest any person without a warrant for suspected commission of a cognisable offence in light of Section 5, which requires handing over the arrested person to the nearest police station with the 'least possible delay'. The Court further stressed that the 'least possible delay' language of the AFSPA reflected the requirements of the Criminal Procedure Code (CrPC) and the Constitution, which

mandate production of a detainee before the nearest Magistrate within 24 hours of arrest.

Similarly with respect to the search and seizure powers granted under Section 4(d) of the AFSPA, the Court interpreted the AFSPA to require the armed forces to transfer custody of seized property to local police forces. Furthermore, in conducting searches and seizures under Section 4(d), the armed forces were bound by relevant CrPC provisions that would otherwise bind civilian authorities....

Following the NPMHR ruling, the Gauhati High Court, which has jurisdiction over the conflict-prone Northeast States, has faithfully applied NPMHR's reasoning to restrict the power of the armed forces to act independently of State authorities. For instance, the High Court held that the armed forces' refusal to involve local police in an operation to track down suspected militants in Assam overstepped the bounds of the AFSPA. Similarly, the Court held that the armed forces' failure to hand over arrested persons to local police authorities represented violations of the AFSPA. In such situations, the Gauhati High Court has insisted that the armed forces demonstrate adequate factual circumstances to justify non-compliance with the requirement of handing over custody to civilian authorities with the 'least possible delay'.[10]

However, on 2 May 2007 in the Masooda Parveen versus Union of India and Ors, it was argued that

It is Mr. Ganesh's plea that despite the fact that police station Pampore was a stones throw away from village Chandhara, no effort had been made by the army to convey the information to the police at the earliest and the police had been called in only on the morning of 3rd February, 1998 after Regoo had been done to death. Mr. Ganesh has also placed reliance on the judgment of this Court in Naga People's Movement of Human Rights vs. Union of India (1998) 2 SCC 109 to contend that while upholding the vires of the Armed Forces (J&K) Special powers Act, 1958, this Court had laid down certain guidelines which would mutatis mutandis apply to a search, seizure and arrest under the Act as well. He has pointed out that the basic principle which governed the exercise of authority under the Act was that the army was to act in aid of the civil power meaning thereby that the pre-eminence of the civil authority had in no way been diluted. He has, in particular, placed reliance on the specific conclusions drawn in paragraph 74 of the Report and has pointed out that this Court had clarified that the civil power continued to function even after the deployment of the armed forces.[11]

Not accepting these arguments, the Supreme Court ruled that what the army did was very much within its authority and therefore no punitive measures were to be entertained. In the Thangjam Manorama case in 2005, the initial ruling of the Guwahati High Court was the following:

> The State of Manipur is not the appropriate Government having any administrative control over the armed forces deployed in the State. On the other hand, the members of the Armed Forces are entitled to protections as per provisions of Section 6 of the Act of 1958 which provide that no prosecution, suit or other legal proceeding shall be instituted, except with the previous sanction of the Central Government. The Central Government being the appropriate Government and having absolute control over the armed forces deployed in a disturbed area has to deal with the report and take follow-up action as may be necessary in accordance with the provisions of law. Since the subject-matter of dispute is a definite matter of public importance, the Union Government is required to take appropriate decision without least possible delay.
>
> In the result, both the writ petitions are disposed of with direction to the State of Manipur to hand over the report to the Union Government in the Ministry of Home Affairs without delay. The Union Home Ministry, represented by the Secretary, will examine the report and pass orders/ take appropriate action against the 17th Assam Rifles personnel, if any, indicted in the report without loss of time. The Union Home Ministry shall also take an immediate decision about publication of the report in tune with the citizens' right to information. The people of Manipur seek justice and it should be done forthwith to restore their confidence in the Constitution and the laws.[12]

A ruling of the principal bench of the Guwahati High Court made on 31 August 2010 clearly said that the state government is competent to conduct inquiry over the armed forces and the inquiry commission set up by the state government to probe the killing of Thangjam Manorama is legitimate. Hence, the state authority and can take up actions against the accused army personnel. This ruling was followed by the Guwahati High Court ruling on 10 January 2011 in which a double bench of Guwahati High Court comprising of Chief Justice Madan Bhimarao Lokur and Justice Ashok Potsangbam issued a notice of motion regarding the case of Thangjam Manorama.[13] It asked the Union of India and 17 Assam Riffles as to why Manorama was not handed over to civil custody. The Assam Rifles filed a petition and took the case to Supreme Court.

The AFSPA created a milieu of uncertainty, fear and violence within states and the spectre of this violence pervaded over the mode of governance and Naga women argue that women are the greatest victim of this violence. Not just the women from Nagaland but much of the women from North East India are of the opinion that the AFSPA should be removed immediately. In Manipur, women had launched a major campaign on this in 2004. In Nagaland also such a campaign is on, merely it is not as dramatic as the one in Manipur. The last few decisions of the courts and the government over AFSPA portrayed that there was a growing ambivalence about the AFSPA and a realization that violence alone is not a problem solvent in the administrative circles. The government therefore changed its tenor and embarked on a program for development of the people, particularly the women. It was slowly taking up the role of champion of Naga women particularly because it found in the women strong supporters of the ceasefire. This was happening exactly at a time when the GoI was opening itself up to the east through the Look East Policy and due to which peace in northeast was becoming a priority.

Impact of Conflict on Women

In the name of territorial sovereignty and integrity, on the one hand, and maintenance of law and order, on the other, both state and non-state actors have resorted to gendered forms of violence such as rape and physical assault. Women have suffered due to their identities as mothers and wives; they have been used as couriers and human shields during the conflict. The violence inflicted on men and women by state and non-state forces reveals the gendered power structures and gender ideologies.

The women in Manipur live with the parallel challenge of being configured both as victims and as agents of community management. Empirical evidence, particularly newspaper reports illustrate the various forms of 'gendered' violence which, according to Rita Manchanda is a continuation of the violence experienced in 'normal' conditions (Manchanda 2005). In the ongoing conflict situations the numbers of violent incidents are constantly on the rise as both state and non-state armed conflict impacts on civilians, particularly women. In North East India, both the state and non-state military forces recognize women as agents of peace. What does agents of peace in conflicts situations imply? Does it merely mean playing the role of negotiator or mediator to resolve immediate conflicts or does it entail engaging with the larger socio-political framework that produces conflicts? The immediate role in resolving conflicts lies in the shoulder of the women of Manipur as the chief minister is quoted in a leading daily,

> [A]s saying Manipur is today veritably on fire and the major onus of dousing this fire rests on the shoulders of our womenfolk who have always taken a major role in the shaping the history of the land. He said there are no sons who will not listen to their mothers, no brother who cannot be influenced by their sisters. (*Imphal Free Press* 2001)

The above statement idolizes women as symbolic bearers of national and ethnic identity, and hence their roles as mothers and sisters are crucial to fostering the feeling of nationality. It is the same ideology that encourages gender based violence during times of war 'to erode the social and moral fabric of entire communities' (Gervais 2007). It is against this backdrop that we need to situate the women's role as peacekeepers in Manipur society. Before revisiting the role of women as peacekeepers, it is also important to understand how women have contributed to the socio-economic and political processes of bringing about peace. In this context, it is important to remind ourselves that the experiences of women as 'victims' and as agents of peace and social organization are varied, owing to their affiliation to various ethnic groups. Women have been marginalized within their own ethnic groups; and they are constantly fighting for their socio-economic and political rights. The rising conflict has made its own demands on the women to take on the role of negotiators which has expanded the role of women not just in the civilian but the political sphere as well. Women from all the ethnic groups party to the conflict have taken part in the resistance movements; and one of the common points of state oppression shared by all the women's groups in the region is the AFSPA (1958) which they are all seeking to have repealed. Similarly, it is important to look at how these women's groups are negotiating with the challenges they face regarding their participation in democratic politics, be it the panchayat, state and general elections, their position in the village councils and apex court (in case of Naga tribes), and the injustices they face regarding the disparity in inheritance practices. Feminist interventions in security discourse have helped us in widening the paradigm of 'security' measures to be taken in conflict zones. Conflict zones, as we are all aware, produce and reproduce hierarchies instead of resolving the tensions. Testimonies bear evidence to the multilayered, gendered nature of violence, be it physical, emotional or social. All these three forms of violence are interrelated and inform political and social issues. The state has often appealed to women to be agents of peace, reasserting their role as mothers and sisters. The evocation of 'feminine' values is couched in the hierarchization and reproduction of the male/female divide, based on masculine and feminine values, a tension which never gets resolved and is only addressed when women's movements resort to patriarchal rhetoric of 'motherhood' and fail to take a political standpoint against patriarchy.

The testimonies of women presented below reveal some of the contradictions of the women's movements, and also highlight how women's political engagement whether in democratic political institutions or in voluntary organizations provides them with a forum in which to bring in their perspective in managing conflict situations. Such political participation by women carries with it the possibility of transgressing the stereotypes which are often the centres of justification of control over sexuality. What follows are the testimonies of women activists in these two states of North East India, Manipur and Nagaland.

I was born after World War II. The Naga Insurgency began during our childhood. When we were in primary schools, we were frightened from all corners. There were frequent encounters between Naga UGs and ARs. Most of the parents warned their children that when you hear gunshots you have to roll down. If Army comes you must not talk too much. For a long time parents advised us to keep our essential commodities ready as at any moment we had to hide in paddy fields. No free movement was allowed in Ukhrul. Ukhrul was declared a disturbed area under AFSPA. My father was called by the Army because he was found in possession of a country made rifle (licensed). He was a government employee in the Health Department. I was in class two when this incident happened. The court case continued for two – three years and my parents spent all their earnings on this case. Government of India has ignored our area as it is a border district. There is hardly any development at all.

In 2004–2005 I personally met some of the key persons of UG groups and urged them to stop killing. It is important to internationalise our women's body of Naga women. We need to form a network of Naga and Manipuri women. Women should come out and talk to their respective groups and bring the UG groups on the same platform to enter into dialogue so that we could achieve our larger goals.[14]

My husband died in January 2006 in a shooting. He went out of the house saying he would be getting money from the bills of his contract work. My house is at Thongu Part II close to Manipur University. I made no demand for ex-gratia. I had never worked before my husband's death as he never allowed me to go outside though I was always interested in social work. I made no demand for ex-gratia. What would I have done with ex-gratia? After I became a Gram Panchayat member, all eyes are on me. I am now a public face. People come to me with appeals of funds release for NREGS jobs card, allocations, pay, and so on. BPL cards do not even reach people. Women should be encouraged to take part in the decision-making process. I have set an example, people say. When I go for Sports.

Meet and share the dais with other members they always point towards me. I feel proud when I hear words of appreciation from school children.[15]

I, as a secretary of the Kwairamband Nupi Kethel Semgat Sagatpa Lup, (Organisation for the welfare and development mother's market) led our organisation in many protest against the human rights violation conducted by the armed forces. In the time of Rabina and Sanjit's killing in July 23rd 2009, six months agitation was done, Rabina was my granddaughter. Eventually the state atrocity claimed by own granddaughter. The protest continues. After the incident of 23rd July and the subsequent agitation, I feel there is a reduction in the number of killings but several other forms of social violence are emerging, we are moving to different direction, drug trade involving high profile people seems like a conspiracy to destroy the people of Manipur in a subtle way.

How can we celebrate republic day? Under the black laws, we suffered a lot. Sharmila, ignored? We want her to stop fasting the government have taken no action. Indian state is biased against us and tries to divide across the ethnic lines. How can we celebrate this as republic day, for us it is black day.[16]

Women's Participation in Decision-making in Conflict Situations

The masculine and feminine roles prescribed by a society in the public and private domains are reconstituted as 'men are expected to withdraw from civic life for compulsions of war and self-defence' (Banerjee 2008, 206). In North East India, with the reorganization of gendered roles in public and private places, women are emerging as important civic actors working through institutions such as the NMA, Naga Women's Union of Manipur, the All Tribal Women's Organisation and Tanghkhul Shanao Long. What follows is a detailed description of how these organizations were established and their current ways of working. This individual description of the different groups is being done here to avoid the tendency in both research and development policy to generalize 'women's groups'. It is by detailed understanding of their different modus operandi, and the other differences between women's groups, that their work can be seen from an appropriate perspective.

Women in North East India have lodged a number of protest movements under the aegis of well-organized groups such as NMA and Meira Paibis. They have negotiated with the power structures for not just their own survival but also the survival of their entire communities. One specific characteristic of women led protest in this area is its widely inclusive character. It is increasingly being recognized by the international community that women can play a significant role in the resolution of armed conflicts and in reconciliation processes. Research has shown that in many countries women have not only proved to be extremely creative in developing survival mechanisms, but they often play important, though unacknowledged roles, in ending organized violence. Current events in Manipur reflect how important women's groups are in civil society movements in North East India. The role of women in peace-making is particularly important in the context of North East because like most other conflict areas the North East has witnessed massive displacement of men from the conflict zones, which has some visibility and women form the major part of the civil society there. Therefore, any comprehensive efforts at conflict resolution in the North East cannot ignore the role played by women. Yet there are hardly any works dealing with the peace efforts made by women in North East India. Hence, even while current events are unfolding in

Manipur portraying that women are in the forefront of protest against violence analysts are at a loss to explain the nature of such mass protests. Some are even trying denigrating the movement by calling it a movement generated by 'insurgents'. Such denigrations, I feel, will only result in shrinking the space for negotiations and dialogues that might lead to peace. To understand the present situation, one needs to analyse how women have been negotiating for an end to violence in the last few decades in not just Manipur but in many part of the North East, including Nagaland.

There are different ways by which women organize for peace in the North East. In Manipur valley, women's activism is symbolized by the activities of Meira Paibis or the torchbearers. Manipuri women today trace their origin from the military deeds of Linthoingambi of Ningthou Khomba, who was known to have saved her palace from attacks by the enemy. During the last century, there were two women-led uprisings in Manipur known as the Nupi Lal. These were against the British. Today, there is a women's bazaar in Manipur known as Nupi Keithel where women meet, sell their wares and discuss problems of the day, including politics. This bazaar has served as a launching pad for collective revolt by women. The Meira Paibis also trace their origin from such organized women's activism in Manipur. According to Yumnam Rupachandra of the *North-East Sun,* the Meira Paibis have become an institution in their own rights today. They started as *nasha bandis* or combat groups for the ever-increasing consumption of alcohol by the men. Slowly they captured the imagination of the People's Liberation Army (PLA). The PLA imposed a ban on bootlegging and booze in January 1990. Two months later, succumbing to this pressure the United Legislative Front government declared Manipur a dry state. This was a victory for the Meira Paibis. The social cleansing drive, it is said, evoked popular support. According to some critics, Meitei militants actively support these women's groups. But recent events portray that Meira Paibis enjoy the support of most of the civil society in Manipur. In the last two years the Meira Paibis have expanded their area of action. Now they campaign against atrocities by the security forces. They also keep nightlong watches to foil raids. They dialogue with security forces and convince them from picking up innocent bystanders for questioning as part of counter insurgency operations. From the month of July of this year they have begun an unprecedented movement against the AFSPA that has captured the imagination of all civil society groups working on peace. They are in the forefront of protest against violence and it is being extremely difficult for the state to ignore their demands.

Other than the Meira Paibis there are the NMA of Nagaland that has been very active in the politics for peace in North East India. The NMA has rendered valuable service for the cause of peace. It came into existence on February 14, 1984, with a preamble that stated, 'Naga mothers of Nagaland shall express the need of conscientizing citizens toward more responsible living and human development through the voluntary organization of the Naga Mother's Association' (*Constitution of the Naga Mother's Association* 1992). Membership of NMA is open to any adult Naga women irrespective of whether she is married or single. Members can join through the women's organizations of their own tribes. The organization encourages human development through education and it efforts to eradicate social evils and economic exploitations and work towards peace and progress. It mediated between the Government of Nagaland and the Naga Student's Federation over age limit for jobs and came to an equitable settlement. An achievement of NMA is the formation of the Peace Team in October 1994 to confront the deteriorating political situation. Their theme was *shed no more blood*. The NMA spoke against killings not only by the army but also by the militants. In a pamphlet released on 25 May 1995, the representatives of NMA wrote that 'the way in which our society is being run whether by the overground government or the underground government, have become simply intolerable'. The NMA celebratesthe 12 May each year as Mother's Day and renew their appeal for peace. Apart from peace initiatives, the NMA has worked for social regeneration. In Nagaland, there is rampant abuse of alcohol and drug. The NMA provides facilities for de-addiction. They collaborate with the Kripa Foundation of Mumbai for rehabilitation of drug doers. The NMA has also started anonymous HIV testing. They are probably the first women's organization in the North East to test pregnant women for HIV virus. The NMA is providing pioneering service for care of patients afflicted with AIDS. An important issue that is preoccupying the doctors of NMA is the increase in HIV-positive cases among pregnant women. NMA's greatest achievement is that most Naga women's organizations are its collaborators. The members of NMA also collaborate with the Naga Women's Union of Manipur. The rallies organized by NMA are always well attended by other Naga women's organizations. The NMA work very closely with the Naga *Hohos* (apex tribal body in Nagaland). That the NMA has assumed enormous influence in Naga politics is borne out by the fact that they are the only women's group in South Asia who has participated in a cease-fire negotiation. In 1997 they mediated between the GoI and the NSCN-IM faction and facilitated a ceasefire.

Tangkhul Shanao Long (TSL)—as its very name suggests—is the women's organization of the Tangkhul Tribe. TSL was formed on 8 May 1974 as a platform to safeguard the rights, modesty and dignity of women. On 3 March 1974, a number of women of Grihang and Kumram (Ngaprum) were sexually assaulted by the Indian Border Security Force (BSF). Among the rape victims was M. N.S. Rose of Ngaprum (now Kunmram). She committed suicide. As Ms P. Veronica Zinkhai (1996) states,

> This was only one out of the many incidents in which security forces had behaved towards Naga women like beasts. I realised that unless a platform of women is formed, the same torture, harassment, assaults and violence against women would continue in the days and years to come.

Initially, TSL was known as the East District Women Organisation. While membership comes from every village, the main concentration is in Ukhrul and Senapati districts. The head office is in Ukhrul District. TSL have been instrumental in lobbying to prevent human rights violation in the hill districts. Soon after 9 May 1994, when armed commandos fired at random killing three people and began destroying property, TSL took a leading role to organize the biggest ever rally in Manipur on 2 June 1994. This rally was attended by activists from both valley plains and hill districts. With the initiative of TSL, the Naga Women Union of Manipur first met at Kohima on 4 December 1993 (Naga week 1–5 December 1993) than at Imphal on 7 January 1994, and resolved to form a union. In addition to lobbying against the AFSPA and the atrocities committed by the security forces, TSL has launched a campaign against illegal liquor sales, human trafficking, and drug peddling. The TSL units in the two villages of Shirui and Lunghar have been instrumental in redefining conflict prevention and peace.

Women as Peace Negotiators: 'Pukreila'

The Siege of Shirui (19 January–2 February 2009)

Shirui village is located about 13 km away from the district headquarter of Ukhrul. Shirui is a popular trekking point and is famous for the world famous Shirui Lily. According to Sorin, President, Shirui Shanao Long, 'NSCN (IM) cadres stayed in the Government Tourist Lodge within the village for almost two years. We had no idea that NSCN (IM) cadres were not allowed to stay here'.[17] On 19 January 2009, reportedly around 2 AM, the villagers realized that the 17 Assam Rifles had laid seize of the village with the jawans surrounding the camp and the village. Their main objective was to pull out the NSCN cadres. The women and men met in the community hall of the village and the women decided to act as a stand-off between the army and the NSCN camp. Just as in the 1990s, women's activism was focussed on forming human shields between the army and the cadres as the army insisted on pulling out the cadres on 20 January 2009.

> We braved the cold winter and kept a vigil near the main thoroughfare fearing every moment that there might be a shootout. Around 2000 women had taken part in the vigil from 20 January–2 February 2009. We took turns to keep a vigil. We walked up and down from the Tourist lodge to the village almost 5–7 times. For the first two days only women from Shirui participated in the day long vigil; later women from other villages also participated. We made repeated appeals to the Indian Army to withdraw to avoid conflict.[18]

Another organization the Naga Women's Union of Manipur (NWUM) has been able work across the boundaries of conflict, and boundaries that exist in post-conflict societies. The first meeting of NWUM formed the union on 7 January 1994. NWUM comprises all the women's organizations of the Naga tribes of Manipur. The Union became operational on 5 October 1994 with the approval and adoption of its constitution during its first assembly-cum-seminar held on 4 and 5 October 1994 at Ukhrul. Ms Gina Sanghkham, President of NWUM, has pointed out that the Union is a membership-based organization that, unlike other women' organizations in North East India has been able to address the injustices women face in their own customary laws relating to inheritance and participation in decision-making. The Union also encourages the participation of women in electoral politics. Ms Aram Pamei (1997) in the annual report of the Union presented in the 4th Annual Assembly on 10–12 October 1997, emphasized the non-violent means that NWUM used to resolve the Naga-Kuki conflict. The Union undertook peace campaigns by conducting seminars in different localities, with the support of the Fraternal Green Cross, and the Legal Education and Aid Society of India. The 1997 annual report also mentions the willingness of NWUM to work with their Kuki sisters to resolve conflict. NWUM has also been engaged in on-the-spot fact finding investigations, together with other NGOs and CSOs involved in human rights issues, particularly the Naga Peoples Movement for Human Rights (NPMHR). NWUM also extended support to the women candidates in the Lok Sabha elections running on a platform to uphold the rights and dignity of women and work for equality. In addition, the Union has stated that

> by Naga custom, whether it is in the general administration of the village, or in the administration of justice, there is nothing which denies women's participation in administrative or judicial decision-making. The Union wishes to claim that this custom of the Nagas should be made to be seen by including women as representatives in their local village councils.

The Union has also demanded equal wages for women and men, and equal inheritance rights of both movable and immovable properties for both female and male children. NWUM clearly approaches securing the rights of women from a different paradigm: their approach is one which ensures and encourages women's participation in decision-making right from village council up to Lok Sabha (the house of the people, the lower house of the Parliament of India). Ms Grace Shatsung, President of NWUM, and Ms Gina Sangkham, former President of NWUM have also reported on the efforts by the North East Network, particularly through peace workshops, to bring all the groups under one umbrella with one platform. There is great need for a sustained effort to stand up for the rights of women on all levels.

From this short analysis, it becomes apparent that women's groups such as Meira Paibis and NMA or TSL who have a broader definition of peace are usually more successful during times of conflict than those who think that peace is only an end to armed conflict. These groups believe that peace can be achieved through dialogue and political negotiations. They believe that only military solutions cannot bring peace. They work towards a betterment of their own society and in this way they equate peace with justice and development. However, post-conflict situations require other skills from women's groups.

Women's Activism Today

With the conflict going into background, new contentious gendered issues are coming up that is putting women and men in contest with each other and the state is appearing as the new arbiter. In the traditional governing system under the village council or informal council of elders, women were excluded from decision making. Today the Village Development Board (VDB) that has governing powers in the villages and forms the village councils has to allocate 25 per cent of its fund for women only and employ female representatives to administer it and that has been ordained by the state powers. In village councils, there are very few female chairpersons. Tokheli Kikon is the first woman village council chairperson in Nagaland. Tokheli Kikon initially started off as a social worker and village council member of Naharbari Village, Dimapur. She recalls that in 2005, when she contested the village council election, she was the only women candidate contesting against three male candidates. She recalls with pride that out of 21 votes, she received 13 votes and there were two absent votes. After she became the village council chairperson, she ensured that 25 per cent of the VDB fund is utilized solely for the women unit of the village. She encouraged capacity building of women. She says her motto is 'work and eat'. Under the National Rural Employment Guarantee Act (NREGA) fund she has encouraged villagers to focus on drainage system of the village. She also restored the water body close to the village and encouraged villagers to take up pisciculture, which is one of the major sources of livelihood for men and women.[19] Women are taking up these examples showing that women in decision-making roles can bring forth real changes. Mrs Vamuza, the Chairperson of Naga Women's Commission, in 2009 also felt that the women's groups need to generate awareness about the Government of Nagaland,

land revenue department's efforts to make participation of women mandatory in village council/VDB. In a memorandum (No LR/1-1/94), the government announced that women will have a separate share in village development board fund. Some women have even used this fund to buy land for themselves and give a rest to the myth that Naga women do not own land.

In Nagaland, the cultivable land is the most valued form of property both for its political symbolism and economic value. It is something that can give people sustainable livelihood. In Nagaland, girl children are equally cared for and infanticide does not exist. There are no dowry deaths and no starvation deaths. Also, women have the right to divorce their husband anytime but they do not have the right to inherit ancestral property. There is a broad debate going on among Naga women about their land rights. Women are claiming that land rights will give them the ability to decide regarding agricultural production and increase their decision making roles in society. It will also give them better economic status, protection from desertion, pauperization and so on. It might also save the land, particularly when men become addicts. Also, rural women totally depend on the land and they also form the main workforce. More often, men migrate from rural to urban centres and when that happens, the women have to protect the land. Also for women with disabilities, it becomes extremely essential that they inherit property to save them from added vulnerability and morbidity.[20] In this newer mode of activism, land has become a contentious issue between men and women today.

Perhaps the most dramatic of women's contests in Nagaland with State support today is over the question of 33 per cent. Women are poorly represented in formal decision-making processes in Nagaland including the village, regional and national levels. To facilitate women's participation in the political process and involve them in decision-making, the Government of Nagaland passed the *Nagaland Municipal Act of 2001*, the *Amendment of 2006* and the *108 Amendment Act*, and the *Women's Reservation Bill of 2008*. The Nagaland State Commission for Women is an apex organization meant to look after the needs of Naga women. In 2009, Mrs Sano Vamuzo,[21] who was the chairperson at that time and who was also one of the founder members of NMA, pointed out that there is a need to generate awareness about women's role in decision making bodies by encouraging them to participate in electoral politics. She cited the state initiative to ensure

33 per cent reservation for women in local bodies as an effort by the state to ensure women's engagement in electoral politics. She recalled the Commission's efforts to bring together various civil society actors on 13 February 2009 and the house unanimously adopted two resolutions: (a) In favour of immediate support for the reservation for Women's Bill and (b) the reservation of seats for women as per the Nagaland Municipal Council Amendment Act 2006.

Yet, during the Mokokchung Municipal Elections of 2008, this bill could not be implemented as women filing nomination papers were stopped by volunteers from 16 wards of Mokokchung town arguing that reservation of seats for women was irrelevant for Ao (Ao is a tribal group) as it was against customary law (Department of Planning and Coordination, Government of Nagaland 2004, 103–04). The situation got so bad the women under the leadership of NMA went in for litigation asking for implementation of the bill. When the municipal and town elections were postponed as a result of controversy over women's reservation bill, the women asked the court to continue with the election and implement the reservation bill under article 243 T(3) of the Indian Constitution and Section 23 A of the Nagaland Municipal (First Amendment) Act 2006. Even the chief minister of Nagaland supported the women in his speech on 8 October 2010 when he said that there is

> a commonly held view amongst some Nagas that traditionally women do not have any role in public governance in Naga society. However, it is also gratifying to note that many enlightened people in the State no longer subscribe to this view. In modern times, societies which do not accord an equitable and honorable status to their women are considered to be backward, underdeveloped or even primitive.[22]

The women petitioners, including Rosemary Dzuvichu and Aboiu Meru representing the NMA, won this case and Article 35 of the court order stated that elections be undertaken by 20 January 2012 honouring the 33 per cent stipulation for women.

Women's activism over 33 per cent portrays the appearance of new form of activism for Naga women. No longer were questions of sovereignty allowed to push questions of women's rights under the carpet. With conflict shifting from people's immediate memory there was no longer any justification to gloss over other rivalries be they on the basis of ethnicity, location or gender. In these contests, the people are going to the state machinery for arbitration and the state is also allying with certain groups to facilitate governance. An IAS officer clearly said that NMA is always welcome in our offices as we think of them as allies in our good work.[23] That is not to say that everything has changed; in a total budget of ₹7,911.85 crores in Nagaland in 2012, only ₹14.98 crores was specially designated for women's development. However, it is possible to deduce that side by side the old form of activism women are developing a new form of activism where they are strategically allying with the state which was almost a taboo in the old form of activism.

This is a tale of how the state came to realize that the answer to the Naga problem is not merely violence but also development. In this way, the state convinced the Nagas to come to a ceasefire. In this, they were aided by Naga women who wanted to end violence. Once state verses community conflict could be put in the back burner, it was possible to convince the younger people what they needed was resources so that they could take their rightful place in the world. This nudge towards resources also brought forth other smaller disparities in society that was not grand enough to threaten the state but large enough to keep the people fragmented. The state could now act as a grand arbiter dispensing resources and justice.

The women for their part, through their lived experiences in conflict, started working for peace. In their activism for peace, they acquired a legitimacy to enter the space for political decision-making that was denied to them earlier. In their commitment for peace, they motivated their society for ceasefire. The state found in them an unusual ally and could see their far-reaching influence in society. When the state decided to move away from their traditional mode of conflict with the Naga people, it reinvented its indispensability by championing the cause of women. It was around the same time that women's activism was going through a generational change. Younger women leaders decided to innovate on the new agenda for women and brought in the question of women's right. In this, they found much of the traditional leadership allied against them. There is one section of the HoHo that is willing to excommunicate women-making alliances with state and raising gendered demands.[24] The women, on the other hand, found the state keen to ally with their cause in its role as an arbiter. This mutual coming together of Naga women and the State of Nagaland is reflected in the activism for Women's Reservation Bill. The women used all government institutions to further the cause for peace, justice and equity. This coming together was timely although the alliance is bound to be fragile. Both the sides are giving lip service to this alliance to further its own interest. For now, this alliance has proved transformative for gender roles in society helping the cause of peace, stability and justice. What is glossed over is the nefarious side to this alliance. Is the state using women to break the strength of secessionist demands of an extremely problematic corner of India? If this happens, then this will not be the first time that the state is using one section of the population to weaken the other. Tragedy will be if the Naga human rights leaders, who have otherwise been wise, keep their eyes closed and exacerbate the situation by denying social justice to women and other marginalized sections of the population. In the recent elections, the women were unable to show solidarity to other women candidates who were otherwise more than qualified. This shows the contradiction within the women's movement. Women leaders who are rightfully demanding 33 per cent should also realize that such demands will come to a nought unless they move one step forward and actually help women to get elected at all levels of law making and representative bodies. Otherwise, they will remain voiceless with either the state or other actors claiming their voices and using it for purposes contrary to their interests.

The success of women's activism in Nagaland and Manipur is not because of UNSCR 1325 but notwithstanding that. The experiences from Nagaland and Manipur portray that communities that have histories of women's activism in different spheres will ultimately have women in political decision making. It might not be through the trodden path of electoral politics. It might even be through non-traditional means. Women face many obstacles in their quest for leadership in the public sphere. Sometimes, the state can act as an impediment and at other times human rights activists can oppose the leadership of women. But women, through their negotiating abilities, try to negotiate with multiple groups including the state. It is to the benefit of the state that their role in peacemaking is recognized. However, if the state does not recognise that there is a conflict that is on, then it is very difficult for the UNSCR 1325 to be affective. This would be to the detriment of women's leadership for peace and the state's quest for peace.

Notes

1. Authors interview with Lourembam Nganbi, Vice President, Apunba Manipur Kanba Ima Lup, President of Apunba Nupi Lup Bishnupur district, former External Affairs Secretary of United Committee Manipur (UCM) on 23 January 2014 in Bishnupur Bazar Imphal.

2. Author's interview with Ema Laishram Gyaneshori Devi (age 63) and Meira Paibi of Nagamapal Lamabam Leikai, Imphal on 22 January 2014 in Imphal.

3. Naga People's Movement of Human Rights vs Union of India 27 November 1997, http://www.indiankanoon.org/docfragment/1072165/?formInput=disturb ed%20area accessed on 10 February 2013.

4. Jammu and Kashmir Disturbed Areas Act 1992, Vakil No. 1, http://www. vakilno1.com/bareacts/Laws/Jammu-And-Kashmir-Disturbed-Areas-Act-1992. htm (accessed on 11 January 2016).

5. Assam Maintenance of Public Order (Autonomous District) Regulation Act 1953.

6. Deputy Speaker, *Lok Sabha Debates*, 18 August 1958.

7. Mohanty, *Lok Sabha Debates*, 18 August 1958.

8. Speaker, *Lok Sabha Debates*, 18 August 1958.

9. Laishram Achaw Singh, *Lok Sabha Debates*, 18 August 1958.

10. Human Rights Features, http://www.hrdc.net/sahrdc/hrfeatures/HRF168.htm and http://www.hrdc.net/sahrdc/hrfeatures/HRF168.htmry (accessed on 12 February 2012).

11. Indian Kanoon, http://indiankanoon.org/doc/745885/ (accessed on 15 February 2012).

12. *Col Jagmohan and Ors. Vs State of Manipur and Ors*, http://www.indiankanoon. org/doc/38473/ (accessed on 25 February 2012).

13. Guwahati High Court serves notices to the accused in Manorama rape and murder case, http://kanglaonline.com/2011/01/guwahati-high-court-serves-notices-to-accused-in-manorama-rape-and-murder-case/ (accessed on 22 February 2012).

14. Ishita De's interview with Janeth Hungyo, former Executive Member of TSL 1974–1982; focus group discussion on 13 June 2009.

15. Ishita De's interview with a gram panchayat member who wishes to remain anonymous in Imphal district, in an interview conducted during the Capacity Building Workshop organized by Women's Action for Development (WAD) on 17 June 2009.

16. Authors interview with R.K. Radhesana, Joint Secretary Khwairamband Nupi Kheithel Semgat Sagatpa Lup and Ema Keithel, Secretary of the organization Apunba Manipur Kanba Ima Lup (AMKIL), on 22 January 2014.

17. Interview with Sorin, President, Tangkhul Shanao Long, Shirui village, Ukhrul district.

18. Interview with Ms Sorin, President of TSL in 2009 in Shirui. Interview taken by Ishita Dey and Chitra Ahanthem on 11 June 2009 in Shirui. The discussions were on recently concluded Shirui seize by the Indian army.

19. Interview of the author with Tokheli Kikon, Dimapur, 30 February 2012.

20. Interview with Gangarani in a capacity-building workshop with WAD, Imphal, 17 June 2009.
21. Interview with Sano Vamuzo, Chairperson, Nagaland State Commission for Women, 6 August 2009.
22. Court Judgment on Women's Reservation Bill Nagaland Guwahati High Court, WP (C) No. 147 (K) 2011, Judgement dated 21 October 2011, 4. The author received a copy of the judgment. Courtesy: NMA.
23. Authors interview with Ramaiah Ramakrishnan, Secretary to the Governor of Nagaland, Kohima, 3 March 2012.
24. Authors interview with a top leader of the HoHo (name not disclosed as per request) Kohima, 4 March 2012.

References

Banerjee, Paula. 2001. 'Between Two Armed Patriarchies: Women in Assam and Nagaland'. In *Beyond Victimhood to Agency: Women War and Peace in South Asia*, edited by Rita Manchanda. New Delhi: SAGE Publications.

———. 2008. 'The Space Between: Women's Negotiations with Democracy'. In *Women in Peace Politics*, edited by Paula Banerjee, 206. New Delhi: SAGE Publications.

Bordoloi, Gopinath. 1946. *The Constituent Assembly Debates*, vol. IX, 4 of 26. Available at: http://parliamentofindia.nic.in/ls/debates/vol9p27a.htm (Accessed on 13 February 2016).

Chaliha, Kuladhar. 1949. *The Constituent Assembly Debates*, vol. IX, 1–2 of 20. Available at: http://parliamentofindia.nic.in/ls/debates/vol9p27a.htm (Accessed on 13 February 2016).

Constitution of the Naga Mother's Association. 1992. Reprint, Kohima.

Hazarika, Joysankar. 1996. *Geopolitics of Northeast India: A Strategical Study*. New Delhi: Gyan Publishing House.

Department of Planning and Coordination, Government of Nagaland. 2004. *Nagaland State Human Development Report*. Department of Planning and Coordination, Government of Nagaland, 103–04.

Gervais, Myriam. 2007. 'Experience of Women During and After Violent Conflict: Implications for Women in South Asia'. In *Women Building Peace Between India and Pakistan*, edited by Shree Mullay and Jackie Kirk, 159. Kolkata: Anthem Critical Studies.

Imphal Free Press. 2001. Imphal Free Press, 17 March.

———. 2005. 'Anti-trafficking Consultation: An Eye-opener'. *Imphal Free Press*, 1 October.

Kikon, Achumbemo. 2003. *In Experiences on Autonomy in East and Northeast: A Report on the Third Civil Society Dialogue on Human Rights and Peace*, edited by Sanjay Barbora, 29. Kolkata: Mahanirban Calcutta Research Group.

Khala, Khatoli. 2003. *The Armed Forces (Special Powers) Act and its Impact on Women in Nagaland*. New Delhi: WISCOMP, 25.

Luithui, Luingam and Frans Welman. 2002. 'Naga History: Chronology of Recent Events', unpublished report circulated by The Naga International Support Centre, Amsterdam, 3. Available at: www.nagalim.nl (Accessed on 14 February 2016).

Manchanda, Rita. 2005. 'Naga Women Making a Difference: Peace Building'. In *Women Building Peace: What do They Want, Why It Matters*, edited by Sanam N. Anderlini. Washington, D.C.: Policy Commission.

Meghalaya Guardian. 2004. 'Trafficking in Women'. *The Meghalaya Guardian*, 13 September 2004.

Prasad, Brajeshwar. 1949. *The Constituent Assembly Debates*, vol. IX, 3 of 20. Available at: http://parliamentofindia.nic.in/ls/debates/vol9p27a.htm (Accessed on 13 February 2016).

8

Women of Manipur: A Space for UNSCR 1325

Asha Hans

Introduction

Manipur is described as a 'disturbed' area by the Indian State and has become a location of civil resistance, which is sometimes peaceful but occasionally violent. The resistance has been a struggle for political change where women have played an important role through direct and constructive non-violent actions. In spite of the peaceful initiatives police induced violence and militarization has been used to suppress the women and taken advantage by non-State actors marginalizing women in this battle for survival. The narratives and discourses about the struggle are changing as is women's space in them. The resistance movement today has many streams with different strategies, goals and methods. We need to ask what cutting edge solutions are needed to keep the women from being marginalized in these movements especially in the context of UN Security Council Resolution (UNSCR) 1325 and its sister resolutions.

Background to a Conflict

The State that literally, has passed through various phases of extreme turmoil and at the same time efforts at peace mostly being local initiatives. The State's political system has changed dramatically within the last century contributing to the anarchy. These shifts have ranged from Manipur being a feudal kingdom and changing to a colonial British subject, to self-governance and a constitutional monarchy, and then joining the Indian political system as a Union Territory and finally as a full-fledged State in 1972. Protests marked this final merger by different parties to the conflict and the open war between the State and its people had begun where women played a significant role in creating spaces for peace.

In any conflict-like situation some groups suffer in a different way than others; the issue of sexual exploitation of women, however, have been an abysmal feature of every conflict, cutting across space and time. The conflict in Manipur has thrown up issues of protection and participation of women, two themes underlying UNSCR 1325. The controlling system of military and security forces has been strengthened by an Act introduced in 1958, the Armed Forces Special Powers Act (AFSPA) discussed earlier, in the chapter by Amrita Patel. It has been observed that over the 20 years from 1951 to 1970, armed forces were summoned as many as 476 times to suppress insurgencies. The frequency of interventions by the armed forces in Manipur increased further when it was declared a 'disturbed area' in 1980 and came directly under the purview of the AFSPA. For instance, during the period from May 1979 to May 2012, 1528 people were killed in Manipur by extrajudicial execution alone (India Supreme Court 2012). In this situation of high conflict, it is recognized that women's bodies are targeted but while trauma occurs, there is also the emergence of strength to challenge the war.

Locating Women's Structural Space in Manipur

In the context of our discourse on using UNSCR 1325 in Manipur, we need to go beyond how many National Action Plans (NAPs) have been adopted across the globe? Which countries have developed them? How many women are there in peacekeeping forces? These numerical analyses do not assist in understanding the ground situation. If we have to think of implementing UNSCR 1325, we need to understand the existing system of social justice and women's space in the country.

Reviewing the social structures and women's position relates to their autonomy and power. With patriarchal norms which have existed for centuries, it is likely that change in their favour would be not be easy to achieve. Women of Manipur like other states of the India/North East are subsumed by patriarchy and thus discrimination, but these would anyway need to be overcome in most states.

Security and Women

Today, Manipur is one of the highly affected states in the North East where the army, security forces, and the police and non-state forces compete for power and control. Evidence of militarization is apparent as Manipur has more than 60,000 military and security personnel and more than 300 security checkpoints (Hayes 2012, 10). Thirty to forty non-state outfits are active at present.[1] A report of the State home department in May 2005 indicated that 'as many as 12,650 cadres of different non-state outfits with 8,830 weapons are actively operating in the State' (Centre for Development and Peace Studies 2011). Village Defence Forces (VDFs) supported by the State are being established and more and more households own a weapon as these have found easy access from neighbouring China and Myanmar (Hayes 2012, 10, 14).

Thousands of people are estimated to have been killed in the last three decades by the armed forces and other law enforcement officials. A civil society report quotes the police figures of 3,000 civilian deaths, 1,500 militants and 1,000 of security members. The figure by civil society in contrast is about 20,000 people (who died). It further claims that: 'These statistics do not include a large number of indigenous women in Manipur who are victims of reported aggressive violence including murder by state forces and unknown persons in a variety of contexts.... These crimes have largely occurred uninvestigated or prosecuted' (CSCOHRM 2013, 3).

The rising crimes against women in the conflict situation has been a cause of concern and in a memorandum submitted to the governor in December 2012 a women's organization—Women's Action for Development (WAD)—had highlighted that in the year 2012 they had collected data on about 264 cases out of which 23 rape cases, four cases of rape and murder, 18 cases of suicides, 61 missing cases and

81 cases of child trafficking.[2] The demands for revival of the Manipur State Human Rights Commission and the establishment of a working committee on VAW have been prominent. The establishment of a fast track court in order to dispose all the criminal cases committed against women has been another major demand of the people. The Incidences of spousal violence has been on the rise so much so that it has been ranked fifth in the national statistics (NFHS 3 2005–06, 519). Domestic violence linked to patriarchal thinking is very high. NFHS (National Family Health Survey) 3 data again shows that the percentage of women who agree with one or more reasons for wife beating ranges from 28 per cent in Himachal Pradesh to 90 per cent in Manipur; the percentage of men who agree with one or more reasons for wife beating ranges from 23 per cent in Uttaranchal to 85 per cent in Manipur (NFHS 3 2005–06, xlvi). The concern in the context of women is due to the fact that being part of a patriarchal system women's health needs are rarely met, they lack information and despite many supportive traditional economic structures their financial independence is limited. While violence is high, there is also low self-esteem.

Charge-sheeting rate for IPC (Indian Penal Code) crimes is the lowest in Manipur (6.5 per cent) against the national average of 78.8 per cent. However the percentage of females arrested under IPC crimes at an all-India level is 6.2 per cent while in Manipur it is 14.1 per cent. Manipur stands at fifth (32.4) ranking in violent crime compared to 21.2 at an all-India level (Ministry of Home Affairs 2011).

The violence is provided legitimacy by an unconstitutional framework. The AFSPA 1958 was a colonial by-product as observed in Amrita's chapter. The earlier law of 1942, on which the law is formulated, had been used by the British to crush the Indian national movement for independence. This law is being used to limit people's demand for autonomy in Manipur. A strong opposition to the law by Manipur politicians who called it a 'black law' did not stop the central government from imposing it. An emergency law came into being when there was no declared war. The law has taken away the constitutional right to life under Article 21. Further, Manipur was declared a 'disturbed area' in its entirety in 1980 and AFSPA was imposed in the whole state on 8 September 1980, which continues to be in place till now. Many attempts have been made by women to repeal it, but they have not met with any success except from the municipal centre of Manipur's capital, Imphal.

The majority of the population suffer the impact of the conflict; however, there are specific indicators that have emerged in the context of women that require an overview. These include an increase in single-headed households, the disappearance of men and boys, sexual abuse, displacement and loss of livelihood.

Women have been observed to take on the role of the head of households; they bear responsibility for the day-to-day subsistence activities that are made more dangerous by the violence. Women complain of mobility restrictions due to many reasons. The first and foremost is the insecurity felt by them due to presence of armed personnel. The armed personnel range from government forces—the army, police—to the various security and other forces. The other threat is by non-state actors who might target them as women, or as women supporters of government forces or women supporters of other armed groups. Their movement is restricted both at night and in the day, imposed by themselves or their families. Women also complain that at the slightest sign of a problem the men run away leaving the women to fend for themselves and the police just stand by and do not provide protection.[3]

The plethora of army and rebel-held security checkpoints has turned traditional jungle subsistence and the collection of food, water and fuel into a day-to-day ordeal. The increase in violence includes strip searches and sexual harassment. Frisking and checking are conducted openly and 'indecent' frisking is common (E-Pao 2009). Police and security forces also enter households without permission for purposes of arrest under AFSPA.

Militarization and Its Direct Impact: Rape, Gun Widows, Orphans and the Disappeared

Rape poses a continual threat to women in conflict zones, while other forms of gender-based violence include prostitution, sexual humiliation, trafficking and domestic violence. Rhonda Copelon has contributed to our understanding of rape as a form of torture and signified its genocidal characteristic (Copelon 1995). Rape by soldiers of vanquished women has a long history. Half a century ago, rape in war was outlawed by the Geneva Conventions but continues even after the introduction of multiple conventions and laws including UNSCR 1325 and following resolutions that focus on protection of women.

In Manipur, rape has been a common occurrence, through use of AFSPA. However post these incidents also has been witnessed an unprecedented civic uprising, including the 'mothers' nude protest' against the Act. On 11 July 2004, on the discovery of the mutilated body of Thangjam Manorama, who had been picked up by the soldiers of the Assam Rifles, raped, tortured and killed by the soldiers, the women of Manipur demonstrated before the army headquarters in nude. The police imprisoned the women who had stripped and kept them in jail for three to four months.[4] On the uproar after her death, General Vij, Chief of the Indian Armed Forces, was to question Manorama's credentials as a 'patriot' and as a 'chaste' woman (*The Times of India* 2004). However, in the eyes of the law neither stands. That she was shot and her genitalia mutilated with the gun shots meant that those who raped her wanted this as a lesson to other women who had been protesting against the state.

Consequent to the public uproar, not only due to the rape of Manorama, but also the shame of women forced to protest in nude in front of the Kangla Fort, the heritage site was returned to the state by the army. The AFSPA, however, was not withdrawn and is still embroiled in a controversy and the people of Manipur continue their protest against the act demanding its repeal. Rape by the armed forces such as the Indian Reserve Battalions continues despite the subdued conflict (*TNN* 2012).

There is also strong evidence that members of the security forces, whether army, other security forces and local police commandos, have used rape as a tactic in an increasingly violent suppression of insurgent movements. Many of these groups claim to be fighting for the rights of the same women they abuse. Women who are supposed to have joined these forces also suffer sexual abuse at the hands of armed forces and police during combing operations (CSCOHRM 2013, 14). Torture has become part of everyday life for women in Manipur and is not an aberration.

Legally, there is immunity in place for security forces provided by AFSPA. The immunity for rape nevertheless exists, whether it is by the government (as for army personnel by AFSPA), non-government forces or community members. As it was conveyed in the town of Morehon, the Manipur—Myanmar border by a woman I interviewed said, 'If someone is raped, a pig is killed and money given and the rapist forgiven'.[5] As non-state actors are part of the community it is a difficult to take a stand on them, but in recent years women's voices against these groups have been increasing.

The existence of the AFSPA means that security forces have the power to use any kind of force against civilians (WILPF India 2014, 5). No laws are for instance observed when arresting women though many are members of very well-known women's human rights group the Meira Paibis. This is possible because of suppressive laws in place. The new war is thus fought differently and targets the insurgents and civilians equally. Large amounts of small arms are not only in the possession of the armed forces but also the non-state actors and the police. India is the largest importer of arms in the world and it is therefore not surprising that weapons find their way to so called 'disturbed areas' such as Manipur (SIPRI 2014, 4). The Indian army is also the single biggest buyer of land mines in the world, many of which have been used in the southern border of Manipur bordering Myanmar. Landmine clearance operations have failed, leave families in vulnerable situations (Hayes 2012, 12). Landmines have a gendered impact as men have better access to health and rehabilitation services, leaving women disabled and excluded from society. These deaths leave behind old mothers, young widows and children, with no means of survival (Nepram 2010).

So many Manipuri men have been killed by the army and non-state groups that the term 'gun widow' has entered the everyday language. Manipur continues to account for the bulk of incidents of violence in the North Eastern region (India; Ministry of Home Affairs 2014–15, 13). Single women, especially conflict widows, lead lives of poverty with little option of livelihood or government support. There are about 15,000 widows in Manipur (*The Telegraph* 2011). The large number of young widows that are seen in Manipur is a testimony of the impact of the conflict. The plight of the young widows is apparent in the narration of a young woman on her condition of having to live in her brother's house with her husband's family not giving her any space to live. In the absence of any livelihood, she has been forced to seek help from her natal family.[6]

This increase in widows has brought civil society organizations together. Among these are the Conflict Widows Forum (COWF) and Extrajudicial Executed Victims Families' Association, Manipur (EEVFAM) that assists many widows to access legal aid (van Lierde 2011). There are also the Gun Victims Survivors Association and the Manipur Women Gun Survivors Network.[7] Another organization working for widows is WAD who are doing victim counselling and providing a monthly pension to the young widows for their survival. They have formed an association known as the Country Widow Forum.

The government in turn runs the Indira Gandhi National Widow Pension Scheme (IGNWPS) where widows above the age of 40 get a meagre sum of ₹200 (US$3) per month. The government with a tendency to measure everything in numbers, even the age of widows (above 40 years of age) who can avail of a scheme benefit is incomprehensible. No official could explain this cut off age of 40 years. With young women losing husbands to the conflict their access to any benefit becomes a challenge. During conflict women in single headed households have to carry the economic and social burden. Desertion is also common as many men deserted their wives to join the non-state armed forces. A major challenge to the people is the enormous number of disappearances. Ima Ngambi, a Meira Peiba, said that she had been involved in campaigns against the state when people started mysteriously disappearing due to the conflict in Manipur. In response to these stories of hurt and violence, Rashida Manjoo, a SRVAW (Special Rapporteur of Violence Against Women), held consultations in Imphal and said:

> I heard anguished stories from relatives of young women who have disappeared without trace or who were found dead shortly after going missing. The lack of response from the police is the norm in such cases, with the attitude being that these are mostly elopement cases. I am deeply concerned about other consequences of such disappearances of young women, including exposure to sexual abuse, exploitation or trafficking. (United Nations Human Rights 2013)

An organization called the Families of the Involuntarily Disappeared Association, Manipur (FIDAM) came up in 1999 with the demand that the large number of enforced disappearance' cases involving security forces be released. The disappeared were both men and women, though most were young men who left behind young wives or mothers to fight for their release. In interviews, FIDAM came out as a weak organization but is starting to make its presence felt. In contrast, the Jammu and Kashmir movement on disappeared has been stronger. The Verma Commission India reminded the government that it had signed the International Convention for the Protection of All Persons from Enforced Disappearance (ICPPED), which had to be honoured (Verma 2013, 149).

Poverty due to conflict and dispossession has been exploited by traffickers of women and children, primarily for domestic labour but also for the sex industry. Anti-trafficking organizations reported instances of women and children from Manipur being trafficked to Singapore, Thailand, Malaysia and Dubai, and internally to places such as Mumbai Goa and Kerala. The families of trafficked children are duped by false assurances about education or training.[8]

The North Eastern part of the country has also acted as a sanctuary for displaced Indians and refugees. The IDPs (internally displaced persons) include Nagas, Kukis, the refugees from Myanmar including Bru and Chakmas who cross either the state or country borders to find refuge. There is also the immigrant issue that becomes inextricably linked to the ethnic. Women and children constitute the majority of those internally displaced or those seeking refuge across state frontiers due to conflicts. The magnitude of internal displacement as a result of the various conflicts in the state has been enormous (Hussain 2002). These IDPs include the Kuki-Naga Conflict of 1992, the KukiZomi, Thadou–Paite and Meitei–Pangal conflicts of 1993 and the Naga ceasefire extension of 2001, which also created displacement.

Refugees, displaced people and sexual abuse are all products of a militarization that impacts women's bodies as well as the quality of their lives and autonomy. UNSCR 1325 recognizes these issues, but while all NAPs mention representation of women and prevention of gender-based violence, they rarely include gendered issues of refugees, IDPS and reintegration processes. With these multiple issues of ethnicity, refugees and lack of justice dispensing structures whether UNSCR 1325 created NAP will bring about peace is questionable unless the region is demilitarized. Women's voices will be important in creating a non-violent society. In this context, whilst it is easier to stand up against the armed forces of the national government in the case of non-state actors and police who are local and members of their own society it becomes problematic for women when attempting to create change. There is, moreover, an absence of national or international law that can support women in bringing these two actors to accountability. There is a need for creating a fair justice system that takes into account the issues of impunity.

The response of the state and judiciary is inadequate as is the role of the Manipur State Commission for Women (MSCW). The Commission has low number of cases reported to it. The total number of cases received during the year 2011 was only 37 while eight cases have been closed and there are 29 pending cases (Manipur State Commission for Women 2011).

In 2013 there was an attempt to link the system of justice to AFSPA. Indicting the government, the Justice J.S. Verma Committee set up to provide quicker trial and enhance punishment for offenders of crime against women stated that that they noticed that impunity for systematic or isolated sexual violence in the process of internal security duties was being legitimized by the AFSPA. They stated that women in conflict areas are entitled to all the security and dignity that is afforded to citizens in any other part of our country (Verma 2013, 149). It recommended that the continuance of AFSPA in conflict areas needs to be revisited. It further recommended that complainants of sexual violence must be afforded witness protection. Special commissioners should be appointed in conflict areas to monitor and prosecute for sexual offences. Training of armed personnel should be reoriented to emphasize strict observance of orders in this regard by armed personnel (Verma 2013, 150–51).

All these recommendations have been disregarded by the justice system. The field interactions revealed that the courts do not push for investigation but only compensation. Justice is monetized and leaves behind the individual right to compensation vis-a-vis the earlier community rights. The new justice system is based on a colonial law that has replaced the Pachaloishang—the traditional justice system run by women that looked after cases related to women. In this woman-sensitive system, women could appeal against injustices and were giving fair hearing (Singh 2001, 5). Today, the justice system in Manipur is based on the colonial system where issues related to women in conflict find no space.

Women and Economies of Conflict: The Shifting Model of State Security Through Economic Militarization

An encapsulated version of todays globalized world and its inherent contradictions of capital and militarization are already visible in the complex socio-cultural milieu in the border town of Moreh on the Indo-Myanmar border. This small town in Chandel district is today the hub of international trade. The average annual volume of trade through Moreh is estimated at ₹250 million but unofficially it may be around ₹15 billion (Ahanthem 2011, 2012). It has destroyed the local economy and brought in drugs, HIV and commercial sex in its most virulent form.

The town has an open border with Myanmar and due to daily cross-border transactions all the people in the area are under the watch of the armed personnel, which affects their physical and psychological security. The women porters can barely make their two ends meet. The lack of health facilities make the women vulnerable to diseases such as HIV/AIDS. The women in poverty situations, therefore, augment their earnings through sex trade, even there they earn only an average five hundred rupees per day. When the army posts harass the women who work on the border, they have to resort to paying them through sexual favours. The town being a trading one on the border attracts traders, drivers and security forces who are customers in the sex trade. The slow expansion of the red light area in the border area on Myanmar side is also an incentive for engaging in this trade. Many businessmen come in from Imphal, Myanmar and Mizoram and pay for sex work that security forces for instance do not pay for. Due to the changes in patterns of economy, more and more women including tribal women are taking up commercial sex and daily wagers where they are increasingly becoming vulnerable to abuse and exploitation. There are many women engaged in commercial sexual activities in Imphal East, Imphal West and Churachandpur. These groups of commercial sex workers are very vulnerable. They are targeted by the state police on the pretext of social policing. Money is also exhorted from them. It is also reported that the widows (whose husband had been victims of extrajudicial executions by the security forces alleging to be a militant) became CSW and they are also assaulted by the Manipur Police Commandos (Sangai Express 2009; *Nagaland Post*).[9]

Today, Manipur is one of the six high prevalence states in India contributing to 8 per cent of India's HIV positive cases and its prevalence rate among pregnant women is a cause of serious concern (Manipur Aids Control Society 2013; DNA 2013).[10] It is the gateway to drugs coming into India, mostly through this town with the police and army fully involved in drug carriage.[11]

The shift today from this small trans-border commerce seen in Moreh to hard core economic transformation is affecting women in many other ways. Whilst there has been serious debate on women and economic globalization and its impact on people, the issue has gone untouched from the perspective of conflict zones where a double jeopardy is in place. Manipur is a stark example where layers of conflict existed, mostly political, and has been studied in detail by many authors. However, the impending disaster of a new burden brought in by economic militarization was not perceived. A link between militarization and development has been emerging recently in the state. Together with AFSPA is the Unlawful Activities (Prevention) Act of 1967 (UAPA) that was amended twice, with Parliament adopting a third amendment in 2012 to expand the scope of the definition on terrorist acts' to include acts that threaten the economic security of India (PRS Legislative Research).[12] This Act threatens Manipur's economic autonomy, the environment and indigenous people's culture.

The linkage between armed conflict and resources is part of the history of colonialism. Modern day wars over resources are more subtle and attempt an overt linkage to the political. Manipur is rich in hydro-power, oil, gas, coal, limestone and uranium and has a huge, forest reserve. This makes it the target of contemporary forces of modernization that take advantage of existing conflicts and have increasingly marginalized indigenous peoples. Manipur is home to over 30 distinct and self-identified indigenous tribes or peoples. Such conflicts have physically displaced them as dams, roads and settlements encroach on their traditional habitat (CSCOHRM 2013: 16). It has been easier to manipulate the economy as the armed forces are already in place.

From political to economic militarization, the pathway is clearly defined as observed in the Loktak Lake that is famous for its numerous floating masses called *phumdis*. In 1999, two thousand soldiers from the Indian Army cordoned off the islets of Thanga, Karang and Ithing in Loktak Lake and detained the local population. During the six days of the 1999 military action, these people were accused of being part of the insurgent group United National Liberation Front (UNLF) and were told to reveal information about the insurgents. They were tortured and subjected to other forms of degrading and inhuman treatment. Local women leaders such as the Meira Paibis, Yumnam Subashini, Ningthoujam Ongi Shanti and Ningthoujam Momon were interrogated and tortured for hours. Fourteen years later, the Loktak Development Authority forcibly removed the villagers living on Loktak Lake floating phumdi masses to profile the Lake as a tourist location (E-Pao 2013). The destruction of the women's fishing industry so that a tourist industry would come up, demonstrated the shift of continuing militarization as it was done with the help of military forces. The Guwahati High Court issued notice to the chief minister and other officials of Loktak Development Authority on this (Schertow 2011; Human Rights Asia 2011).[13]

Linked to the use of force in Loktak is the Mapithel Dam located on the Thoubal River in Ukhrul district. It is a project being undertaken by the Government of Manipur's Irrigation and Flood Control Department (IFCD), with assistance from the central government. Construction began in 1989, amidst heavy protests from those to be affected by the dam. The Mapithel Dam Affected Villages Organisation (MDAVO) formed, mostly by villages that fell within the submergence area and later the Mapithel Dam Affected Ching-Tam (hill-valley) Organisation (MDACTO), are spear heading the resistance and appropriate compensation. Militarization has resulted in the denial of rights as security forces are being used to implement the government's 'development' agenda. In the North East, development sites such as dams are manned by armed forces to suppress protest. For example, the Mapithel Dam area is one of the most militarized zones in Manipur (CSCOHRM 2013, 17–18).There are many more examples of development-induced displacement in conflict areas.

Besides water, minerals have been another attraction in Manipur. New ventures of oil exploration, chromium mining, among others are in the offing. The impact of this neo liberal industrialization without any social security for the affected persons will be devastating as narrated in the resistance movements on displacement to the author. Also the engagement of the security apparatus in guarding these sites of conflicts has enlarged the presence of the armed forces. These are glaring evidences on the use of military forces in conflict areas for resisting people's voices of resistance on crucial issues as land acquisition, loss of livelihood, and just compensation and rehabilitation. In recent years, the Government of India (GoI), has been assisting Manipur and other states to augment and upgrade their police forces to deal with insurgency. Of the 51 reserve battalions sanctioned for the North East, nine are for Manipur (Ministry of Home Affairs 2014–15, 16).

Displacement has added to the existing conflict and the burden on women doubles. Besides violence that restricts their mobility and livelihood, the patriarchal structures of the indigenous societies further restrict them. Civil society considers these changes as 'leading to deep agrarian crisis, intensifying militarization processes, conflict within communities and increasing violence against women' (CSCOHRM 2013, 17).

Women's Contribution to Peace

Women have contributed significantly to the peace movement in Manipur. With a history of women's role in protests against the British, the movement moved appreciably towards a role defining them as major actors (Devi Binarani 2011; Devi, Helen 2012; Gangte 2011).[14] We began by seeing what happens to women in conflict situations. There is the violence syndrome and use of women's bodies both for iconization and desecration, at the same time, we cannot overlook the agency factor that is also a product of conflict.

The Manipur situation in relation to AFSPA brought forward a nuanced and rarely understood aspect in the context of women's political autonomy. The young Manipuri woman stands out today, as one of the world's greatest icon representing non-violence. Known locally as Mengoubior—the fair one—Irom Chanu Sharmila, a poet, a writer and a rights activist, has been on hunger strike since 4 November 2000.[15] She straddles the world of peace activism, but her contribution has not been recognized in the manner it should have been by the women's or the peace movement either in India or globally. There are few global examples of women who have stood firm against the strength of a large and powerful nation such as India. Sharmila's stand against militarism should have sent a powerful message to Indian society, but in comparison to the ongoing corruption issue in India the peace initiative did not draw the young to it.

The Meira Paibis, as we observed, have been active in protesting human rights violations and unjustifiable arrests by the security forces since a long time. It was not an individual organization but 32 women's groups who came under one platform called the Apunba Lup. Women in Manipur are known for taking up cudgels against social issues and taking action against social ills such as drug abuse, alcoholism and other social problems such as HIV/AIDS. The Meira Paibis did this work voluntarily without any payment or any honorarium. The mothers had a community history where mothers hared shared responsibility of breastfeeding with women neighbours and relatives when the mother is new to child care or lactates late (Lalit n.d.). Pateman argues that women are differently incorporated in the political system and their bodies have symbolized everything to the political (Pateman 1989, 7). This is true of the women's inclusion in the conflict situation where the Meira Paibis found space as they were mothers and not political actors. The motherhood does not convert into political power. The group has not played a significant role in formal peacekeeping. Even though the moral authority of Meira Paibis was at its peak after the Manorama protest in 2004 and members of the Apunba Lup were imprisoned for many months, when it came to sharing political power they were excluded. The Meira Paibis are facing a diversity of changes and the movement is on the decline. As their concerns transform and fluctuate they transform their priorities and identities. In recent days Meira Paibis have little funding to run the organization and as one of them mentioned, 'We are all getting old'. The old movement with the strong Meira Paibis and women of the Ima Market who together fought all sought of violence no longer has the same power. During the height of conflict this was the place where women could meet openly without drawing attention of the state/security forces. The markets remained the central point of women's response to the conflict, a place where many protest movements were born. It was the place for discussions on the situations and what could be done. Unfortunately the market space of women's solidarity has changed. In the place of older women, younger women have started to join the market place moving it from a socio-political and socio-economic to an economic space alone. The space for discourse and revolutionary change has given way to a competitive market place. In any peace-making efforts women will no longer be able to provide a traditional platform for discourse or decision-making. They are an aged group out of touch with the changing situation. The women in the Ima markets are reducing and their economic power is on the decline. This weakening of the movement and its fractured characteristic has marginalized the earlier groups. It is perhaps due to this lack of social support and money that some may have taken to collaborate with non-state armed groups such as the Revolutionary People's Front (RPF) of which they may be members (*One India News* 2012).

Marginalized and excluded from the mainstream and no replacement of new members, an essential element in the continuity of the movement there has been little to highlight in the work they carry out. The crumbling of social traditional structures does not help them. Other linked changes include the disappearing women's social structures such as the Khutlang[16] (Wahengbam 2009). Women used to work together in their fields, not on the basis of payment but work repayment. This age old system of collective work brought in a culture of merging the social with the economic. It was a platform that contributed to women's solidarity during conflict. In the modernization process the Khutlangs are disappearing, giving way to the state-sponsored self-help groups (SHGs) that are dependent on state aid that is erratic and dependent on bureaucratic structures. Unfortunately, with simultaneous structural change in the armed conflict and intrusion of non-state actors, the traditional economic structure is breaking down strengthening the patriarchal forces and keeping out of the peace processes.

As Jennifer Nedelsky claims,

> We come into being in a social context that is literally constitutive of us. Some of our most essential characteristics, such as our capacity for language and the conceptual framework through which we see the world, are not made by us, but given to us…through our interactions with others. (Nedelsky 1989, 7)

Subsequently, they have turned inwards and the gaze of the public shifted to this new identity. In any fluctuating situation, to manage new situations, they have to forge new commitments that transforms their priorities and identities.

While the state has excluded women in any peace initiatives, some women have at times taken over the role of interlocutors on their own. This process has been mostly between private actors such as the NSCN-IM (National Socialist Council of Nagaland—Isak Muivah) and the NSCN-K (National Socialist Council of Nagaland—Khaplang). In 1999, four women of the NMA (Naga Mothers Association) and NWUM (Naga Women's Union Manipur) crossed into Myanmar to hold discussion with Khapalang, the head of NSCN-K, and discussed the creation of a peaceful dialogue.[17] Though they conveyed the message to NSCN-IM leaders, peace was still a long distance. Three years later, they went international participating in the Bangkok People's consultations. The women's solidarity movement has however been declining. As to the unity among the women's movement, there is an emerging distancing as in the case of the entry of Naga leader Muhiava when he was not allowed to visit his home in Manipur. The NMA, with thousands of other Nagas in Manipur protested. However, in discussions with them they said that where peace was concerned they supported the women's organization. It is also visible that the NMA, though remaining a leader of the women's movement, is working mostly in Naga-dominated areas and has shifted back to working on social issues such as climate change. The areas of common action for feminist critical engagement have changed since the ethnic demands from across-State borders.

The new groups fighting militarization are formed of academics, professionals and urbanized NGOs. The major role that women have played is to talk to the different non-state armed groups in bringing about peace. In the changing situation the younger women want good jobs and go out to big cities in India and work (Phanjoubam 2008). One of the Meira Paibis we met remarked that many women from Manipur, especially unmarried ones, have left to seek a better life in the larger towns and cities. Every year, the numbers who leave is increasing. The flight goes beyond the state's boundaries. Their ethnic identity follows them to the mainland where in recent years they have been assaulted in various parts of the country such as Delhi, Pune and Bengaluru (*The Indian Express* 2012).

It needs to be emphasized that it would be dangerous to even attempt to club all women into one homogeneous category. Their experiences, even as women, are varied. Another central concern, related to the above mentioned conceptual and practical (i.e., political) challenges, is the issue of women's solidarity. The complex and sometimes contradictory dynamic of solidarity among women is related to the conceptualization of their identity. Some conceptual issues regarding the definition of common avenues for both feminists and policy-makers to address gender issues is crucial to ethnicity. These are diversity of experiences and solidarity despite diversity.

Thus, at issue here is a debate on the situation of women that recognizes differences among women, without fixing the boundaries between them. This conceptual approach, we believe, has opened up space for dialogue across differences; as well as providing an avenue to define politics and policies that address the situation and needs of women in a changing conflict situation. Economic equality and justice is rooted in women's Constitutional rights. The differentiation in the state's and women's ideology of control and independence is essentially distinctive. The increasing use of militarizism combined with capitalist policies by which the state and corporate interests are protected while women are rendered powerless the act itself creates solidarity.

The Manipur situation is thus very complex. It is no longer a political conflict with women's participation in peacekeeping being questioned. The process of militarization ends in normalizing the role of the military and shifting its use to another parameter such as the economy is simple. There has emerged a clear linkage between the militarization and state use of force in control of natural resources. Women in areas affected by economic militarization illustrate shifting images. Starting with images of the raising of their voices against the process, to one of poverty, indigence and destitution to other images of using of bodies to overcome the poverty of trafficking, migration and forced sex work. Despite this evidence of the state repression, the identity-based formations of womanhood remain. Even if they join the state or non-state actors their roles are circumscribed by the feminist standards. The use of violence by the state and by the patriarch in society and within the home is restricted only by their continuous advocacy and lobbying against militarization. Their fight against so called democratic institutions who in alliance with military structures and anti-terror laws lead to authoritarianism and are difficult to stand up against. The non-state actors who start as supporting populations end up as authoritarian and violent as the state create a dilemmas in women's ideologies and actions. With the failure of the justice system and national or transnational action, the women in Manipur stand alone in their fights against injustices committed against them. However, women's own resilience assists them in confronting challenges in ending gender-based violence, especially when the violence is used by the security forces as a mechanism for obstructing women's challenges for political change.

Violence against women who protest for autonomy has been documented, but not the recent opposition to corporate greed. The change from armed forces violence 'development' and corporatization have created change. A shifting from a political movement to NGO supported approach is visible. However, the issues aggravated by the new crisis confronting society have consolidated women and innovate against the consolidated power of State and global forces. NGOs (non-governmental organizations) who led the movement are, like elsewhere in India, building solidarity in transnational geopolitical spaces. However, women remain as the spearhead in the field but there is little space given to them at the international level even when they join NGO-led protests. The only space they have been able to achieve is in India through CEDAW (Convention on Elimination of Discretion Against Women) reporting and whenever a UN Special Rapporteur arrives.

UNSCR 1325 and Developing a National Local Plan

UNSCR 1325 can play a major role in Manipur. As the chapter unveiled old and new reasons of why we need the resolution, attempts were started by civil society on this 15th anniversary. Recently in 2014–15 as a prelude to the anniversary, the Manipur Gun Survivors Network organized a meeting to create a network of states in the region on UNSCR 1325. There is, therefore, a response to the felt need and a space created for the resolution (E-Pao 2014; *Manipur Times* 2015).

Strengthening these demands is the India Alternative Report to CEDAW in 2014 that recommended that the State should honour its international commitment to women in conflict transformation and peace-building under UNSCRs 1325, 1820, 1888, 1889, 1960, 2106 and 2122 (National Alliance of Women India 2014, 19). In this context, the report has one full chapter in an attempt to link the CEDAW recommendation 30 to the resolutions as it has a broader dimension that fits into a changing world and pays due attention to development (Chapter 11, 11, 159–84).

The chapter has reflected on both the cause and effects of the conflict on Manipur. The cause is very clear. The increase in arms in the region has contributed to women's insecurity, and this domination of the state in the political arena through militarization was strengthened by the state infiltrating into new areas of economic militarization. While the immediate effect of conflict included sexual abuse and other bodily harm, the long-term use of armed forces resulted in women's loss of livelihood and independent living. Women's initiatives towards peace at grass root level that is essential for formation of local action plans suffered as traditional and recent networks broke down. It is obvious from this chapter that the growing political and economic militarization of the State affects women's lives, while the issues of impunity has always remained and, unless challenged, the abuse of women's rights will continue.

In the absence of an NAP or a civil society, peace initiative groups have approached the UN through many forums especially the Special Rapporteurs. As a result, Margaret Sekaggya, the Special Rapporteur on Human Rights Defenders, as well as Christof Heyns, the Special Rapporteur on Disappearances, and Rashida Manjoo, the Special Rapporteur on Violence Against Women, have all reported that rape and sexual abuse have been reported in areas where there are armed conflicts in India such as Jammu and Kashmir, Assam and Manipur, among other regions. Women of certain ethnic minorities appear to be at risk as they are targeted by the police and security forces who use torture—including rape and other sexual violence—against them. In regard to women, Radhika Coomaraswamy, former Special Rapporteur on Violence Against Women, said: 'Rape and sexual abuse have been reported in areas where there are armed conflicts in India such as Jammu, Kashmir, Assam and Manipur, among other regions. Torture, including rape and other sexual violence, is also reportedly used by the police and security forces. In certain reports that the Special Rapporteur has received with regard to custodial violence outside the armed conflict areas, women from certain castes and ethnic or religious minorities appear to be at risk of being targeted by the police' (United Nations 2001). The recent (2013) visit by

Rashida Manjoo took place because of an invitation sent to her by Civil Society in Manipur. However none of the Rapporteurs have been able to influence government policy. NAP remains a distant goal on a horizon ruled by military power.

The question of arms infusion into Manipur by both state and non-state actors remains an issue outside the regular discourses. That armaments brought in for political control are being used for economic control is yet to be recognized. The connection between economic militarization has also not been recognized as an issue in the UNSCR 1325 discourse. This is a new complexity that requires a further investigation. It is therefore imperative that we discuss the formulation of local action plans before going to the level of an NAP. The local action plan has to be devised as per needs of the women at the local level, because it is they who are affected. The local women's movement needs support to revive. Though the Meira Paibis and NMU headed by Gina Shanghkham have played important roles in conflict management and peace resolution at local level, and their role at grass roots cannot be minimized, to survive they require sustenance from various local and national actors. Then only can UNSCR 1325 become a reality.

Notes

1. There is no record these figures are quoted by human rights activists. As per the South Asia Terrorism Portal there are six proscribed, seven active and 25 inactive groups (South Asia Terrorism Portal). In discussions with local human rights groups, this figure is incorrect, as many lie low for some time and then come back. (South Asia Terrorism Portal (http://www.satp.org/satporgtp/countries/india/database/indiafatalities.htm).
2. Personal Communication on 20 December 2012.
3. Personnel communication from women in Bishnupur, Chandel, Churachandpur, Tamenglong, Senapati, Ukhrul and Imphal Field Work March 5 to 19th December 2012 and 2 February to 4 March 2013.
4. Interview Imphal on 18 December 2012.
5. On 19 December 2012.
6. Interview of a woman in Imphal on 18 December 2012.
7. For details see VanLierde (2011).
8. Interview with secretary, New Life Foundation, Bishnupur district on 19 December 2012.
9. Also visit to Moreh by author on 19 December 2012.

10. According to independent estimates, there are an estimated 38,000 IDUs in Manipur, a state of around 2.5 million people. These drug users mix heroin with water and inject it in their arms with a syringe. Manipur, with a population of 2.8 million, has an estimated 38,016 people infected with HIV, including 10,109 women and 2,578 children (DNA 2013).
11. Deputy Chief Minister Gaikhangam who is also in charge of the Home Department has admitted that lack of discipline among police personnel led to involvement of some cops in transportation of illegal drugs towards Moreh (E-Pao 2013).
12. It expands the definition of 'terrorist act' to include Acts that threaten the economic security of India and damage its monetary stability by production, smuggling or circulation of 'high quality' counterfeit currency.
13. Numerous cases of impunity and violence have been targeted towards women including Ms Lungmilla, who is in a vegetative state when a tear gas canister fractured her skull during a rally to submit a memorandum stating their grievances against the construction of the Mapithel Dam (Thoubal Multipurpose Project) on 3 November 2008 by the Indian Reserve Battalion and the Manipur Police (Human Rights Asia 2011 quoted in CSCHR 2013, 17).
14. Women of Manipur have historically too been resistant against the colonial rulers and in 1904 and 1939 the uprising known as Nupi Lal or the women's war is testimony to their organizational skills in resistance. The Meira Paibis constituted one such force that resisted the violence due to militarization.
15. Sharmila started a fast when an Assam Rifles battalion killed 10 civilians in a village near Imphal. Three days later, Sharmila started her fast, demanding revocation of the AFSPA. Since then, every fortnight she travels from hospital to court to reply to the magistrate's query if she is willing to break her fast and her response till date has been no. She is then taken back to hospital to be force-fed through a nasal tube.
16. *Khutlang* in Meiteilon is a multiple synonymous term, literally, *Khut* means hand and *lanba* or *lanthokpa* means to lend out expecting something in return.
17. Interview with NMA past president Kheshli Cheshli.

References

Ahanthem, Chitra. 2011. 'Sanitised Societies and Dangerous Interlopers: Women of a Border Town—Moreh'. CRG Policies & Practices No. 33. Kolkata: CRG.

Centre for Development and Peace Studies. 2011. *Overview: Insurgency & Peace Efforts in Manipur*. Available at: http://cdpsindia.org/manipur_insurgency.asp (Accessed on 7 June 2016).

CSCOHRM (Civil Society Coalition on Human Rights in Manipur and the United Nations). 2013. *Violence Against Indigenous Women Perpetrated and/or Condoned by the State During Armed Conflict Manipur: Perils of War and Womanhood*. Memorandum to Rashida Manjoo Special Rapporteur on Violence Against Women, Its Causes And Consequences United Nations. Imphal: Civil Society Coalition on Human Rights in Manipur and the United Nations.

Copelon, Rhonda. 1995. 'Gendered War Crimes: Reconceptualizing Rape in Time of War'. In *Women's Rights, Human Rights: International Feminist Perspectives*, edited by Julie Peters and Andrea Wolper, 197–214. New York: Routledge, Chapman & Hall, Incorporated.

Devi, Helen R.K. 2012. *Women and Socio Political Movement in Recent Past and Present*. Manipur: Sunmarg Publication.

Devi, Thockchom Binarani. 2011. *Women's Movement in Manipur*. New Delhi: Concept Publication.

DNA. 2013. 'Manipur's HIV-affected Women Suffer for Husband's Sins'. *DNA*, March 31.

E-Pao. 2009. 'Indecent Frisking Draws Flak: Rights Panel Fumes'. Available at: http://epao.net/GP.asp?src=1..140509.may 09 (Accessed on 7 June 2016).

———. 2012. *Spotlight on Women Khutlang*. Available at: http://e-pao.net/epSubPageExtractor.asp?src=features.Spotlight_On_Women.Khutlang_Genesis_of_all_womens_organisation (Accessed on 17 May 2013).

———. 2013a. 'Gaikhangam Talks Tough, Assures Action, Again'. e-pao.net/ge.asp?heading=22&src=010513 (Accessed on 7 June 2016).

———. 2013b. *Repeal the Manipur Loktak Lake Protection Act 2006*. Available at: www.epao.net/epSubPageExtractor.asp?src=news_section.News_Links. News_Links_2013.Repeal_the_Manipur_Loktak_Lake_Protection_Act_2006_20130402 (Accessed on 18 December 2013).

———. 2014. *Women Leaders of Manipur Form Alliance on Women, Peace and Security*. Available at: http://e-pao.net/epSubPageExtractor.asp?src=news_section.Press_Release.Press_Release_2014.Women_Leaders_of_Manipur_forms_Alliance_on_Women_Peace_and_Security_20140509 (Accessed on 8 June 2016).

Gangte, Priyadarshini M. 2011. *Women of North East in Present Context*. New Delhi: Maxford Books.

Hans, Asha. 2012 and 2013 visit to Manipur districts of Bishnipur, Chandel, Churachandpur, Tamenglong, Senapati, Ukhrul and Imphal, March 5 to 19 December 2012 and 2–4 March 2013.

Hayes, Ben. 2012. *The Other Burma: Conflict, Counter Insurgency and Human Rights in North East India*. Amsterdam: Trans National Institute.

Human Rights Asia. 2011. *INDIA: Manipur Police Assault Protesting Women at Loktak Lake*. Available at: http://www.humanrights.asia/news/urgent-appeals/AHRC-UAC-251-2011 (Accessed on 8 June 2016).

Hussain, Monirul. 2002. 'State Development and Population Displacement in North East India'. In *Dimensions of Displaced People in Northeast India*, edited by Joshua Thomas and C. Joshua Thomas, 282–98. New Delhi: Regency Publications.

India Supreme Court. 2012. The Supreme Court Of India; Criminal/Civil Original Jurisdiction Writ Petition (Criminal) No.129 Of 2012 ExtraJudicial Execution Victim Families Association (Eevfam) And Another Petitioner(S) Versus Union Of India & Another Respondent(S) With Writ Petition (Civil) No.445 Of 2012 Suresh Singh Petitioner(S) Versus Union Of India & Another Respondent(S), 2.

The Indian Express. 2012. 'Attack on North East Students'. *The Indian Express*, 12 August 2012.

Lalit, Pukharambam. n.d. *Learning from Manipuri Women*. Available at: http://themanipurpage.tripod.com/culture/women.html (Accessed on 8 June 2016).

Manipur Aids Control Society. 2013. *History of MACS Executive Summary*. Available at: http://manipursacs.nic.in/ (Accessed on 8 June 2016).

Manipur Times. 2015. 'NE India Women's Peace Conference'. *Manipur Times*, 25 March. Available at: http://www.manipurtimes.com/events-pr/1344-first-northeast-india-women-peace-congregation (Accessed on 7 June 2016).

Manipur State Commission for Women. 2011. Statistical Statement Showing Total No. of Complaints Received. Available at: http://manipurwomencommission.gov.in/complaints2011.html (Accessed on 7 June 2016).

Ministry of Home Affairs. 2011. *National Crime Records Bureau*. Government of India.
———. 2014–15. *Annual Report*. Government of India.

Nagaland Post. 2011.'Sexual Harassment of Csws. Widows Whose Husbands Have Been Extrajudicially Executed by the Security Forces are Further Harassed When They Take to Sex Work. Sex Worker Hospitalized After Police Assault'. Available at: http://www.nagalandpost.com/ChannelNews/Regional/RegionalNews.aspx?news=TkVXUzEwMDAxMDA3Mw%3D%3DaNfu1Mt1Wqw% (Accessed on 7 June 2016).

National Alliance of Women, India. 2014. 'Chapter 11'. *India 4th and 5th NGO Alternative Report on CEDAW*, 159–84. New Delhi: National Alliance of Women, India.

Nedelsky, Jennifer. 1989. 'Reconceiving Autonomy: Sources, Thoughts, and Possibilities'. *Yale Journal of Law and Feminism*, 1 (1): 7–36.

Nepram, Binalakshmi. 2010. *Gender-based Violence in Conflict Zones Case Study of Impact of Ongoing Armed Conflict, Small Arms Proliferation and Women's Response in India's Northeast*. CEQUIN India.

NFHS 3 (National Family Health Survey). 2005–06. 'NFHS-III: 40% of Indian women face domestic violence'. Available at: http://infochangeindia.org/women/news/nfhs-iii-40-of-indian-women-face-domestic-violence.html (Accessed on 7 June 2016).

One India News. 2012. 'Meira Paibis Link with Militant Outfits Exposed'. *One India News*, 10 October. Available at: http://news.oneindia.in/2010/10/06/meirapaibis-link-with-militant-outfitsexposed.html (Accessed on 7 June 2016).

Pateman, Carole. 1989. *The Disorder of Women: Democracy, Feminism and Political Theory*. Stanford: Stanford University Press.

Phanjoubam, Pradip. 2008. 'Challenges Before Women's Movement in Manipur'. In *Women and Peace: Chapters from Northeast India*, edited by Anuradha Dutta and Ratna Bhuyan, 101. New Delhi: Akansha Publishing House.

PRS Legislative Research. 2011. The Unlawful Activities (Prevention) Amendment Bill. Available at: http://www.prsindia.org/billtrack/the-unlawful-activities-prevention-amendment-bill-2011-2159/ (Accessed on 8 June 2016).

Schertow, John Ahni. 2011. *Urgent Appeal: Manipur Police Assault Indigenous Women at Loktak Lake*. Available at: http://intercontinentalcry.org/urgent-appeal-manipur-police-assault-indigenous-women-at-loktak-lake/ (Accessed on 8 June 2016).

Shakti, Vahini. 2004. *Trafficking in India Report*. Faridabad, Haryana. Available at: http://www.crin.org/docs/traffickingreport.pdf (Accessed on 8 June 2016).

SIPRI. 2014. *Fact Sheet*. Available at: http://books.sipri.org/files/FS/SIPRIFS1403. pdf (Accessed on 20 January 2015).

Singh, Kulachandra B. 2001. 'The High Status that the Law of Mani Accorded to Meitei Women'. Manipuri text, MachaLeima, No. 15.

The Telegraph. 2011. 'Manipur "Gun Widows" Call for End to Violence'. *The Telegraph*, June 18. Available at: http://www.telegraphindia.com/1110618/jsp/ northeast/story_14126459.jsp.

The Times of India. 2004. 'Manorama Not Raped: Army Chief'. *The Times of India*. 16 September.

TNN. 2012. 'Women's Panel Seeks Report On Bishnupur Gang Rape'. *TNN*, 28 March.

VanLierde, Frank. 2011. *We, Widows of the Gun, Manipuri NGO Governance (WinG), Gun Victims Survivors Association, Human Rights Alert, Extrajudicial Execution Victim Families Manipur and CORDAID*. Available at: https://www.cordaid.org/ media/publications/We-widows.pdf (Accessed on 7 June 2016).

Verma, Justice J.S., Justice Leila Seth and Gopal Subramanium. 2013. Report of the Committee on Amendments to Criminal Law. Submitted to Prime Minister, 23rd January 2013 see http://www.prsindia.org/uploads/media/Justice%20verma%20 committee/js%20verma%20committe%20report.pdf)

WILPF India. 2014. *Caught Between Arms: The State of Women's Rights in India.* Shadow Report to CEDAW 58th Session. Geneva: Women's International League for Peace and Freedom. Available at: http://www.wilpfinternational.org/wp-content/uploads/2014/07/CEDAW-WILPF-India-shadow-report.pdf (Accessed on 8 June 2016).

United Nations. 2001. *E/CN.4/2001/73, Paragraph 85*.

United Nations Human Rights. 2013. *Special Rapporteur on Violence against Women, its Causes and Consequences Finalises Country Mission to India*. Office of the High Commissioner for Human Rights. Available at: http://www.ohchr.org/EN/ NewsEvents/Pages/DisplayNews.aspx?NewsID=13282&LangID=E (Accessed on 8 June 2016).

Wahengbam, Sushma Devi. 2009. *Khutlang: Genesis of All Women's Organisation of Manipur-E-Pao*. Available at: http://e-pao.net/epSubPageExtractor. asp?src=features.Spotlight_On_Women.Khutlang_Genesis_of_all_womens_ organisation (Accessed on 8 June 2016).

9

Conflict and the Peace Process in Jammu and Kashmir: Locating the Agency of Women

Rekha Chowdhary and Vibhuti Ubbott

To address the question as to why women should be in the peace process in the particular context of conflict situation of Jammu and Kashmir, it may be pertinent first of all to refer to the question as to where women are located in the context of conflict. There is not much presence of women in the discourse related to conflict, except as victims. In the core area of conflict, that is, in the Kashmir valley and the militancy infested parts of Jammu, women attain visibility mainly as victims of violence. Their victimization has resulted from the overarching role of violence. Most of what has been documented about the women, therefore, is in relation to the various ways women have borne the impact of violence—women caught in the militarized context of conflict; their bodies having become the site of war with both security forces and militants being guilty of sexually abusing women; facing the burden of destitution in the absence of their men who are either killed or disappeared; and facing the psychological trauma and manifold health-related problems.

Though their victimization remains a reality in the conflict situation of Jammu and Kashmir, however, the emphasis only on victimization portrays women in a very limited manner. The assumptions that the men are responsible for conflict situation and women are passive recipients of this situation and are caught in it involuntarily not only denies agency to women but also portrays them as 'apolitical' members of society. The stereotyped distinction between men 'who make war' and women who are merely sufferers, ignores the possibilities of women being actors in their own rights. Referring to women's agency in 'managing survival and reconstruction and women's notions of security of peace' in the context of South Asia, Rita Manchanda notes that:

> Beyond the icon of Mother Sorrow, there are many faces of women in conflict in South Asia. Women have negotiated conflict situations by becoming citizens, combatants, heads of household, war munitions workers, prostitutes, producers of soldiers and war resisters and political leaders at the local and national level. In South Asia, at one end is the Women of Violence represented by the Armed Virgin of the Liberation Tigers of Tamil Eelam (LTTE), at the other end is the Woman of Peace, symbolised by the Naga Mothers Association (NMA) in the nationalist struggle for independent Nagaland. (Manchanda 2001, 10–11)

In Kashmir also, women have reflected various dimensions of their agency. They have shown a very strong sense of identification with the political movement as it has been manifesting itself during last six decades, but more particularly in the last two and half decades.

In order to assess the role of women in the separatist movement of Kashmir, it may be pertinent to locate the movement in the broader context of conflict situation of the state.

I. Locating Women in the Context of Conflict

Though the conflict situation in Kashmir is an old one, which started in 1947 when the tribal invasion took place and the state came be partitioned between Indian-administered and Pakistan-administered sides, the recent phase of conflict situation started in late 1980s with the onset of armed militancy and separatist upsurge. The background to the militancy could be traced both to the long-term political discontent that had remained more or less unaddressed since early fifties, as well as the immediate political situation as it had been evolving a few years prior to the onset of militancy. While the loss of political and constitutional autonomy of the state, the excessive intrusion of the centre in the politics of the state, the absence of democratic space and the lack of legitimacy of the electoral and power politics since 1953, had led to the accumulated discontent which got intensified in the post-1984 period. What triggered the unrest was the renewed intrusion by the Centre in the politics of the state generating a very strong sense of political alienation.[1]

What was peculiar about the phenomenon of militancy that erupted in 1989 was that it was supported by common people and enjoyed a high level of legitimacy. However, apart from armed militancy, Kashmir witnessed massive protests on a regular basis. By the turn of 1989, the intensity of protests was so high that it seemed to have swayed all sections of society. This was the time that the whole of Kashmir was reverberating with the slogans 'Hum kya chahte? Azadi' (What do we want? Independence).

The mass demonstrations had the presence of large number of women. In fact, due to the very high visibility of women in the demonstrations, they had become the public face of the popular unrest. However, this was not the first time that women had come on the streets of Kashmir to make a political statement.

Kashmir has had a tradition of protest politics in which women have been quite visible. Thus, women were actively involved in the first-ever series of mass protests in the post-accession period in 1962 when Kashmir erupted around the issue of theft of the holy relic in the famous Hazratbal shrine in Srinagar. The emotional outburst in the form of massive processions of men and women, almost on daily basis, was a manifestation of the political discontent of the Kashmiri society. The tradition of mass protests continued in the later period. Women were on the streets in the period 1976–77 when Congress had withdrawn its support from Sheikh's government and it was rumoured that Sheikh was severely indisposed. They were also part of the huge crowd that celebrated the victory of Sheikh Abdullah in the 1977 assembly election. Throughout the period of unrest after 1984, women were visible in most of the popular protests.

What is important about the role of women during the period of militancy, however, is that in the early period they played a very crucial role in legitimizing the armed militancy. Though the cadre of militants was comprised mainly of men and women did not participate in militant activities, yet they were the backbone of militancy as such and glorified the militants. They considered the militants as their heroes, called them 'our boys', sung songs in praise of them and were ready to provide whatever support they could. They gave them shelter when required and felt a sense of pride in having contributed to the 'cause'. To quote Prashar:

[W]omen did not pick up arms or engage in arms training during the popular militancy in the early 1990s, but were instrumental in acting as support groups for militant men. They nursed and shielded the militants, and carried messages and arms. As mothers, they sang praises of the martyrdom of their sons, showered their dead bodies with dried fruits and inspired the men in their family to take up arms against the Indian state. Younger women romanticised the mujahidin and an aggressive and gun-wielding masculinity was embraced and legitimised by a society otherwise known for its pacifist and Sufi values. (Prashar 2011, 438)

While women were the force behind the legitimization of armed militancy, they were also instrumental in de-legitimizing it in the later period. By the middle of the 1990s, violence had so deeply impacted the Kashmiri society that the earlier romanticization of militancy had given way to a sense of fatigue. Women particularly had to bear the major burnt of this violence including sexual violence. To quote Ramachandran and Jabbar, 'Hundreds of women are believed to have been raped by militants and security forces…. Militants have raped women as a way of punishing other family members believed to be informers or suspected of opposing the militants. Soldiers rape women to punish, intimidate and humiliate' (Ramachandran and Jabbar 2003, 19). The armed militancy led to the militarization of society and deeply impacted the social and cultural processes. With an overwhelming influence of 'gun-wielding' people and their intervention in cultural, religious and social matters, and the assertion of the masculinized discourse, women found space shrinking for them. Basically, it was the change in the nature of militancy that resulted in a change in their attitude towards violence as a means of political resistance. As compared to the committed and ideologically oriented first group of militants, many of whom were educated and even drop-outs from the professional institutions, many militants during the period of the mid-1990s were lured by exterior motives including money, status and power. Meanwhile, there was the factor of jihadi groups who had come from outside Kashmir and saw the Kashmir conflict in religious terms—in terms of the global Islamic agenda. Not being aware of local religious sensitivities located in Sufi tradition, the jihadi militants alienated women. The capturing of Chrar-e-Sharief—the shrine of the patron saint of Kashmir, Sheikh Noorud-din-Noorani—by jihadis and its destruction during the encounter between the militants and the army was particularly responsible for turning Kashmiri women away from militancy in general and jihadi militants in particular. By the mid-1990s, the shift in societal response towards militancy could be clearly seen. The militants were no more celebrated as 'heroes' and were not welcomed at homes and streets the way they were in the earlier period of militancy. It was only during the death of any local militant that one could see the emotional response of women. This response continues to be visible even in the post-militancy period. It is in the act of mourning that the political response of women is manifested. A local militant is still a 'martyr' and gets respect from the society, but there is overall rejection of armed militancy.

The withdrawal of societal legitimacy of militancy was so unambiguous that by the end of the decade of nineties there was sufficient pressure on the separatist leadership to take a position against it. In 2000, a debate took place between Syed Ali Shah Geelani and A. G. Lone, two top-most separatist leaders representing two different ideological positions. It was during this debate that Lone declared that not merely were the jihadi militant unwelcome in Kashmir but that the armed militancy per se had lost its relevance (Chowdhary 2002).

Women have been using their agency in many more ways. As reported by many, women have been negotiating for their husbands and sons. It has been a common situation of Kashmir where the men had been picked up by the security forces and women had to visit the police station or the army camp and plead for the release of their men. To quote Ahmad:

> Illiterate women, whose sons, spouses, brothers or fathers were serving jail sentences in different parts of Kashmir and India, began to follow their legal suits, contacted lawyers, got to learn about the draconian laws under which their beloved ones were imprisoned, got exposed to the legal clauses and knew which judges were hearing their cases. They began to visit various jails, torture and detention centers and traveled to alien places, which provided them diverse exposure, and they are well aware of the location of prisons, courts and cheap hotels to stay during which the trial was going on. Thus, their personal tragedies made them emerge as empowered women, who control the lives of

their kith and kin, despite the impediments of education, gender and birth. (Ahmad 2011)

In the same vein, Manchanda notes:

> In protracted conflict situations like Kashmir where the cultural space for women in the public sphere is highly restricted, women's political mobilisation has been manifested in domestic activism. In their everyday life, ordinary women forged survival strategies for their families and communities, they entered into negotiations of power with the security forces and the administration for the rescue and safety of their families. Their traditional roles as mothers and wives were 'stretched' as they emerged as agents of political resistance. The collapse of the divide between the public-private sphere following the societal upheaval attendant on conflict pushed women into negotiations of power in the public sphere as the management of survival became politicised. Indeed, the political mobilisation of the domestic sphere challenged the dichotomy between the domestic and public sphere of politics. (Manchanda 2001, 43–44)

In asserting their agency, women have not necessarily been vocal. In the kind of the situation in which they were caught up, they asserted their agency very silently. There are many examples where, in the face of pressures placed by the extremist and fundamentalist forces to impose moral codes on them, women forcefully, though silently, offered their resistance.

As it happens in many situations of conflict, women are seen as the bearers of the identity of community and, hence, come to be placed under cultural pressures. To quote Prashar, 'women as the cultural bearers of national identities become upholders of the key values of the conflicting sides. In other words, women's bodies and gendered identities become the territories on which militants and counter-militants wage their wars and play out their ideologies'. During the early period of armed militancy, a number of fundamentalist elements, which were otherwise on the fringe of Kashmir's politics, gained visibility through their dictates. Invoking religion, these elements sought to control the cultural and social space and impose restrictions on women in many ways—by banning beauty parlours, imposing dress codes and asking women to veil themselves; banning the use of contraceptives and abortions; and imposing codes of sex-segregation in public spaces.[2]

II. Agency of Women

How did women respond to these pressures? There was certainly no visible and organized resistance of women. Throughout the period of armed militancy, women have not been able to organize themselves under a common platform to speak on their own behalf or to confront the issues from a gender perspective in the form of collective resistance. The political movement has been so overarching in Kashmir that it has not left much space for women's movement and gender politics. In clear terms, every other movement or struggle has to be subsumed in the larger struggle and, according to the separatist leadership, will have a place only after the political struggle is fully accomplished. In this context of lack of space for gender politics, the women responded in the only way they could be most effective—silently rejecting the pressure of fundamentalist politics. This becomes clear from the response of women to veiling. Whenever a dictate to cover their faces was issued, women would strategically follow it but would discard it when they got the first opportunity. In the end, they did not make it a part of their routine life. Two decades after the militancy started, one can see that women have continued with their own cultural traditions. For most of the women, veiling is still a 'non-Kashmiri' phenomenon. They proudly inform that Kashmiri women were never traditionally veiled and had the freedom of mobility. In rural areas, the women were involved along with their men in the agricultural activities and could not have afforded to veil themselves. Even in urban areas, there was no tradition of veiling women. So when the pressure was exerted by the militants, they adopted various strategies to cope with the pressure.

Interestingly, there was no organized resistance, not even a campaign in Kashmir against the fundamentalist forces. It was, therefore, at the individual level that the women offered their resistance to any attempt to intervene with the traditional freedom that they used to enjoy. Referring to the nature of their resistance and the problems related with the overarching patriarchal nature of society, Dasgupta notes:

> [E]ven amidst this atmosphere of violence and terror the women of Kashmir have shown resistance and a sense of discrimination. They have refused to give up their traditional value system and cherished heritage. Had they not resisted the pressures to succumb to social customs that were alien to the Kashmiri way of life, perhaps Kashmir would have gone the way of Afghanistan. (Dasgupta 2001, 20)

The fear of Talibanization of Kashmiri society was always alive. However, it was mainly due to the determined, though silent resistance of women that this fear could not take the shape of reality. Women, while being very much part of the movement and identifying with it saw to it that they are not adversely affected by the campaign of the reactionary forces.

Going beyond the perspective of victimhood, one can see as to how women have coped with the complex consequences of conflict and how they have survived. The vibrant educational sector of Kashmir specifically provides a very impressive picture of women being survivors. They have shown their resilience through the period of conflict. The number of girls in all educational institutions is increasing and even within the co-educational institutions, there is large number of girls. Various universities in Kashmir provide a very clear reflection of the interest taken by women, not only in conventional fields of education but also in the new scientific, technical and management-related fields. Women are competing for professional courses and opting for technical lines not only near home, but in various parts of the country.

Besides, the silent resistance offered at the individual level, the agency of women has been reflected in collective actions as well. One very often quoted instance of women rising above their situation of victimization and using it for the collective resistance, can be provided through the example of Association of Parents of Disappeared Persons (APDP). It is a purely indigenous organization formed by women who are the relatives of the people who disappeared during the course of conflict. The Chairperson of this organization, Parveena Ahangar, lost her own son during the conflict and has no clue about what happened to him since he disappeared.

> Parveena succ[e]eded in assembling the relatives of persons who had been subjected to torture, death, solitary confinement and other brutal methods while in the custody of the police or military forces in various parts of the Valley. In the course of foregrounding their trials and tribulations, she participated in conferences on human rights violations in the Philip[p]ines, Thailand and Indonesia and organized peaceful demonstrations in the backyard of India's political gurus and masters, New Delhi. (Khan 2009, 102–03)

This organization with a cadre and membership of many women similarly placed has succeeded in giving voice to the voiceless.

The women who became associated with it belonged mostly to the vulnerable sections of society and were not only victimized by the security forces but were also marginalized by the society and the separatists. Documenting the cases of the disappeared, the organization has brought focus on the issue of disappearances in Kashmir at the national and international levels. Referring to their role, Manchanda notes:

Women have innovated forms of resistance grounded in the cultural space of women, especially around mourning, for example, the Association of the Parents of the Disappeared (Kashmir's Mothers Front), which politicises the women's traditional motherist role by taking the private act of mourning into the public space. Women's ways of acting are increasingly challenged the notion of what political activity can be.' (Manchanda 2001, 44)

III. Patriarchy, Gender Context and Women

Despite the fact that women have been very much involved in the movement in their own right and have exercised their agency in a variety of ways, they are not central to the peace processes. There is almost no visibility of women in the dialogues, negotiations and other formal processes of peacebuilding. One of the major reasons for the absence of women from the peace process is the absence of women in the leadership position when it comes to anything political. Whether it is the mainstream politics or the separatist politics, women are not able to attain positions of significance.

In any case, the absence of women in the leadership position reflects the lack of equality between men and women in Kashmiri society and the social, financial, emotional and psychological dependence of women over men. The gender hierarchy that operates in the social sphere also gets reflected in the political sphere—whether it is the mainstream politics or the separatist politics. To quote Manchanda, '[f]ear of social censure in a deeply conservative society has inhibited the organized activism of women and prevented many from assuming political roles' (Manchanda 2011).

Nyla Ali Khan notes the impact of patriarchal structure and gender hierarchy on the perpetual subordination of women in various fields of life. She links the structures of patriarchy not only with the absence of women in public space but also in their subordination in the context of conflict situation as well. 'Ironically, women in J&K have not yet found niches in the upper echelons of decision-making bodies—political, religious or social. Asymmetrical gender hierarchies legitimized by the forceful dissemination of fundamentalist and militarized discourses portend the debasement and prostration of women' (Khan 2009, 123).

Though women have been active supporters of the separatist politics, there are not many women visible in the leadership position. Seen from that perspective, the separatist leadership seems to be all male-dominated. There are exceptional cases of women leaders such as Aasia Andrabi or Zamruda who have some presence in the separatist politics but generally there are no women, not just in the higher leadership position but also in the lower or middle level of separatist cadre.[3]

It is the traditional patriarchal culture with a demarcation of roles for men and women that keeps women away from politics. Women, despite being educated and pursuing careers, are essentially seen as home makers. The political roles that fall within the confines of the public roles are not, therefore, easily accessible for women unless there is familial support. With the exception of certain 'political families' which provide such a support to women, generally women are not encouraged to be visible in the public space. And in the extraordinary circumstances such as the conflict situation, when women attain visibility, this is mainly in relation to the roles that can be seen as extension of the familial roles. That is why it is the 'motherhood' that gets celebrated. Alternatively, women are visible as 'widows' or 'half-widows'—again a reflection of their status not as individuals but in relation to men in the family. The domestic space arguably is the 'private' space where women are supposedly 'protected' and 'secure' and, therefore, even when they enter the 'public space' it is for the specific purpose of getting educated or for the purpose of working or pursuing their careers. Beyond this purpose, the public space is not considered 'proper' for women and in the general social understanding carries all the possibilities not only of endangering the 'security and safety' of women but also upsetting the social and ethical order.

Even for few women who have entered the leadership position, it entails lot of problems. They feel that they are seen as insignificant actors not equal to male leaders. There is the typical case of Anjuman

Zamrud who joined the separatist organization—All Parties Hurriyat Conference (APHC)—in the initial stage of its formation. She was later jailed on the charge of being involved in hawala transactions. She was almost left alone to fight for herself. Referring to her case, Manchanda notes:

> Zamrood is particularly bitter because, as a constituent member of the Hurriyat since 1993, she had expected that when she was arrested in 2003 and jailed for allegedly receiving monies from the Pakistan High Commission for the Hurriyat, the top leadership would defend her against the charges of being a 'terrorist'. However, as she reveals in her memoirs Qadi no 100, the Hurriyat disowned her and left her to be beaten and mentally tortured in Tihar jail for five years. (Manchanda 2011)

What remains problematic for women, in the gender context, is that women and their issues do not form the central core of the discourse of conflict. This is despite the fact that issue related to the sexual abuse of women by the security forces has been the major issue raised by the separatists. However, rather than the issue being raised from gender perspective, is raised from political perspective and has at best an instrumental value for the separatist politics. This is despite the fact that the cases related to sexual abuse of women by the security forces are the major issues raised by the separatists. Nyla Ali Khan reflecting on the instrumental use of the issue of sexual abuse both within the separatist and mainstream politics, asks this question about the victimized women, 'Will the grievances of such aggrieved and powerless people ever be redressed. Will the violated women of Kashmir ever have the satisfaction of knowing that those who wronged them did not go unpunished?' And then she goes on to explain:

> Women representatives of the then ruling PDP and those of its ally, the Congress Party, were quick to make visits accompanied by their entourages to isolated villages or town in which the Indian army has trammeled upon the sensibilities of the female population. The PDP, while in opposition, raised the issue of human rights abuses which, until then, had not been given much credence by the NC government. But they were unable to advocate reforms that were specific to women, and no stringent and timely measures were taken to redress those wrongs. (Khan 2009)

One can see that issue of sexual abuse of women is raised more from a political perspective rather than from a gender perspective. Despite the fact that cases of 'rape' evoke emotional response in Kashmir and protests against the cases rapes of women by the security forces are the common occurrences, yet, the issue of rape is not seen from the gender perspective. The issue is highlighted to refer to the atrocities committed by the security forces but not much attention is paid to the women who are so victimized. Referring to the infamous Kunan Poshpura case that in the separatist discourse is one of the worst cases of gang rape in Kashmir, Bhasin Jamwal, thus, notes:

> As in case of Kunan Poshpura…women of the village do not only reel under the trauma of what happened but also face the brunt of an apathetic society—stigmatized and abandoned forever, by their husbands, government and the civil society. No woman in the village was married after the incident for several years. Some victims were also abandoned by their husbands. For several years no schools were opened in the village. (Jamwal 2010, 329)

One of the reasons as to why the gender concerns are not at the centre of the discourse of conflict is that women themselves have failed to assert their own gender-related politics. The phenomenon of women's movements that caught the imagination of the women at the global and the national level during and after the 1970s, just bypassed the state of Jammu and Kashmir. It is ironical that, despite multiple issues related to women, not only in the context of conflict but even outside the conflict politics, one cannot name a woman's organization that is seen to be playing an effective role in this state. What is the matter of greater concern is that the women within the state are fragmented on the basis of community, religion, region and other fault lines. They are compartmentalized on the basis of these identities.

IV. To Conclude

In the context of the centrality of women in the conflict situation, and more so in the context in which they are able to act in political manner in their own way, there is great prospect of women being in the centre of peace process. With women having asserted their agency in a very effective manner, their potential to act as a pressure group is immense. Already having an informal role in combating violence and de-legitimizing violence, they can be involved in the formal processes in effective manner. It is important that the voice of women be given a pivotal space and, learning the lessons from their silent resistance, they be involved in the more formal and organized processes of peace-building.

Women have the potential of breaking the barriers not only of borders but also of regions, religions and communities. Gender provides a common identity to women and through this common identity they can not only become the bridge-builders between the communities and the regions but also give a new direction to the political discourse that till now remains militarized and masculinized.

One may conclude by referring to the UN Resolution 1325 that emphasizes on increasing 'the number of women at all decision-making levels in conflict management and resolution', increasing 'the support for women's peace-building activities', supporting 'equal participation for women in peace negotiations at all levels', and addressing 'the specific protection needs of women in conflict situations' and prosecuting 'war crimes against women'.

Notes

1. The political situation in Kashmir became quite volatile after 1984 when Farooq Abdullah's legitimately elected government was overthrown due to the defections engineered by the Congress that was the ruling party in the Centre. Farooq Abdullah who had succeeded his father as the leader of NC had won a very keenly contested election against the Congress in 1983. The removal of Farooq Abdullah from power had psychological impact on people of Kashmir. For them it was a substantiation of the fact that governments in Jammu and Kashmir rather than being based on the mandate of people, were based on the pleasure of the 'Centre'. Farooq-led NC meanwhile got convinced that to sustain its power it needed to align with the Centre and entered into an alliance with the Congress Party. The NC-Congress alliance was not received positively in Kashmir and led to a wave of anger against this party. It was in this situation that the Muslim United Front emerged as a political force. The MUF had so mobilized the popular responses that it was expected to win a large number of seats in the Assembly elections of 1987. Failure to attain more than four seats by this party led to a wide-spread feeling that the elections were rigged. Post-1987 situation in Kashmir was very explosive and gave rise to mass protests and by 1989, the armed militancy overtook the valley.

2. Ramachandran and Jabbar state that 'People especially in the villages were told that the Central government was trying to alter the Muslim Majority nature of State and so Muslims should have more children. Besides, the armed struggle needed more fighters. The sale of contraceptives was sto[p]ped and family planning procedures were not performed, at least openly in the hospitals'. She further notes, 'Members of the Jamaat-i-Islami and the Banat-ul-Islam (its women wing) would tell women that they were life givers and so should not kill their unborn children', recalls a doctor in a government hospital (Ramachandran and Jabbar 2003, 21).
3. To quote Ramachandran and Jabbar 'the militant groups were all-male fighting units. According to former militants of Hizbul Mujahideen, the Hezbollah and al-Jehad, there are no women in the militant groups. Women were not among those trained in Pakistan, they say' (Ramachandran 2002).

References

Ahmad, Mushtaq ul Haq. 2011. *Has Conflict Empowered Kashmiri Women*. Available at: http://www.countercurrents.org/sikander050911.htm (Accessed on 21 March 2015).

Chowdhary, Rekha. 2002. 'Kashmir: Lone's Liberal Legacy'. *Economic and Political Weekly*, 37 (25, June): 22–28.

Dasgupta, Sumona. 2001. *Breaking the Silence: Women and Kashmir*. New Delhi: WISCOMP.

Jamwal, Anuradha Bhasin. 2010. 'Women's Identity and Politics in Jammu and Kashmir'. In *Identity Politics in Jammu and Kashmir*, edited by Rekha Chowdhary. Delhi: Vitasta.

Khan, Nyla Ali. 2009. *Islam, Women & Violence in Kashmir: Between India and Pakistan*. New Delhi, Tulika.

Manchanda, Rita. 2011. 'Kashmiri Women Demand Participation in Peace Process'. *Peace Talks*. Available at: http://peacetalks.hdcentre.org/2011/02/kashmiri-women-demand-participation-in-peace-process/ (Accessed on 8 April 2015).

Manchanda, Rita, ed. 2001. *Women, War and Peace in South Asia: Beyond Victimhood to Agency*. New Delhi: SAGE Publications.

Prashar, Swati. 2011. 'The Sacred and the Sacrilegious: Exploring Women's "Politics" and "Agency"' in Radical Religious Movements in South Asia'. *Totalitarian Movements and Political Religions*, 11 (3): 435–55.

Ramachandran, Sudha and Sonia Jabbar. 2003. *Shades of Violence: Women and Kashmir*. Delhi: WISCOMP.

Ramachandran, Sudha. 2002. 'Women Lift Veil on Kashmir Struggle'. *Asia Times*, 7 March 2002. Available at: http://www.atimes.com/ind-pak/DC07Df01.html (Accessed on 8 April 2015).

10

Whither Peace? A Discussion on Violence, Impunity and 1325 in Light of Communal Violence

Ila Pathak and Saumya Uma

Editors' Note

Ila Pathak sent in a draft chapter in 2012 and passed away before this volume approached publication. We are deeply grateful for her presence in this conversation. We have edited this chapter based on our understanding of her draft. We are also grateful to Saumya Uma who took on the challenge of updating the chapter and explicating Ilaben's point.

Although UNSCR 1325 addresses conflicts that involve the state, we invited Ilaben to write a chapter based on her involvement with religion-based riots. We were interested in learning about the utility of the 1325 framework for conflict situations involving non-state actors.

Ilaben's descriptions of the two cases flag several of the issues that the WPS (Women, Peace and Security) resolutions seek to address: listening to women, creating accountability, ending impunity for sexual and gender-based violence, and including women in decision-making. The narratives in Ilaben's draft raise these questions, but as part of a broader discussion of the politics of communal violence in India. In this edited version, we have sought to highlight these issues.

Ilaben's brief discussion of why the Women's International League for Peace and Freedom (WILFP) thought it important to be part of the fact-finding mission offers us a glimpse into how local events and global values connect. It also offers an example of the role that the transnational women's movement, along with its local linkages, has played in creating normative regimes around women's rights.

The one direct reference Ilaben makes to the relevance of 1325 and its utility for better access to justice comes where she says that a National Action Plan (NAP) would have offered a reference point in the many sexual violence cases, including Bilkis Bano's, lawyers are fighting in the aftermath of both riots. Adoption of a 1325 Action Plan would signal government acceptance of these gender justice norms, while a People's Plan would assert consensus around a normative agenda for inclusion and access to justice in the context both of traditional conflict and conflicts involving private actors.

We have edited Ilaben's draft to succinctly set the stage for a clearer exposition of these ideas by Saumya Uma, who has written a postscript and conclusion. The chapter is now structured as follows. It opens with some general observations about violence, the normative framework of 1325 and women. The next section highlights gendered aspects of the violence in two selected riots and their aftermath. Finally, the chapter closes with Saumya Uma's postscript and conclusion.

Ilaben wrote in her draft:

> Other cases are still to be heard, justice is awaited. Justice gives hope that such beastliness may not be unleashed again. It provides sense of security. It asserts equality of citizens. Somewhat under that assertion is the assertion of gender equality. That leads to peace. The beleaguered may feel relieved that the massacre will not be repeated.

A Women's Movement Intervention

When violence occurred in Kandhamal in August 2008, I was dumbstruck when I realized that these happenings bore a close parallel to those in Gujarat five years earlier. At my behest, the WILPF studied both the Gujarat riots and the Kandhamal riots.[1] This was important not just because women are the worst sufferers in any troubled situation but also because India has been a signatory to a number of international covenants. The WILPF International president and WILPF India president decided to research the riots and consequences of violence. They were specifically interested in the plight of women and children, both in camps and rehabilitation.[2]

A number of well-meaning organizations had already visited the scene of the riots and subsequent sites of relief camps. They had made several recommendations and prayers to the High Courts of Odisha and Gujarat and to the Supreme Court of India. However, WILPF found that these recommendations and prayers did not include the specific demands of women. There is no gainsaying the fact that men do suffer in such violence, but women are more vulnerable and their specific demands may not be realized when the generalized demands of men are being fulfilled. Such demands ought to be responded to and this is the theme of the previously cited international covenants. The WILPF chose to focus on them.

The team went to Kandhamal in January 2009 and made a rapid survey of three relief camps that were still operational and were at that time sheltering more than 8,000 people. The drive to send back the displacement was in full swing. The team became intimate with the goings-on in the camp during the past four months. The way the displaced were accommodated, fed and provided with basic necessities was not as per law. There was a wide schism between what should be and what was actually there, and no possibility of improvement was left because the camps were being wound up under pressure from the local government. The team also met various government officials and politicians in order to impress upon them the sorry predicament of the victims of the riots, especially the women and children.

The visit to the camps made it clear to the WILPF team that the rights of the victims to life, liberty and freedom of religion were jeopardized. The State had failed to protect their human rights. The team also noticed that women were the worse off; their specific rights such as rights to privacy and freedom from sexual assault were undermined.

The WILPF team went through the prayers made to the Supreme Court in earlier petitions and recommendations made to the state government but it appeared that none of them had specifically mentioned women or their rights. It is true that demands for protection and compensation were meant for both men and women, yet specific mention of women's needs was nowhere noticed. This is what has been happening over the years, women-specific demands are subsumed within general demands. Therefore, the WILPF team thought it necessary to raise women's issues separately.

Two petitions with reference to Kandhamal riots were already lying with the Supreme Court of India. The WILPF team decided to make a special petition to the apex court. The petition was based on the international conventions. Indian women expect that India acts in accordance with the promises made internationally. The documents that recognize and support women's human rights, namely, Universal Declaration of Human Rights (UDHR), Vienna Declaration 1993, Convention on the Elimination of all forms of Discrimination Against Women (CEDAW) and Security Council's Resolutions 1325 and 1820, are to be referred to towards making specific provisions for women in the wake of such eventualities as rioting, armed conflicts and so on in relief camps and such other shelters. The prayer in the petition was:

> Indian women need a mechanism, which could be activated in times of need to protect women's human rights, demand special provisions that ought to be made for women and to ensure thorough monitoring that such provisions are made and continued as long as needed. (Ebbe and Pathak 2009, 69)

Of Women, Violence and Impunity: Some General Observations

During riots, the basic rights of victims to life and property are snaffled. Thereafter, if they do not get immediate relief and complete rehabilitation, their desolation is compounded. Finally, in a civilized society, it is imperative that the perpetrators are caught and punished appropriately.

In these riots, violence related to women is based on perceptions of patriarchy. Women were gang raped in front of the men of their own family and neighbourhood symbolizing the dishonour of the whole community. Children of all ages were killed before the eyes of their parents. In conflicts such as these, women lose their right to life and right to equality.

When we turn our attention to relief camps, we feel that patriarchy holds its sway here also. It was apparent that women were ignored; their needs not catered for, though a facade of concern for them was kept up. If a covered bathing space was not thought of to be important, what other care could have been taken of women's needs is difficult to comprehend. Their rights to privacy, health and security were compromised, shattering their mental peace.

When survivors of the riots were looking for justice they were thwarted from registering complaints by the police. Women's complaints were added to other complaints; separate FIRs (First Information Report) were not made. Such approach of the police made women feel oppressed. If the perpetrators of crimes are not brought to book, the apprehension that those crimes would be committed again with impunity is reinforced. Life for women in displacement camps or thereafter remains one of struggle, trying to escape unhurt from their tormentors. Trained personnel need to help victimized women in both uncovering and registering crimes as well as in soothing the women who felt stigmatized as victims of sexual crimes.

To establish rule of law, to provide justice to those who were victimized, to prosecute those who had indulged in criminal acts and subverted legal system in their favour, and to fix the accountability of those who committed these crimes with impunity were topmost priorities. The arduous task of getting complaints registered, the insistence on naming leaders of violence in the complaints and so on had to be performed. Teams of NGOs helped victims; teams of the accused were no less active. Simultaneously, charge sheets were changed and justice for the victims did not remain a matter of course, it became complex.

Apart from these, the judges had to contend with specific issues raised during and after the riots. Reports of rapes did not indicate rapes as are ordinarily described in law books. In addition to rape, women were stripped, humiliated further by parading them naked and brutalized further by mutilating their bodies after gang rape. These were much more grievous crimes than their definitions in the Indian Penal Code (IPC). The quantum of punishment for such crimes needed much deliberation. Leaders of large crowds of killers are hardly ever brought to book or punished. Foot soldiers are usually caught by the law but the political leaders get away with impunity.

A Normative Framework

India has ratified a number of international conventions and signed many instruments. WILPF's focus was to check if women's rights were protected as spelt out in the 'Universal Declaration Of Human Rights' (UDHR 1948), the 'Vienna Declaration' (1993), 'Convention on Elimination of all kinds of Discrimination Against Women' (CEDAW 1986) and Security Council Resolutions 1325 on Women Peace and Security and 1820 on Sexual and Gender-based Violence during Armed Conflict. CEDAW, UDHR and the Constitution of India uphold the rights to live, to access food, pure water, health and other ingredients that make for good quality of life.

To compel State governments to be gender sensitive and to adopt gender perspective an instrument with its mechanism appeared to be lacking. UNSCR 1325 (2000) took note of such eventualities with reference to women subjected to armed conflict. UNSCR 1325 refers to armed conflict between nation states, here the conflict is within a country but undoubtedly 'arms' were used to subjugate 'the other' and women were subjected to unprecedented violence. In the preamble of UNSCR 1325, concern is expressed, 'that civilians, particularly women and children, account for the vast majority of those adversely affected by armed conflict, including as refugee and internally displaced persons and increasingly are targeted by combatants and armed elements'. 'The consequent impact this has on durable peace and reconciliation' is recognized. Further, 'the important role of women in the prevention and resolution of conflicts and in peace building' is reaffirmed. 'The importance of their equal participation and full involvement in all efforts for the maintenance and promotion of peace and security, and the need to increase their role in decision-making with regard to conflict prevention and resolution' was stressed.

UNSCR 1325 asserts equality of women whose equal participation in prevention and resolution of conflict is encouraged. Gender perspective is sought to be adopted that could replace patriarchal perspective that inflicted misery and pain on men, women and children, all. Article 13 of UNSCR 1325

> calls upon all parties to armed conflict to respect the civilian and humanitarian character of refugee camps and settlements and to take into account the particular needs of women and girls, including in their design and recalls its resolutions 1208 (1998) of 19 November 1998 and 1296 (2000) of 19 April 2000.

UNSCR 1325 in Article 6 'requests the Secretary General to provide to Member States training guidelines and materials on the protection, rights and the particular needs of women' and 'invites Member States to incorporate these elements as well as HIV/AIDS awareness training into their national training programmes for military and civilian police personnel in preparation for deployment'. Had the national action plan been in place, the victimized women could have registered their complaints in police stations and awaited law take its own course.

Article 6 of UNSCR 1325 also draws attention to 'the importance of involving women in all peace-keeping and peace building measures' and 'further requests the Secretary General to ensure that civilian personnel of peacekeeping operations receive similar training'.

Article 9 of UNSCR 1325 'calls upon all parties to armed conflict to respect fully international law applicable to the rights and protection of women and girls, especially as civilians'. The article also refers to the obligations under the Geneva Conventions of 1949 and the Additional Protocols thereto of 1999, and other UN conventions and protocols. Article 10 of UNSCR 1325 'calls on all parties to armed conflict to take special measures to protect women and girls from gender based violence, particularly rape and other forms of sexual abuse, and all other forms of violence in situations of armed conflict'.

Article 11 of UNSCR

Emphasizes the responsibility of all states to put an end to impunity and to prosecute those responsible for genocide, crimes against humanity, and war crimes including those relating to sexual and other violence against women and girls, and in this regard stresses the need to exclude these crimes, where feasible from amnesty provisions.

The commitments to which UNSCR 1325 leads the nation are important to uphold human rights of women. Anwarul K. Chowdhury has often reminded us that adoption of 1325 opened a much-awaited door of opportunity for women, who have shown time and again that they bring a qualitative improvement in structuring peace and in the post-conflict architecture.[3]

It is important that states strengthen and uphold their 1325 commitments, through national and regional plans. Indian women reaffirm the call to all governments to get their act together and work towards the elimination of violence against women and ensure that victims have full access to justice and that there is no impunity for perpetrators.

The Need for a National Action Plan

In order that India as a nation and Gujarat as well as Odisha as its states act upon the above-cited 'call', India has to have a National Action Plan (NAP) that makes it mandatory on its constituent states to follow when such unfortunate eventualities occur and displaced camps are set up. Looking at conditions prevailing in both the states, particular needs of women and girls in settlements (which came up after the relief camps were closed) are still to be taken into account. A NAP as per the UNSCR 1325 needs to be formulated and implemented.

The Supreme Court of India had to intervene to ask the Central Bureau of Investigation (CBI) to step in, or to appoint a Special Investigation Team (SIT) in Gujarat or to shift hearing of cases outside Gujarat. But for the Supreme Court of India's intervention, Gujarat's Bilkis Bano, a pregnant woman subjected to gang-rape, could not have secured justice done to her. Lawyers could have referred to the Articles 9 and 10 of UNSCR 1325, had there been a NAP in place, based upon UNSCR 1325 in her case and other cases as well.

Introduction to the Cases

As early as 1992, following the demolition of Babri Mosque at Ayodhya, Muslims were killed in a communal violence in Surat, which is another major industrial city of Gujarat. From the reports published thereafter, it was clear that the massacre was pre-meditated and affected women and children. Hatred for the 'other' became an important issue in this communal fight.

Ten years later, in 2002, after coach S6 of Sabarmati Express was burned at Godhra station and five years thereafter, Christians, the other minority in Kandhamal, Odisha, became targets. Such sudden, apparently meaningless violence, making the victims lose loved ones in the family, home and hearth, and physical and moral strength, strikes at the core of human value. Suddenly, the victims' rights to privacy or to non-interference in family life were just blown away. What can bring peace to them?

During the peace committees formed in Kandhamal, the bias against women again came to light. Among the 50 members who formed the Kandha side of the committee, only three–four were women and that too because the meetings took place in their respective villages. While on the Pano side, the women were conspicuous by their absence. In Kandhamal, peace committees were organized with the Kandhas on one side and Pano displaced on the other.[4] In some committees, the displaced were outnumbered by their counterparts. It was reported that in a large group of more than fifty men, three or four women were noticed. It appeared that even this small number participated because the meetings were held in their villages. However, no woman displaced participated in any peace committee.

The communal attacks were represented as spontaneous reactions to actions, such as the burning of coach S6 in Gujarat and the murder of Swami Lakshmananand Saraswati in Kandhamal. It was to be decided by the judge whether the riots were 'reactions' only or were part of a conspiracy.

Comparison

When we examine the epidemiology of the riots, we come to the conclusion that there are a number of similarities between the riots in Gujarat and those in Kandhamal. As in Gujarat, dead bodies were used to rouse the passions of right-wing Hindu forces. In doing so, Kandhamal acted in an exaggerated fashion in comparison with Gujarat. While the procession in Gujarat moved a much shorter distance, the procession in Kandhamal moved along a zigzag path through the whole district. In both the states, the local administration, that is, the state, sided with the aggressors facilitating the riots. The first successful experiment of violence and torture was made in Gujarat, and it was replicated in Odisha.

About violence in Gujarat in 2002, it is said that Godhra or no Godhra, the riots would have taken place. The same can be said about Kandhamal, 2008 too.

> The mass-violence of the years 2007 and 2008 was started on the premise of flimsiest of reasons, false accusations and was executed with brutal aggressiveness. They had to get it on somehow, as it were. Once started, however, it took the victims unaware and totally unprepared by its instantaneity, speed, simultaneity, meticulous planning, and thoroughness and disciplined implementation. The violent incidents were like so many military like operations. The organized and well thought out character of the mass violence has been its most important hallmark, but often missed or under played by observers. (Aloysius 2010, 2)

Every word and phrase penned by Aloysius in the preceding para is applicable to what happened in Gujarat 2002 too. Mobs in both places comprised local villagers joining the members of different Hindutva organizations. In Kandhamal, support to the attacking crowds was provided by immigrant traders who made their trucks and incendiary material available to the marauders. Assailants were all armed with swords, rods, scythes sticks, pipes, farm implements and incendiary material. They approached in large crowds, killed, molested and raped women, quartered bodies and burned them.

Ten Years Later

At the end of 10 years, in response to untiring legal activism pursued by 'Citizens for Justice and Peace' (CJP), the Supreme Court intervened and got SITs appointed so that some victims found their claims vindicated. For Sardarpura Massacre case, there were 73 accused out of which 31 were convicted. They were all awarded life-terms.[5] In Malav-Bhagol Ode-1 case, out of the 40 accused, 10 got life imprisonment and one got six months in jail. In Pirawali Bhagol massacre Ode-2 case, 46 were accused, out of which 23 were convicted, 18 got life imprisonment and five got rigorous imprisonment for seven years.[6]

At Naroda Patiya, 97 Muslims, including 36 children and 35 women were murdered. In a landmark judgment, the judge identified the incident as 'a cancer for our cherished constitutional value of secularism'.[7] The judge rejected the 'reaction' theory, and held that the motive of the convicts was to commit crime by taking law in their hands. Out of the 61 persons tried, 32 were held guilty. This judgment is seen as remarkable also because it held a member of the legislative assembly (MLA) responsible. A leader of a right-wing party, the Bajrang Dal (BD), was also convicted. Criminal liability of the leaders was established, which was unprecedented so far in riot situations. While the MLA was awarded 28 (10+18) years of jail term, other 30 were awarded 31 (10+21) years of jail term and the BD leader is to spend his remaining life in jail. Complicity of the state and police disappeared as the Supreme Court-appointed SIT took over. In Kandhamal too, an MLA was convicted and punished along with the others.[8]

Analysing Riots: 2002

It was on 27 February 2002 that Gujarat woke up to the death of 58 Hindu *Kar Sevaks* (volunteers). They were torched alive when travelling in S6 coach of Sabarmati Express at Godhra. An unnatural brooding sense of calm and foreboding pervaded the city. Calls for Gujarat bandh on 28 February and Bharat bandh on 1 March followed immediately. All usual activities came to a grinding halt for the next two days and were replaced by crowds of thousands roaming the cities and villages of Gujarat shouting '*maaro, kaapo, baalo*' (kill, hack, burn), unleashing unprecedented violence that specifically targeted Muslims. In 19 of the 25 districts, the marauders slaughtered 950 as per official figures and 2,000 as per estimates made by others filing reports. Initial estimates were that 150,000 Muslims were driven from their homes, but in May 250,000 Muslims were reported to have been displaced. For the next 72 hours the violence continued. The state was culpable in its failure to protect the lives and property of the Muslim community and its reprehensible role in provoking the violence. There is also evidence that the local media played a partisan role in riots as well and incited the Hindu community to violence.

Sexual Violence

As mentioned before, the hate campaign against Muslims continued, especially against women. A report clearly says the following:

> After raping them, the attackers inserted sharp swords, knives or hard objects into their bodies to torture them before burning them alive. In the many bouts of communally incited riots that have taken place in different parts of the country, never has there been this depth of perversion, sickness and inhumanness. (Concerned Citizens Tribunal 2002, 40)

A daily newspaper, *Sandesh,* with a large circulation published from Ahmedabad came out with inflammatory stories. On 28 February a story was as follows: '10–15 Hindu women were dragged away by a fanatic mob from the railway compartment'. The same story was repeated on page 16 with the heading, 'Mob dragged away 8–10 women into the slums'. A day later, on 1 March, this newspaper carried a follow up to this story on page 16 with the heading, 'Out of kidnapped young ladies from Sabarmati Express, dead bodies of two women recovered—breasts of women were cut off' (Vardarajan 2002, 230–31). This news story inflamed public opinion and to stop it, a fact-finding women's team was sponsored by Citizens' Initiative, Ahmedabad, which said:

> met Aziz Tankarvi, editor of '*Gujarat Today*' known to represent the Muslim voice. He stated, When someone is murdered you are hurt. But a man can bear it quietly, it is when your mothers and daughters are violated, then he definitely responds, takes revenge *(Murder ho jata hai, chot lagti hai, to admi chup sahan kar leta hai lekin agar maa, bahen beti ke saath zyadati hoti hai to woh jawab dega, badla lega)*. (Vardarajan 2002, 232)

The impact was obvious as even a Muslim was convinced that the violence against women was justified because this was first undertaken by Muslims. The only real losers here were women. Rape is, thus seen as violating the honour of men and not the dignity and integrity of women.

Different sources produced near-similar incidents such as:

1. S, a rape survivor from Village Delol, Kalol Taluka, Panchmahals District (Vardarajan 2002, 223):

> On the afternoon of 28 February (2002) to escape the violent mob, about forty of us got on to a tempo, wanting to escape to Kalol. My husband Feroze was driving the tempo. Just outside Kalol, a Maruti car was blocking the road. A mob was lying in wait. Feroze had to swerve. The tempo overturned. As we got out they started attacking us. People started running in all directions. Some of us ran towards the river. I fell behind as I was carrying my son, Faizan. The men caught me from behind and threw me on the ground. Faizan fell from my arms and started crying. My clothes were stripped off by the men and I was left stark naked. One by one the men raped me. All the while I could hear my son crying. I lost count after three. They then cut my foot with a sharp weapon and left me there in that state.

2. Madina, a survivor from Eral, Kalol block (Hashmi 2002, 20):

> Many Muslim families left Eral on 28 February on hearing rumours of large scale rioting. Madina's father-in-law believed that he was respected in the village so they did not leave. But their house was stoned and they were abused on that very day. The family hid in a neighbour's house but they had to flee from there the very next day. On 1 March at around 5 PM a mob of 400–500

men armed with sharp weapons, petrol and kerosene came and first looted then burnt the houses of Muslims. Madina's family hid in an empty hut in the village but again the next morning, on Sunday, 2 March, at about noon, the mob attacked the hut. Madina and the family ran helter-skelter and hid in a maize field. The mob followed them and started searching for them. The crowd managed to pull her daughter Shabana and niece, Suhana. Madina could hear their screams begging for their 'izzat' and life. She and her youngest daughter were hiding nearby and could see the two girls being dragged and gang raped. Then they cut off their breasts and then burnt them off before the very eyes of the hiding mother.

3. Shamin, a survivor from Randhikpur (PUDR 2002:14):

In Randhikpur, when large mobs attacked them, 100 to 150 women and children had run for their lives. A group of 17 ran from village to village. Shamin delivered a baby girl at a mosque where they had taken shelter for a night. The next morning they again set out. On the way, they were confronted by groups of men who gang raped the women and then killed them. Shamin and her day old baby were also not spared. Bilkees, a five month pregnant young woman was gang raped by three men from her village. Her three-year-old daughter was snatched away from her and was killed in front of her. She was left for dying and was the only survivor of the group of 17. When the police came to check the corpses, they took her to Limkheda. She went to lodge an FIR at the police station the next day. But the police did not mention rape.

The most shocking comment about the subjugation and humiliation of women during the riots came from the then Defence Minister, George Fernandes. On 30 April 2002, he spoke on the floor of the parliament during the debate on Gujarat, in defence of the Bharatiya Janata Party (BJP) government headed by Vajpayee. Citing the instances of rape and foetus being taken out a mother's womb, he asked if this was unusual. He implied that such things had happened before. His words, in English translation:

All these sob stories being told to us, as if this is the first time this country has heard such stories—where a mother is killed and the foetus taken out of her stomach, where a daughter is raped in front of her mother, of someone being burnt. Is this the first time such things have happened? Didn't such things happen on the streets of Delhi in 1984? (Vardarajan, 2002, 12)

Fernandes brushed away the sufferings of women of Gujarat and refused to look at the widespread violence that had occurred. With both the state government and Central government turning a blind eye to the crimes committed against women, the victims found it difficult to get complaints filed the first step towards getting justice.

Reluctant Relief

On 28 February, terrorized Muslims fled their homes. They were led to the then newly setup relief camps in the city of Ahmedabad by their community leaders. These camps were not organized by the state government but by religio-political organizations who had taken up the task of protecting, feeding and housing victims. Since there were no specific orders issued to the collectors to organize relief camps, the collectors interpreted the absence as specific orders not to organize the camps. The police directed victims to those camps but the officers did not take cognisance of the existence of the camps and, thus, felt no need to provide help or protection.

When asked why the government had not taken over the administration of the camp, the reply was that it could not provide separate camps for Hindus and Muslims so could not provide security. Camps, thus run by religious trusts, further divided and communalized society.

It was clear that the government abdicated its constitutional responsibility to protect the basic rights of every citizen when it is duty bound to do so. A petition was then filed by six relief camps supported by CJP in the High Court of Gujarat (Special CA no. 3773 of 2002) and the government, as per the order dated 22 April 2002, accepted responsibility to provide adequate relief to the camps like food, water, public toilets, medical aid, dole of ₹5 per person per day, shamianas for protection from heat and army protection for security.

A committee on empowerment of women, headed by Margaret Alva, Chairperson, noted among other complaints: 'At Shah Alam Camp (Ahmedabad), beddings especially for pregnant and confined women were not provided and there was shortage of milk for children and nursing mothers. The living condition was poor' (Alva 2002, Para 9). Such conditions prevailed in all camps.

In the few camps recognized by officials, the supply of rations was irregular and short of the amount needed. There was a mismatch in the number of inmates as reported by the camp officers and that cited by the camp managers. The officers would count the numbers in the afternoon when the inmates moved out to find relatives or to try to return to their homes or find work in nearby areas. In the evening most returned and some others also came seeking shelter. The number counted by camp managers in late evenings or early mornings was not acceptable to officers. They kept track of people moving out but not of those who came in. No appeal was possible against anything; neither in the matter of counting of numbers nor in shortfall of rations.

> The Collector at Anand informed the team that there is no mechanism to sort this out. The decision of the government is final. In effect, then, a system was in place aimed to deny relief through non-registration of the camps, through faulty recording of the number of inmates and through the lack of a system of redress. (PUDR 2002, 42)

Again, CJP approached the Gujarat High Court to get an assurance from the government that the camps would not be forcibly closed down. On 4 June the advocate of the state assured that there would be no closure of the camp until 30 June. Soon the officers started pressurizing camp managers who 'voluntarily' signed 'affidavits' expressing their wish to close the camps. The Concerned Citizens Tribunal report notes that 'actions of the state government on the ground, therefore, run contrary to their assurances made to the court'.

> The reluctance of the Gujarat government to provide relief to the inmates of these camps (where even water and food grains had to be obtained through court orders) and its subsequent use of coercion to close them down, is intrinsically connected to an abject and crude refusal to concern itself with rehabilitation of its citizenry (Concerned Citizens Tribunal Report. (Concerned Citizens Tribunal Report 2002, 125)

It can be safely concluded that the government did not settle the victims so that they might live without fear and earn their livelihood. Nor did it want to continue the camps that gave them some relief and security.

Moreover, it is linked to the issue of the refusal of the government to rehabilitate the victims of the carnage. Both are violations of the just and humane principles underlying Indian constitutional law and international covenants related to violence, refugees and state responsibility. (Concerned Citizens Tribunal 2002, 125)

Justice? Who Cares?

It is very clear from the foregoing discussion that the police remained inactive, like mute spectators, neither stopping the attackers, nor helping the victims. Did the police have specific orders to do nothing?

Concerned Citizens Tribunal report condemned the complicity of the government and the police, stating that there was absolute failure of large sections of Gujarat police to fulfil their constitutional duty and prevent mass massacre, rape and arson in short, to maintain law and order. The Tribunal began by asking why there was no police force on Godhra station since the climate in the country was tense and the police either did not act or acted on behalf of the rampaging mobs. So the complicity of police could be easily discerned in the report that of the 40 persons shot dead by the police on 28 February 2002 in Ahmadabad, 36 were Muslims. This happened despite the fact that attackers were Hindus, and Muslims were the targets. After the riots, a police report said that, 'Of the 184 people dead in police firing since the violence began, 104 are Muslims (Concerned Citizens Tribunal 2002, 81–84)'. This reflects the existence of partisanship.

The law of the land requires that separate FIRs be filed for each incident. In the report 'Maaro! Kaapo! Baalo!' of PUDR (People's Union for Democratic Rights), details of police manipulating FIRs is recorded in detail. Separate crimes committed by different groups of attackers at different places were clubbed together as a single FIR:

[One] example is FIR 36/2002 of P.S. Kalol, Panchmahals, which strings together (a) one incident of a 5000 strong Hindu mob confronting a 2000 strong Muslim mob at 4 p.m. on 28 February at Rabbani Masjid, (b) an incident on March 1 in a hospital compound in which one Muslim was killed by a different mob, (c) the killing of 10 Muslims fleeing from Delol by a large Hindu mob at Ambika Society on 1 March, and (d) arson and attack on Boru village on 1 March. (PUDR 2002, 36)

Such an FIR cannot stand in a court of law and so no justice could be done on its basis.

Another form of distortion in the FIRs came to light when Muslims tried to fight back the attacking mob. When a large mob of unidentified Hindus attacked and looted homes, shops and religious places of Muslims, they offered resistance by pelting stones at their attackers. The FIR then made had no Hindu names on it but a few Muslim names were recorded, Ludicrous as it may seem, these named Muslims were rounded-up and charged with looting their own homes, burning their own shops and desecrating their own place of worship. Other similar FIRs of the same type are registered whenever Muslims tried to oppose their attackers. In some instances, both Hindu and Muslims were arrested for rioting. However, Hindus got bailed out quicker than the Muslims as their bail pleas were not opposed by the public prosecutors.

The entry point to justice is to get an FIR registered first. Attempt to get justice was thwarted at the first step for many. A few, with the help of NGOs like 'Citizens for Justice and Peace,' could approach higher courts and get justice. However, the majority of the victims were denied justice.

In the preceding section, the testimony of S is reported. The report further states additional facts. These combined with details from another report, point out that S's aunt Haleema Reshma Abdul was hiding in the nearby bushes and was an eyewitness to the happenings (PUDR 2002, 12). When S regained consciousness, she moved to Delol with her son and aunt. No medical examination within 48 hours of the gang rape was possible in the circumstances and none was conducted. But the survivors recognized some of the attackers, and named them in their complaints to the Kalol police station. The accused were local leaders and economically well-off persons. Consider their occupational profiles: One of them was a manager at a bank, another was an owner of a cinema, still another was the Public Distribution System (PDS) shop owner and still another was a local leader. However, the above mentioned incidents are clubbed together in the FIR for a tempo that was burnt near Ambika Society, Kalol. This FIR mentions only 10 killed while according to eyewitnesses at least 13 persons were killed and two raped with one of the rape victims surviving. No crime of rape was registered with the police despite written complaints and it does not even find mention in the combined FIR. Two persons were arrested in connection with the tempo attack but none of the main accused was arrested.

Having gone through this, one realizes that it is well-nigh impossible for women to have access to justice. When a serious charge such as rape is dropped from a FIR, it clearly signals that the doors of justice are closed for the victim. Bilkis could get justice as she was heard by higher courts and her case was shifted out of Gujarat. But many others are not likely to get justice in a state that has become intolerant of minorities.

Ten years later, the Muslim community has reacted to rapes in a progressive way. Ayesha Khan, a journalist, writes:

> Rape is a double edged sword, first leading to physical violation and second to social ostracization in most societies.... Strangely during the 2002 riots, Muslim women...never betrayed the kind of shame or guilt that rape victims are expected to show. What was their fault? Why should the victim feel shame and guilt? And so it was that many of them did not cloak their identities, and instead chose to come out publicly to demand justice. (Khan 2012, 1)

It is a progressive step forward for the community. Yet demand for justice remains. How do all women secure justice when the state and Central governments do not want to acknowledge that crimes were committed? Denial of justice means denial of security and peace.

Analysing Riots: 2008

When Swami Lakshmanananda Saraswati was murdered along with four of his associates in his Ashram in Jalespeta on 23 August 2008, a Maoist group claimed responsibility but it was widely rumoured that Christians had murdered the Swami. This was a handy provocation for the violence that followed. The murdered body was taken in procession across the district with the permission of the local administration, and supporters organized a virtual bandh and road block in the area (Aloysius 2010, 9). During the two days it took for the procession to reach that place, violence broke out.

> This organised mayhem lasted for more than three full months, wielding effective force in the entire region, affecting more than one lakh people

in more than one way, rendering more than ten thousand families homeless, leaving hundreds, including Christian religious personnel dead and several women, including a nun, raped and disgraced. (Aloysius 2010, 9)

Aloysius, who studied the Kandhamal violence, sees it as 'basically casteist in character'. He says:

It is clearly a reprisal against the so-called lowest castes who have dared to move out of the caste order. The reprisal has been particularly vicious because the caste oppressed people have decided to reach out to appropriate and rally around a supposedly foreign religion. (Aloysius 2010, 4)

This is an unexplored area and needs further research as it will give as an understanding of the social prejudices inherent in the region complicating the already Panna-Adivasi divide.

The violence that rocked Kandhamal in the aftermath of the murder and the funeral procession of the dead body of the Swami has been recorded as noted with destruction of houses, killings and attacking of churches across the state. The government, in which BJP was a coalition partner, appeared to consistently support the Hindutva forces in permitting procession with dead bodies or in allowing the announcement of bandh. It appeared that the state had abdicated its constitutional responsibilities. This was also evident in not only permitting but also joining the call for bandh and allowing the 150 km long zig-zag funeral procession of the dead body of Swami Lakshmanananda. The central forces arrived late and to neutralize their presence they were put under the police. Local administrative officers did not come forward to help.

The official statistics, as reported in 'The Ugly Face of Sangh Parivar' point to the magnitude of the violence.

At the end of December 2008, the government of Odisha says that 698 FIRs have been registered, naming 11,348 accused and eight times that number of 'unknown' participants in the attacks. The number arrested is just 700. As for deaths, the Government adamantly sticks to the number 39 though concerned activists put it at 58. The number of displaced persons has been reduced from the high of 23,000 to no more than 10,000 but that is by forcing them to leave the relief camps without ensuring that they can go back and live with dignity in their villages professing the faith of their choice. The number of the displaced is no less than 40,000. (PUCL 2009, 39–40)

Among the first victims was a nun, Sister Mina, who was dragged out by a mob and raped in Divyajyoti Pastoral Centre, Nuagaon block, Kandhamal district. In Bargarh district, another woman, Rajni Majhi, was burnt alive as the missionary school hostel in which she was working was set on fire.

Unimaginable Terror and Sexual Violence

When our WILPF team visited the camp sites and met the victims, we were overwhelmed with their tales of unimaginable terror. We present them here so that the reader may form an idea about the barbaric intensity of the religious zealots.

> A man was talking about one of his relatives, who was out to graze his goats, was chased and had his head smashed with a stone. A widow narrated the pathetic fate of her husband who had managed to run away initially and hide in the forest behind his home. Two days later when he decided to get away from the forest to safety; he was caught, attacked and hacked into two. His body was later burnt. (Ebbe and Pathak 2009, 36)

> In Tikabali camp, we came across a woman whose house was burned and her husband murdered before her very eyes. The body of her husband was thrown into fire. Along with him, she saw numerous others killed. She described how their church was set on fire and told us that rioters systematically burned down the Bible, furniture, idols of mother Mary, and everything else that she had valued. She reached this point in her recital when she pronounced the word '*marilae* (beaten), then pausing a bit and biting her quivering lips she murmured 'lae marilae'... then halting again, she repeated in a heart wrenching voice, 'marilae... marilae...', and then finally she bent down her head and wept. (Ebbe and Pathak 2009, 37)

Irrespective of which camp we visited, their tales of death and destruction were similar. Men were beaten and killed in front of their terrified families. A young man, 33 years of age, was tied up together with his son and made to watch his house burn. Then he was beaten with sticks and swords till he died. Others were killed during the night as they fled from their burning houses. There were incidents of execution of men who had taken refuge in the forest. Several other people who had taken refuge in homes of Hindus were dragged out and killed. Even when they escaped to the forest, they were not completely safe because they had to survive without food and water for days before they were able to reach the relative safety of the relief camps. Some of those who escaped the mayhem walked 150 km to reach the relief camps.

When some families exhumed some of the corpses, they found that there were not only sword wounds on the corpses, but also signs that they had been physically tortured. This indicated that the 'executions' were carried out with extreme violence and great hatred. The dead were dumped pell-mell in ditches while some were burnt. Houses, churches and institutions were set on fire using petrol and gas cylinders. Such goods are so uncommon among the locals that it was apparent that they were supplied from outside. The arson continued unabated for several days. Buildings were turned to rubble while valuables inside the buildings were broken or stolen beforehand. While travelling in the area, we could see blackened desolate homes and stone columns standing as mute witness to the gory crimes of religious frenzy.

The Spartan Life of Relief Camps

Odisha government had organized 18 relief camps, which sheltered more than 25,000 affected people. Information was conveyed to the WILPF team that the camps were set up after the eruption of violence on 26 August 2008:

> By the 30th there were 7500 persons in camps. By 1st September, there were 12,500 and, by the next day the number was to 19,642. By 3rd September, the numbers rose to 23,746. The rapid increase of displaced persons located in the identified camps in a matter of hours is the best indicator of the monumental scale of the tragedy.

> By the time we went to Kandhamal on 20th September, the numbers had come down to 13,000 though the basic impediment issued by the

attackers that Christians must agree to give up Christianity and practice Hinduism, had not changed. The secret behind this sleight of hand was revealed when we spoke to the Relief Commissioner (Southern Region). He explained the Government's stated: only those whose houses have been destroyed have a right to be in the relief camps. Those whose houses are intact but have run away from the village out of fear have to go back because their houses are intact The government sent them away ignoring their trauma, their dignified decision to continue with their faith and risk to their lives for what they considered important. This is perversity with a vengeance. (PUCL 2008, 37–38)

Another ostensible argument doing the rounds was that the government wanted to vacate the school buildings where the camps were run because exams were fast approaching.

The WILPF team visited three camps in total—one at Tikabali, one at G. Udaigiri and one at Mondasoro. When the team reached Tikabali camp, approximately 1,200 victims were still taking refuge there. As the team started sharing experiences with them, the first impression that got carried across was that they were still apprehensive about returning to their homes and villages. This awareness lingered with us throughout all the three camps that we visited. In G. Udaigiri, there were about 3,000 displaced, while in Mondasoro there were about 650 of them.

While talking to residents in these three camps, we came to know that Hindu extremists were holding ceremonies to purge tribal communities of Christian influence in the district's indigenous belt for past several years. It is impossible to know how many may have been re-converted here in the wake of the latest violence, though a three-day journey through the villages of Kandhamal turned up plenty of anecdotal evidence.

Most of the houses in Kandhamal sported saffron flags. They were a means to differentiate the Hindu households from the Christian ones. The colour of some of these flags had faded while the rest were bright and new. The bright ones were of households who had been recently re-converted. Once a family got re-converted, Hindu neighbours promised to protect them. The re-converted families were not allowed to share their experiences with anyone but if they disobeyed, they were fined ₹501 by the Hindu leaders. Some displaced in G. Udaigiri camp stated that, even after their houses were looted and burnt, they could not breathe easy as they had not yet converted to Hinduism. Hindu fundamentalists believed that the war was not over until the spirit of the Christians was broken and the proof that it was so was in their conversion to Hinduism. People were thus, trapped in an utterly defenceless position where they had to choose between life and property on one hand over religion and faith on the other.

People from camps had made several attempts to return to their villages. However, when the Hindu residents of the village saw them they raised an alarm by beating drum and had gathered other villagers. Then the returning Christians were asked to convert to Hinduism. If they did not agree to convert to Hinduism, they were chased out of the village. According to people in camps, villagers under the guidance of fundamentalist groups were forcing the Christians to sign papers saying that they were 'freely' returning to Hinduism. Those who refused were beaten and driven away. They were also ordered to attack churches and to burn the Bible to prove their loyalty towards Hindu faith.

It was clear that the displaced at the camps were haunted by the fear of conversion and death so instead of going back to their homes, they preferred to stay in the makeshift shelter. To give them confidence, they set up peace committees. We learnt from victims who took part in peace committee meetings that Hindu majority had placed many preposterous conditions, which had to be met before they would be allowed back into their own homes. The conditions that numbered from 9 to19, included reconversion to Hinduism, voting for the BJP, making a commitment not to eat beef, not to indulge in cow slaughter, abide by everything else that Hindu villagers wanted them to do and so on. Victims were also asked to withdraw FIRs that they had lodged against the perpetrators of violence. In such cases, victims naturally remained unwilling to go back.

The peace committees that were formed were ineffective at brokering peace. In some peace committees, the displaced Christians found that they were far outnumbered by the opposite group. They would be 15 while the Hindus facing them would be 50. In some cases, we were told that a few victims did re-convert to Hinduism before they were allowed to return to their homes in the villages. In some peace committees, people were asked to move back to their houses without any conditions. It was reported that the district collector and other officers usually attended these committees and in such meetings there were equal numbers on both sides.

In Dire Straits: Women in the Displaced Camps

Women as usual were the worst sufferers here too. We, the WILPFers narrate our first hand experiences here.

1. Accommodation

The displaced were accommodated in tents as well as school buildings. Displaced of the Tikabali Relief Camp said that in the initial days, there were approximately 6,000 persons living in 110 tents. So 50 to 55 persons belonging to 9 or 10 families including all, men, women and children, were huddled together in a single tent, 15' × 15'm in size. When our team reached there, the situation had eased with only about 1,200 people still in the camp. People had begun migrating in search of work or to relatives, or settling in another district or in a nearby state. The government had also initiated rehabilitation so a sizable number had left from Tikabali and G. Udayagiri. Mondasoro camp was established as a halfway camp in late November and had sheltered 650 persons in a large school building.

2. Food Supplies and Nutrition

Every day in the morning, each displaced was given *chura* with jaggery. This team found the jaggery to be of extremely low quality almost unfit to be consumed by anybody. For lunch and dinner, rice and *dalma* were served. Initially *dalma* was not cooked with vegetables. However, these were added later but the *dalma* remained watery. The main diet of the people in the state is rice, but that is not the only food they eat.

For young children in the age group of one to five years, a packet of biscuits (brand 'Tiger', made of fine wheat flour and sugar as major ingredients) was given every morning as nutritional input. A packet of 'Tiger' biscuits was also given every morning to pregnant women as well as lactating mothers towards providing nutrition to them.

When the team visited Mondasoro camp in the morning of 24 January 2009, it was reported that for the past four days, no breakfast was served. Ostensibly, it was due to supplies not reaching in time.

3. Kitchen and Water

The makeshift kitchen in a corner of the camp appeared to be unhygienic for it was surrounded with dirt and slush. In two camps, we saw cows wandering around the kitchen area.

Drinking water source was either a tube well or a tanker. The daily supply for a family was a bucket that had to be left uncovered in a room/tent. Our team examined a sample and found that it was so filthy that it clearly was not potable.

4. Sanitation

Neither in Tikabali camp nor in G. Udayagiri camp were there any toilets. Whatever was put up in August/September 2008 had not survived. The team could only see pieces of flex/jute cloth, which would have served as screens of the toilets, blowing in the wind. The officers said that the toilets were redundant as the displaced never use them but went out to the forest in order to relieve themselves. In an affidavit submitted to the Supreme Court of India by the State of Odisha, they said that the United Nations Children's Emergency Fund (UNICEF) had donated to the district administration for erecting toilets. The conditions of the toilets were so pathetic that the UNICEF authorities could not even have imagined them.

Wash places were not marked and people bathed wherever the main supply of water was. There were no curtains whatsoever. There were no separate wash places for women. A specific time was decided beforehand for them, but they also had to bathe in the open. Naturally, one could not risk going nearer because of the slush around the waterspout/hand pump.

5. Relief Material

In one of the camps, a woman was dressed in a nightgown. She said that it was in the early morning that she had to flee the attackers so did not have time to change or carry any other garments with her. On asking them whether they had received any garments from the government or the local NGOs, they responded that they had received just one pair of clothing from the government. Some other woman pointed to a towel that she had received as a gift.

6. Risk of Sexual Abuse

Electrical supply was not provided for the vast open area of the camp. Total darkness at night must have bred fear in the minds of those who had just fled violence. Furthermore, there was a much bigger risk of getting raped or sexually abused in other ways for women who had to go to the forest to relieve themselves.

When talking to the director general of police and the collector, the team asked if there had been incidents of sexual violence or rape. We gathered from these talks as well as from conversations with victims that there had been some incidents that had not yet come to light.

7. Health

Complaints of dysentery, diarrhoea and recurring cough were common. There were complaints of fever and typhoid too. Older persons were losing weight and complaining of weakness. Mothers were worried about lack of nourishment to children. A medical officer from the nearest Primary Health Centre (PHC) looked after their health.

8. Education

It was reported that books were distributed among children in the camps and that the teachers among the displaced were asked to look after their studies. The *Anganwadi* worker also ran Anganwadi in the camps. Yet none of the young men spoke of study or examination. Moreover, when the displaced shifted to halfway camp at Mondasoro, books were not given in that camp. Also, these students apparently did not bring any books with them from their previous camp.

After witnessing such violence and living in a transit camp as has been described, students could hardly have concentrated on studies. That voluntary activity does require a secure home and a warm family. Parents who were themselves torn in many ways could hardly have provided necessary succour to their children, which is, of course, bad not only for the children but also for their mothers who are traditionally the ones supporting their children.

9. Counselling

Nobody ever seemed to have had any sort of counselling support in any of the camps. Reports were later heard that some NGOs had provided counselling support to the affected. At Mondasoro, the Bishop claimed that the first Mass held on 23 December 2008, was a very moving experience. Their prayers healed them.

10. Improvement in the Conditions of the Relief Camps

In the affidavit made by the principal secretary to the Government of Odisha, with reference to the petition made by Archbishop of Cuttack, Raphael Cheenath, it was stated that the state had taken steps to bring 'improvement in the condition of relief camps'. Unfortunately, the team noticed nothing that could be described as 'improvement'. Details previously noted do not indicate any improvement in any of the sectors.

Generally speaking, while the gate and area surrounding the gate were swept clean, the places where food and water were stored were very dirty. Food was nothing more than survival diet reduced to the barest minimum. It is difficult to imagine how the people in the camp could have consumed chura and jaggery day after day in the morning and that too of such low quality.

The women had run away from arson and killings, with fear and agitation experiencing trauma that whether they received a sari or two might not have been important. However, it is well known from other displacement camps in the world that women in the camps try to retain their dignity by keeping clean, wearing clean clothes, and by using jewellery and make up. In all three camps it was very obvious that they tried hard to be clean and well dressed.

11. Trauma

Both during the mayhem and in the camps, women appeared to have suffered the most. The sudden uprooting, the mad helter-skelter for shelter and the insecurity of the family weighing heavily on their hearts and shoulders must have been unbearable for many. Total lack of privacy in the tents shared with men of other families could not have allowed them to relax. Worries about their children's hunger, their demands and lack of nourishment compounded by inability to fulfil their needs personally must have kept them on the edge. What they needed most was counselling and a bit of privacy to relax. Their trauma seemed to have been deepened and not lessened. The feelings of guilt and inadequacy added to the trauma as well as their experiences in the camps, for instance the risk of water being poisoned in the half-way camp in Mondasoro. Many behaved abnormally. Some also indulged in self-harming behaviour. These were signs of mental disorders. We had talked about how a woman who was so traumatized that she could not go on further with our conversation and choked on the word 'marilae'. Most, like her, spoke shrilly, trying to get the attention of whoever would listen to them because they wanted to unburden themselves by speaking of inhuman acts of violence that they had witnessed, suffered and dreaded. The fear was in their eyes as well as in their voices.

At the half-way camp, the group of women appeared to be highly traumatized. They seemed to be quieter. The secretary and commissioner in the Revenue and Disaster Department wondered what it would take to make these women return to their homes. After having seen the ghostly villages with burned down houses, it was obvious that memories of their traumatic experiences would be triggered in the minds of the inhabitants trying to return to their houses. They needed proper trauma treatment and continuing counselling. Such treatments would cost a lot, and yet they could probably not be enough.

The (In)justice of It All!

We saw how the government tried to wind up the camps despite the sorry plight of their victims. Its complicity with the attackers was clear right from the beginning. It was evident in not only permitting but also joining the call for 'bandh' and allowing the 150 km long zig-zag procession of the dead bodies. Complicity is also reflected in police inaction. Prohibitory orders under Sec. 144 Code of Criminal Procedure (CrPC) were promulgated all over the district on 25 August and curfew was in force but that made no difference to the attackers. Trees were felled, roads were blocked, burning of Churches and brutal killings continued.

The report, 'The Ugly Face of Sangh Parivar' raises the question: 'What were the police doing?' and answers it: 'Almost nothing.' It states further, 'The local police ignored, not merely complaints of offences that have taken place, which they have to register as offences and investigate, but even more unpardonably complaints of impending assault that it is their duty to prevent. The Christians were left to the mercy of the marauding Sangh Parivar mobs. Perhaps the police approved of the Sangh Parivar ideology, or that they were not sure whether they could go against the arms of the BJP, Sangh Parivar member organizations like the Vishwa Hindu Parishad (VHP) and the Bajrang Dal (BD) as the BJP was one of the parties in power. Perhaps they were afraid of the fanatical crowds themselves, and did not want to take risk of stopping the killers. It is also reported that the police used to say: 'Our lives are as precious to us as yours are to you' (PUCL 2009, 36).

The director general of police of Odisha had defended his force by arguing that the police force deployed at the time of outbreak of violence was quite inadequate. 'The collector supported the thesis and added that in every place there were crowds of 400–500 people armed with sticks or weapons while the district had only 71 policemen. So they were forced to wait for the paramilitary forces to arrive' (Ebbe and Pathak 2009, 35).

The Odisha government announced the setting up of two fast track courts in Kandhamal for expediting the trial of the cases related to violence. When 698 FIRs are registered naming 11,348 persons as accused and only 700 are arrested, the chances of getting justice are almost non-existent. Fast track courts were established, but they came to be seen as sites of speedy injustice. Victims and witnesses were intimidated. Seven cases were disposed of in a routine manner without attaching any gravity to the nature of the complaint and orgy of violence. The sentences pronounced were light and lenient compared with the havoc wrought by the accused in the lives of the victim-survivors.

Postscript by Saumya Uma

This postscript is being written to update as well as elaborate upon some of the contents of Ilaben's article. The attempt here is to complement her article, and highlight the importance of her work and her writing in the discourse on justice for women in conflict situations, and in relation to the Security Council Resolutions 1325 and 1820.

Updates on Justice Processes

Ilaben has elaborated on the justice processes for the Gujarat carnage. There were many challenges to justice faced by human rights lawyers and activists in the courts of Gujarat, such as non-registration of FIRs, shoddy, callous and biased investigations, incompetent and deliberately inadequate prosecution (due to the collusion of many prosecutors with the perpetrators), and unsympathetic judges. Despite such challenges, there has been a better record of justice for the Gujarat riots as compared to the Nellie massacres of 1983, anti-Sikh violence of 1984 or communal violence in Mumbai/Surat in 1992–93. At least part of the credit for this ought to be accorded to ground-level activists such as Ilaben, who have worked untiringly towards justice, particularly for women, at various levels—local, national and international.

The Naroda Patiya judgment is popular for the fact that Maya Kodnani and Babu Bajrangi—who wielded political clout—were convicted. However, the Naroda Patiya judgment also has immense significance for its discourse on issues of sexual and gender-based violence. The charge sheet listed various offences such as murder and causing grievous hurt, but prominent among them was the offence of gang rape. Judge Yagnik, who delivered the judgment, was faced with a situation where there was very little evidence left of gang rape of women due to deliberate destruction of evidence by the perpetrators. Many of the women were subsequently killed and their bodies partially/ fully burnt. Post mortem reports were not available, and where they were, they were not accurate. In such a context, the Judge used an extrajudicial confession by an accused, Suresh, who boasted of having raped Nasimo and then cutting her body into pieces, to convict him. Another witness, Zarina, had been gang raped by four men but was unable to identify them, as in most contexts of mass violence. She described the incident in detail in her testimony in court. The judge observed as follows:

> When PW-205 is not implicating any of the accused, it is clear that she does not have any other intention in her mind for narration of this incident, except ventilation of tremendous violation of her human right and constitutional right before the Court. The loud cries of such victim of crime if not heard by the system, it is mockery of justice. Here, it sounds quite fitting to record the deep concern of the Court about violation of human rights and constitutional rights of the victim who was subjected to gang rape.

The Judge acknowledged the anguish of women like Zarina, and gave them a patient and dignified hearing, so that the confidence reposed by them in the judiciary is not crumbled. Even if no conviction was possible as the perpetrators could not be identified, the sensitive gesture on the part of the Judge is likely to bring a sense of closure to the violations experienced by women, and is nothing short of an exercise in implementing Resolution 1325 in its true spirit.

Although Maya Kodnani—a sitting member of legislative assembly belonging to the BJP and former minister for women and child development of Gujarat—was convicted and sentenced to 28 years imprisonment for the Naroda Patiya judgment, she was granted bail in July 2014. Her appeal against the Sessions Court judgment is presently being heard by the Gujarat High Court. Babu Bajrangi—a BD activist who was convicted of murder in the Naroda Patiya massacre—was granted 15 days' temporary bail.

Sexual and Gender-based Violence in Kandhamal

In the initial months after the Kandhamal violence, there were three incidents of gang rape that came into public knowledge: the gang rape of Sister Meena, a nun; a mass murder and probable sexual brutalities against an adivasi girl Rajni Majhi; and the gang rape of a young Hindu woman in revenge for her uncle's refusal to convert from Christianity to Hinduism. Ilaben, in her present article, makes mention of the first two. The lower portion of Rajni Majhi's body was totally (and deliberately) burnt, and, hence, it was not possible to determine if she had been subjected to sexual violence. In the case of Sister Meena and the Hindu woman, they are alive and continue to engage with the legal system in their quest for justice and accountability.

The WILPF's rapid assessment survey of Kandhamal in January 2009, four months after the violence, was significant in highlighting and indicating the possible extent of sexual and gender-based violence in Kandhamal. The reports prior to that, written by human rights groups, were unable to capture the women's experience and did not elaborate on the status of women. In contrast, the WILPF report observed:

> When talking to the DG and the Collector we asked if there had been incidents of sexual violence, and if so also rape. It seemed from those talks as well as the interviews with the victims that there had been such incidents.... It is well known that many women are too traumatized to even mention let alone report a rape to the police. The shame and also stigmatizing from the society is a huge hindering, and the victims need to get help by trained people. We strongly recommend that resources are allocated to this important purpose. (WILPF 2009, 29)

> During the team's visit to the camp, such crimes were not spoken of. Sexual crimes carry such stigma that these are not discussed in the open. Yet it is necessary to get such complaints registered. (WILPF 2009, 49)

The report was the first indication that rape and other forms of sexual violence were not isolated incidents, as many had believed, but were widespread and endemic during the Kandhamal violence. The affected women's mental health status was highlighted in the report in the following words:

> Their traumas seemed to have been deepened and not lessened. The feelings of guilt and inadequacy add to the traumas as well as the experiences in the camps, for instance the risk of water being poisoned in the halfway camp in Mondasoro. It was noticed that some of them behaved curiously. One very young woman was noticed hurting the inside of her elbow with her own fingernails over and over again. Another was seen drawing her sari repeatedly as if to cover her eyes. The example which has already been mentioned with the woman who had

reached a certain point in her recital when she began to pronounce the word 'marilae' (beaten)—she had said 'lae marilae...' and she stopped suddenly and bit her quivering lip, 'marilae...' she went on—and then, putting her head down she wept. Most of them spoke shrilly, trying to get the attention of whoever would listen to them because they wanted to speak of inhuman acts of violence that they had suffered, seen and dreaded. The fear was in their eyes as well as in their voices. (WILPF 2009, 30–31)

Psychological impact of violence is often ignored as compared with the physical impact, which is more obvious and tangible. The WILPF report played a crucial role in highlighting the psychological impact of the violence on the women adversely impacted by the Kandhamal violence.

In the year following the WILPF report, a national people's tribunal on Kandhamal was held in Delhi. It consisted of a 13-member jury headed by Justice A.P. Shah (retired). The tribunal heard 45 victims, survivors and their representatives, and 15 expert testimonies based on field surveys, research and fact-finding. Ilaben, as one of the 15 experts, presented the WILPF report before the jury. I was the rapporteur for the tribunal and I recall the passion with which Ilaben highlighted a gender perspective of the violence. Her presentation was complemented by a study on the condition of women affected by the violence, undertaken by Nirmala Niketan College of Social Work, Mumbai (College of Social Work, Nirmala Niketan 2010). The two reports—in addition to references to sexual and gender-based violence in testimonies by survivors and their families—led the jury to state that unreported cases of sexual and gender-based violence should be identified and the offence of sexual assault included in FIRs, in cases where it has been ignored, and further to ensure that they are effectively investigated and prosecuted. It further observed:

> During the attacks, women and girls were targeted for sexual violence, humiliation, brutal physical assaults or threats thereof. The jury observes, with deep concern, the silence that prevails in matters of sexual assault, at various levels including documenting, reporting, investigating, charging and prosecuting cases. Though witness testimonies indicate that sexual violence was rampant during the attacks, there are very few reported cases, and an even smaller number that have been registered and are pending in the courts for prosecution. It is the

duty of the State and members of civil society to document incidents of violence against women and seek legal redress for them. (National Solidarity Forum 2011, 173)

It is not surprising that Ilaben's article mentions only two incidents of sexual violence in Kandhamal. As in most contexts of mass violence, where women and girls are targeted for brutal forms of sexual violence, silence prevailed over the attacks on women. It was an open secret among victim-survivors of the violence. The Gujarat case was an exception to this trend, possibly due to the unprecedented scale, nature and brutality of the sexual and gender-based violence. After the 2008 violence in Kandhamal, it took the affected women almost six years to break this silence. This too was after years of persistent conversations with them by researchers from National Alliance of Women's Organisations (NAWO), Odisha chapter, along with me. The report 'Breaking the Shackled Silence: Unheard Voices of Women from Kandhamal', authored by me, is a culmination of conversations with affected women to inquire into their present status (Uma 2014). The report documents 41 incidents of varied forms of sexual and gender-based violence that women in Kandhamal were subjected to, such as threat of rape, threat of rape of daughters of women survivors, threat of mutilation of breasts and other body parts of women, pulling of women's clothes and attempts at forced nudity of women, attempt to rape, rape and gang rape, with or without murder. This too, as we all know, is only the tip of the iceberg and not an exhaustive list. Twelve out of 17 narratives of dissimilarly placed women, reproduced in the report, based on individual in depth interviews, refer to sexual assault, threat/fear of the same (Uma 2014, 12–28).

Justice initiatives for the gang rape of Sister Meena in Kandhamal has some parallels with that of Bilkis Bano during the Gujarat riots. Both belong to religious minority communities that were targeted during the communal violence. Both were attacked due to an intersection of their gender and religious identity. Both were gang-raped. Both cases were fraught with difficulties in the pursuit of justice, due to callous police and investigators. Both cases were transferred from the initial court where the trial began—to another state (Maharashtra) in the case of Bilkis, and to another district (Cuttack) in the case of Sister Meena. Both the transfers were due to the hostile atmosphere in court as well as other reasons, in the interests of justice. Both cases have had success due to the unstinted support given to the courageous women by civil society—by feminist activists in the case of Bilkis, and by the Catholic Church in Odisha in the case of Sister Meena. In Bilkis's case, 13 out of 20 accused persons were convicted by the Sessions Court in Mumbai, and the appeal is pending in the High Court. In Sister Meena's case, three persons were convicted and six were acquitted by the Sessions Court at Cuttack in March 2014.[9] Trial remains pending against 23 accused persons. In short, the attacks on Bilkis and Sister Meena have become symbolic of the targeting of religious minority women in contexts of communal violence; securing justice in both these incidents is crucial not only for the women concerned, but due to the wider implications—the women survivors' confidence in the system of justice delivery, and an end to the widespread climate of impunity that presently prevails over sexual and gender-based violence in contexts of communal violence.

The impunity that exists is further illustrated through the use of sexual violence during the attacks on Muslim community in Muzaffarnagar, Uttar Pradesh in September 2013. Seven victim-survivors of gang rape and other forms of sexual assault petitioned the Supreme Court against police inaction, for compensation, witness protection and an independent investigation (*The Times of India* 2014). In the trajectory of justice for sexual and gender-based violence in contexts of communal violence, the Muzaffarnagar cases have reached a new milestone, as, for the first time, a compensation of ₹5 lakhs was awarded for each of the seven women who complained of gang rape through a Supreme Court order (Supreme Court of India 2014).[10] The grant of compensation is symbolic of an acknowledgement of state responsibility for its failure to protect women and girls targeted during communal violence. The Supreme Court observed:

> No compensation can be adequate nor can it be of any respite for the victims but as the State has failed in protecting such serious violation of fundamental rights, the State is duty bound to provide compensation, which may help in victims' rehabilitation. The humiliation or the reputation that is snuffed out cannot be recompensed but then monetary compensation will at least provide some solace...(para 87) the obligation of the State does not extinguish on payment of compensation, rehabilitation of victim is also of paramount importance. The mental trauma that the victim suffers due to the commission of such heinous crime, rehabilitation becomes a must in each and every case. (para 88)

Sexual and Gender-based Violence: Responses of the International Law

Mass sexual violence perpetrated against women constitute offences under the IPC, however, they did not reflect the gravity of the context or the intent with which such crimes take place or the complicity of state institutions and functionaries. The sexual assault on one woman by a man in 'normal/peaceful' circumstances is vastly different from the commission of the same offence in a context of mass crimes, where the intention is to systematically subjugate, punish or teach a lesson to vulnerable communities by violating the bodily integrity of the women concerned. It is with this intention that when the Criminal Law (Amendment) Act 2013 was enacted, women's rights activist rallied around the inclusion of rape in contexts of communal violence as an aggravated offence, carrying a higher punishment. The 2013 amendment included commission of rape during communal or sectarian violence, as an aggravated circumstance, entailing more stringent punishment.[11] The same law also dispensed with the need for sanction for prosecution of public officials, where it pertains to certain sexual and related offences.[12] Further, a public servant's act of disobeying direction under law has been specifically made an offence. These are significant amendments brought about through the concerted efforts of women's rights activists and others for several decades, setting new normative standards in Indian law.

The campaign for reforming rape law drew inspiration from international normative standards on sexual and gender based violence.[13] The judgment of the International Criminal Tribunal for Rwanda (ICTR) in the case of Jean Paul Akayesu, advances the treatment of rape and sexual violence in mass crimes contexts. The tribunal stated: 'Like torture, rape is used for such purposes as intimidation, degradation, humiliation, discrimination, punishment, control or destruction of a person. Like torture, rape is a violation of personal dignity (International Criminal Tribunal for Rwanda 1998, 687). It stated that where rape is used as a method to destroy a group by causing serious bodily or mental harm to members of the group, it constitutes genocide (International Criminal Tribunal for Rwanda 1998, 731).

The inclusion of rape and other forms of sexual violence within the gamut of 'war crimes,'[14] 'crimes against humanity'[15] and 'genocide'[16] in international law are potentially relevant to Indian efforts at legal recognition of gender-based violence in contexts of mass crimes. The International Criminal Court (ICC) statute explicitly recognizes rape, sexual slavery, enforced prostitution, forced pregnancy, enforced sterilization and other grave forms of sexual violence as war crimes in international and non-international armed conflict as well as crimes against humanity. In addition, persecution is included in the ICC statute as a crime against humanity. It specifically includes, for the first time, the recognition of gender as a basis for persecution. The ICC statute also includes trafficking as a crime against humanity as among the crimes of enslavement.[17] The Elements of Crime of the ICC, which lay down the elements for genocide by causing serious bodily or mental harm, states in a footnote: This conduct may include but is not necessarily restricted to, acts of torture, rape, sexual violence, or inhuman or degrading treatment. Thus, sexual and gender-based violence as a method of committing genocide is given legal recognition.

Concerted efforts have been made by women's rights activists in engaging with the ICC to secure justice for sexual and gender-based violence. For example, Women's Initiatives for Gender Justice (WIGJ), based in The Hague and in New York, advocates for gender justice through the ICC and through domestic mechanisms, including peace negotiations and justice processes.[18] While setting normative standards are very important, those alone do not guarantee access to justice for women, as the international experience shows. Hence, groups such as the WIGJ work closely with women affected by the conflict situations that are under investigation by the ICC, namely, Uganda, the Democratic Republic of Congo, Sudan, Central African Republic, Kenya, Libya and Kyrgyzstan. A need for a persistent engagement of women's rights activists, both with women survivors and their struggles at the ground level as well as judicial institutions at the domestic and international levels, is indispensable.

Inter-linkages Between the ICC Standards and Security Council Resolution 1325

The UN Security Council Resolutions 1325 on Women, Peace and Security and 1820 on Sexual and Gender Based Violence During Conflict, are in many ways connected to and complement the development of international law through the ICC. In fact, Resolution 1325 refers to the relevant provisions of the Rome Statute of the ICC in para 9, and emphasizes the responsibility of all States to put an end to impunity and to prosecute those responsible for genocide, crimes against humanity, and war crimes including those relating to sexual and other violence against women and girls, in para 11.[19] In June 2008, UNSC Resolution 1820 reaffirmed the political commitment of the Security Council to protect women and girls from sexual violence in conflict by demanding the 'immediate and complete cessation by all parties to armed conflict of all acts of sexual violence against civilians'.[20] This resolution too recalled the inclusion of a range of sexual violence offences in the Rome Statute of the ICC and the statutes of the ad hoc international criminal tribunals.[21]

While the ICC focuses on making the perpetrators accountable for heinous crimes, including that of sexual and gender based violence, and awarding reparations to the attacked women, the Security Council Resolutions that are mentioned aim at requiring parties to a conflict to prevent violations of women's rights, support women's participation in peace negotiations and post-conflict reconstruction, and protect women and girls from sexual and gender-based violence in armed conflict. The ICC's role is to provide justice, while the resolutions' role is to enforce the obligation to protect, prevent, ensure participation, and facilitate relief and recovery. The two sets of normative standards are two sides of the same coin, aimed at one goal—ensuring women's safety and security in present and in future, and upholding women's human rights.

Relevance of Resolution 1325 to the Aftermath of Gujarat and Kandhamal Violence

While other countries have formulated a NAP, outlining the policies that they will formulate and steps they will take to implement the standards set by the Resolution, the Indian government is in a mode of denial, stating that there is no armed conflict in India. Hence, it is perhaps premature to expect an official NAP from the government. However, the civil society in India is not precluded from using the resolutions as guiding principles in their peace initiatives among women subsequent to an incident of communal violence. The resolutions also carry with them the potential to be used to negotiate with the central/state government and the district administration on inclusion of women and women's concerns in peace initiatives at the ground level.

NGOs' efforts at peace and reconciliation among women from the religious majority and minority communities (Hindu–Muslim in the context of Gujarat and Hindu–Christian in the context of Kandhamal) have implicitly incorporated the spirit of the Security Council Resolutions within their work. For example, groups such as Sahr Waru and SAFAR in Gujarat, and Sansristi in Odisha have undertaken initiatives for social reconciliation among women of the two communities.

In the context of Kandhamal, the resolutions have been used for advocacy as well, to persuade the state government and district administration to include women in peace initiatives and to bring their experiences and concerns to the centre stage of peace negotiations. For example, a study on the status of affected women in Kandhamal six years after the violence, commissioned by the NAWO, Odisha chapter, and undertaken by me, stated one of the rationales for the study, in the following words:

> Additionally UN Security Council Resolutions 1325, 1820 and other related resolutions were framed to ensure women's voices in situations of conflict, and to reassert the importance of women's participation in conflict resolution and management. However, the Government of India has been slow in the application of these resolutions to India, on the ground that technically there is no 'conflict' in India. As a result, the standards set by these resolutions have not been integrated into government policies, programmes and schemes and remains only on paper. This study is an attempt to operationalise the essence of such resolutions, by emphasizing the need for participation of women in conflict resolution and peace in Kandhamal. (Uma 2014, 6)

The study enquired from the affected women as well as government officials about the existence of peace initiatives and the participation of women in such initiatives. It said:

> We also queried the District Collector on what effort was being taken by the administration to ensure women's participation in peace

initiatives. He admitted that it was not 50%, and that the participation varied, depending on where the peace meetings were being held. At the village level, many women participate in the peace meetings because of easier mobility, he opined, while at the block level and district level, the participation was minimum. He assured us that continuous efforts are being made in this regard. He also said that there is an in-built mechanism to ensure women's participation. PRI members automatically become peace committee members. Since PRI has 50% women, automatically women's participation is ensured, he explained. (Uma 2014, 69)

It concluded that state-led peace initiatives had largely excluded women (Uma 2014, 74). The report's recommendations to the state government, for immediate consideration and action, included the following:

- Identify unreported cases of sexual and gender-based violence, and ensure their registration, investigation and prosecution;
- Take proactive measures to prevent threat of sexual and gender-based violence to women survivors and their daughters, involved in various proceedings related to the Kandhamal violence, as well as to women human rights defenders/social activists who assist them;
- Compensate and rehabilitate women and girls subjected to varied forms of sexual assault; and
- Take a concerted effort to include and facilitate participation of women in peace committees and peace-building initiatives at the village, block and district level. (Uma 2014, 81)

Thus, Resolutions 1325 and 1820 are potential tools to strengthen advocacy initiatives for women's rights in contexts of communal violence, at the preventive, protective and the curative levels.

Notes

1. As far as the study of Gujarat riots was concerned, it was decided that WILPF India president and author of this article will be in the best position as she is a resident of Ahmadabad, Gujarat. However, to fully understand the riots at Kandhamal, Odisha, WILPF decided to set up a team. The team that went

to Kandhamal was led by the president, WILPF-International jointly with the president WILPF-India section and Dr Mujbur Rehman of Jamia Milia, New Delhi.

2. Hans and Rajagopalan add that the WILFP reports form an important resource for the case accounts that follow, especially on Kandhamal, where Ilaben often draws verbatim from the report she co-wrote with Annelise Ebbe.

3. Anwarul K. Chowdhury. '10 years on, the promises to women need to be kept', NATO Review, available at http://www.nato.int/docu/review/2010/Women-Security/Women-resolution-1325/EN/index.htm (accessed on 6 August, 2016).

4. In Kandhamal district of the state of Orissa, the *Panas* are designated as scheduled castes, comprise about 17 per cent of the district population and hold 9 per cent of the cultivable land. By contrast, the tribal *Kandhas*, who are designated as scheduled tribes own about 77 per cent of the cultivable land. Both the marginalized communities were, in some ways, competing with each other for government benefits. The dynamic of *Kandha–Pana* tensions were manipulated to serve the purposes of religious fanatics, through communal attacks on Christian dalits and adivasis, and then claiming that the violence was ethnic (Panas vs Kandhas) and not communal in nature.

5. The Sardarpura judgment, delivered by a special court at Mehsana district, was historic as it was the first conviction in the context of the Gujarat riots, hence, it was the first whiff of justice for the victims (*The Hindu* 2011).

6. The Ode 1 and Ode 2 judgments are for brutal killings of Muslims in Ode town of Anand district, Gujarat (*The Indian Express* 2015).

7. *State of Gujarat vs. Naresh Agarsinh Chara and others* Sessions Case Nos 235/09, 236/09, 241/09, 242/09, 243/09, 245/09, 246/09 and 270/09. Common judgment., dated 29 August 2012.

8. In September 2010, BJP MLA Manoj Pradhan, who was accused of leading mobs that committed brutal killings, arson and other offences, was convicted for murder of Bikram Naik from Tiangia village in Kandhamal district. At least 12 cases were registered against him in relation to the violence in Kandhamal.

9. *State vs Santosh Kumar Patnaik alias Mithu and 8 Others*, S.T. Case No. 243/2010; judgment delivered by Shri Gyanaranjan Purohit, sessions judge, Cuttack. Santosh Patnaik alias Mithu, Gajendra Digal and Saroj Badhai were held guilty for the offences under S. 148, 354/149, 355/149, 294/149, 506(II)/149 IPC, and awarded two years rigorous imprisonment on each count; Santosh Patnaik was also convicted under S. 376(2)(g) IPC and awarded rigorous imprisonment of 11 years. Juria Pradhan, Kartika Pradhan, Biren Kumar Sahu, Tapas Kumar Patnaik, Muna Badhei and Jaharlal Behera who were prosecuted were given benefit of doubt and acquitted.

10. Judgment of the Supreme Court, delivered on 26 March 2014 by P. Sathasivam, Ranjana Desai and Ranjan Gogoi JJ, in *Mohd. Haroon & Ors. vs. Union of India & Another*, Writ Petition (Criminal) No. 155 of 2013 with Writ Petition (Criminal) Nos. 158, 165, 170, 171, 179, 181 196, 206 of 2013, Writ Petition (Criminal) No. 11 of 2014, Contempt Petition (Criminal) No. ... of 2014 (D1372) in Writ Petition

(Criminal) No. 155 OF 2013, Transferred case (Civil) Nos. 123, 124 and 125 of 2013, Transfer Petition (Civil) Nos. 1750, 1825, 1826, 1827, 1828, 1829, 1830 of 2013 and Special Leave Petition (Civil) No. 35402 of 2013 Supreme Court of India).

11. S. 376 (2)(g) of the IPC, inserted by the Criminal Law Amendment Act 2013. It states: the section states, 'Whoever commits rape during communal or sectarian violence shall be punished with rigorous imprisonment for a term which shall not be less than ten years, but which may extend to imprisonment for life, which shall mean imprisonment for the remainder of that person's natural life, and shall also be liable to fine'.

12. Explanation to S. 197(1) of the CrPC, inserted by the Criminal Law Amendment Act 2013.

13. S. 166A of the IPC, inserted by the Criminal Law Amendment Act 2013.

14. War crimes include crimes committed in contexts of international and non-international armed conflict. Common Article 3 to the Geneva Conventions lays down acts that are prohibited during non-international armed conflict. Article 8(2)(c) of the Rome Statute of the ICC likewise prohibits certain acts from being committed during an armed conflict not of an international nature, including violence to life and person and committing outrages upon personal dignity.

15. Crimes such as murder, torture and sexual assault would be construed as crimes against humanity if committed as part of a widespread or systematic attack against a civilian population in pursuance of state or organizational policy, with the perpetrator possessing a general knowledge of the attack, as stated in Article 7 of the ICC Statute.

16. Article 6 of the Statute of the ICC defines genocide as follows:
For the purpose of this statute, 'genocide' means any of the following acts committed with intent to destroy, in whole or in part, a national, ethnical, racial or religious group, as such:

    (a) Killing members of the group;
    (b) Causing serious bodily or mental harm to members of the group;
    (c) Deliberately inflicting on the group conditions of life calculated to bring about its physical destruction in whole or in part;
    (d) Imposing measures intended to prevent births within the group;
    (e) Forcibly transferring children of the group to another group.

    The definition is reproduced verbatim from Article II of the Convention on the prevention and punishment of the Crime of Genocide, 1948.

17. Articles 7(1)(h), 7(1)(c) and 7(2)(c).

18. Article 6(b) of Elements of Crimes of the ICC.

19. For more details, see http://www.iccwomen.org/index.php, accessed on 9 April 2015.

20. Resolution 1325 (2000) was adopted by the Security Council at its 4213th meeting, on 31 October 2000, S/RES/1325 (2000).

21. Resolution 1820 (2008) was adopted by the Security Council at its 5916th meeting, on 19 June 2008, S/RES/1820 (2008).

References

Aloysius, G. 2010. *Kandhamal: An Interpretative Reading of The District's Recent History of Violence*. New Delhi: NCDHR NDM.

Alva, Margaret. 2002. *Composition of The Committee on Empowerment of Women (2002–2003)* (para 9/xiv). Committee on Empowerment of Women. Available at: http://cjponline.org/gujaratTrials/statecomp/pdf%20files/pdfs/Report%20of%20Wom%20Par%20Com%20Aug%202002.pdf.

College of Social Work, Nirmala Niketan. 2010. *Study of the Conditions of Women Affected by Communal Violence in Kandhamal District, Orissa*. Available at: http://www.countercurrents.org/ORISSA_TRIBUNAL.pdf (Accessed on 9 April 2015).

Concerned Citizens Tribunal. 2002. *Crimes Against Humanity, Vol. II: An Enquiry into the Carnage in Gujarat: Findings and Recommendations*. Mumbai: Citizens for Justice and Peace.

Ebbe, Annelise and Pathak Ila. 2009. *"Whither Women's Rights?": A Report from Kandhamal*. New Delhi: WISCOM.

Hashmi, Shabnam. 2002. *Break the Silence: Stories and Testimonies from Gujarat. An Attempt to Share the Pain and Grief of the Victims*. Available at: http://www.onlinevolunteers.org/gujarat/reports/sahmat/index.htm (Accessed on 15 June 2016).

International Criminal Tribunal for Rwanda. 1998. Prosecutor vs. Akayesu, Case No. ICTR 96-4-T. Judgment dated 2 September.

Khan, Ayesha. 2012. *Three Stories of Resilience from Gujarat*. Available at: https://kafila.org/2012/03/02/three-stories-of-resilience-from-gujarat-ayesha-khan/ (Accessed on 15 June 2016).

PUCL (People's Union for Civil Liberties). 2008. 'From Kandhamal to Karavali: The Ugly Face of Sangh Parivar'. A Fact-finding Report of Nine Human Rights Organisation that visited Orissa and Karnataka in Sept–Oct. Available at: http://www.indianet.nl/pdf/TheUglyFaceOfSanghParivar.pdf (Accessed on 15 June 2016).

———. 2009. *Crossed and Crucified, Parivar's War against Minorities in Orissa*. Bhubaneswar and Kashipur/Delhi: PUCL/Solidarity Group.

PUDR (People's Union for Democratic Rights). 2002. *Maaro, Kaapo, Baaro: State, Society and Communalism in Gujarat*. Report published on 1 June 2002. Available at: http://www.onlinevolunteers.org/gujarat/reports/pudr/ (Accessed on 15 June 2016).

National Solidarity Forum. 2011. *Waiting for Justice: Report of the National People's Tribunal on Kandhamal*. New Delhi, 173. Available at: http://works.bepress.com/saumyauma/36/ (Accessed on 9 April 2015).

Sahrwaruindia. Sahr Waru-Women's Action and Resource Unit: An Awakening for Equality and Justice. Available at: www.sahrwaruindia.org (Accessed on 15 June 2016).

Supreme Court of India. 2004. *Mohd. Haroon and Others vs. Union of India and Another*, Writ Petition (Criminal) No. 155 of 2013, judgment delivered by the Supreme Court of India on 26 March 2014 by P. Sathasivam (Chief Justice of India), Justice Ranjana Prakash Desai and Justice Ranjan Gogoi. Available at: http://supremecourtofindia.nic.in/outtoday/41339.pdf, (Accessed on 9 April 2015).

The Hindu. 2011.'First Whiff of Justice for Gujarat Victims'. *The Hindu*, 17 November.

The Indian Express. 2015. 'Godhra Riots: Epicentre 2002'. *The Indian Express*, 28 February.

The Times of India. 2014. 'Muzaffarnagar Gang Rape Victims Move SC Against Police Inaction'. *The Times of India*, 18 January.

Uma, Saumya. 2014. *Breaking the Shackled Silence: Unheard Voices of Women from Kandhamal*. Bhubaneswar: National Alliance for Women–Odisha Chapter. Available at: http://works.bepress.com/saumyauma/40/ (Accessed on 9 April 2015).

Vardarajan, Siddharth. 2002. *Gujarat: Making of a Tragedy*. New Delhi: Penguin Books India.

WILPF (Women's International League for Peace and Freedom). 2009. *Whither Women's Rights?* Report on Behalf of the Women Who Were Part of the Minority Community That Was Attacked in Kandhamal, Orissa, India (WILPF). Available at: http://webmail.wilpfinternational.org/PDF/publications/WhitherWomen%27sRights.pdf (Accessed on 9 April 2015).

Glossary

1. *Adivasis*: Tribals.
2. *Agarbatti*: Incense stick.
3. *Anganwadi*: A nursery school.
4. *Ashram*: A Hindu monastery.
5. *Ashtaprahara Mahayagyas*: mega religious congregations.
6. *Baalo*: burn down.
7. *Bajrang Bali ki Jai*: Salutation to the monkey god, Hanuman, also known as Bajrang Bali. According to Ramayana, he is said to have single-handedly burned down the city of the demon king Ravana.
8. *Bandh*: A form of agitation where shopkeepers down their shutters, public and private transport stay off the road and usual civilian life is brought to a standstill.
9. *Bharat Mata Ki Jai*: Salutation to Mother India.
10. *Chaudharys, Kadava or Leuva Patels*: Sub castes of the Patel community.

11. *Chura*: Smashed or ground chapatti.
12. Crore: 10 Million or 10,000,000.
13. Dal: cooked from pulses.
14. Dalit: A designation for a group of people traditionally regarded as untouchable.
15. *Dalma*: pulses cooked with vegetables.
16. *Devipujak*: Name for Waghri community.
17. *Diksha*: preparation or consecration for a religious ceremony.
18. *Ghar*: Home.
19. *Ghar wapsi*: Return home, by implication, return to Hinduism.
20. Gujarati: A native of Gujarat.
21. *Kaapo*: mow down or hack.
22. *Karsevak*: name given by Hindu right-wing organizations to their workers. *Kar* means hand and *sevak* means servant; so it is for those who will manually build the temple of Sri Ram at Ayodhya.
23. *Kholi*: plate made with leaves.
24. *Kikiyari*: peculiar ear splitting, blood curdling, heart-wrenching screams.
25. Lakh: One hundred thousand or 100,000.
26. *Maaro*: kill.
27. *Marilae*: Beaten.
28. Masjid: Mosque.
29. *Panchnama*: A first listing of the evidence and findings that a police officer makes at the scene of a crime. The document has to be signed by the investigating officer and two supposedly impartial witnesses.
30. Puja: Worship.
31. *Rakta Sindoor*: Red coloured powder.
32. Ramjanmabhoomi: Birth place of Lord Ram.
33. *Ramsetu*: Lord Ram's bridge. It was a bridge used by Ram to reach Lanka in order to defeat the demon king Ravana and free his abducted wife.
34. *Rashtra*: Nation; Hindu-Rashtra is the concept of a theocratic state where only one religion, i.e., Hindu religion is acceptable.
35. *Rathyatra*: Travel on chariot/wheels.
36. *Rau Raksha Abhiyan*: Movement to save the cow.
37. Sadhu: saint.
38. Satsang: Religious congregation.
39. *Shaasan*: Administration.
40. *Shaivites*: Sect that worships Lord Shiva.
41. Shamianas: Make-shift shelter built with poles and overhead cloth.
42. *Shilapujan*: Stone laying ceremony or ceremony to anoint bricks with one's blood to be used in building the temple for Sri Rama at Ayodhya.
43. *Sindhur*: Red-coloured powder.
44. Sri Rama: Lord Rama, the mythological king who was an incarnation of Lord Vishnu.
45. Swami: Religious/spiritual leader.
46. *Trishul Diksha*: Gifting *trishuls* after religious ceremony to participants.
47. *Trishul*: Trident (weapon of the past).

48. *Vanvasis*: Those who reside in forests.
49. *Vishnuites*: Sect that worships Lord Vishnu or Lord Krishna.
50. *Wapsi*: Return.
51. *Yagya*: A religious ceremony around a fire pit.

11

Peoples' Action Plans: Pursuing Human Security with Local Civil Society Actions to Implement UNSCR 1325

Betty A. Reardon

Introduction and Rationale: Implementing 1325 for the Empowerment of Women to Protect Their Daily Local Security and That of Their Communities

'*We the Peoples of the United Nations*' are called to exercise our rights and responsibilities as global citizens in undertaking to assure the implementation of the UN Security Council Resolution 1325 on Women, Peace and Security, a major landmark in the assertion of the human rights of women to live in dignity and security. There are few threats to the dignity and security of all the earth's peoples as severe as those wrought by war and armed conflict. It was with the intention of taking steps toward 'end[ing] the scourge of war' that women peace activists, members of the CSO (civil society organizations) community associated with the UN undertook the lobbying and drafting process that produced 1325.

It appears now that the best hope for bringing the provisions of 1325 into full realization also lie with global civil society, in particular local peace and women's human rights activists throughout the world.

This article is an argument for such civil society undertakings. It suggests a framework and a process for designing and drafting peoples' plans to empower women in decision-making and action regarding all peace and security issues in their local communities. The process is suggested mainly in the form of guiding questions to assess local security threats and to identify ways to apply 1325 to enable women to bring their experiences and perspectives to overcoming them.

As we approach the 15th anniversary of the adoption of this UN Security Council Resolution, women peace activists confront new challenges and new opportunities. The drafting of national action plans (NAPs) for its implementation would, on the face of it, be a cause for satisfaction and optimism about the capacities and willingness of member States to take direct and specific action to assure the achievement of the groundbreaking goals of 1325.

The reality is, however, that most NAPs have thus far been all plan and no action. The operative term for this reluctance to accept breaking the ground beneath the traditional patriarchal power hold over all matters of peace and security is 'lack of political will'. I fear, however, that that term makes light of what is, in fact, political will to obstruct the achievement of gender equality in this the most sacrosanct of patriarchal preserves, militarized security systems. Not simply reluctance, but outright opposition to opening possibilities for non-violent alternatives to that system continues to inflict unnecessary and unbearable suffering on women and the vulnerable of the world. Some member States continue to reinforce the perception of women only as victims of armed conflict rather than as agents of conflict resolution and peacebuilding. Further, women peace activist themselves might be more effective in attempts to empower women to eliminate armed conflict, were they to refocus their efforts to take into account on the entire system of militarized security and its overall negative impact on communal, quotidian human security. More peace scholar-activists are coming to advocate a comprehensive view of national and global security as conceptualized in a feminist human security paradigm that has been referenced for over a decade.

During the 15 years since its adoption in 2001, the human security of women has not become more assured; and the fundamental intention of the civil society initiators of UNSCR 1325 has been diverted from their core purpose, the prevention of war through the empowerment of women. A business as usual attitude still prevails among most member

States and to some extent within the UN itself. Indeed, the potentially transformative power of the resolution as attested to by the delay of so many states to formulate and implement a NAP to bring it into full force—only 47 national plans have been adopted and none of them vigorously implemented. And those have come about only as the fruit of vigorous and tenacious civil society women's groups. Clearly, 1325 represents a potentially transformative challenge to the patriarchal state and its militarized security apparatus. From its inception, the provisions calling for women's full participation have been largely overlooked or impeded. For women, seeking to fulfil the right to participate in all matters of peace and security integral to and interrelated with all other provisions of the resolution, importuning their national governments to propose actions for the full implementation of the resolution has too often proved futile. As argued in the chapter by Asha Hans, other strategies are called for. Those strategies, we believe, lie within the purview of global civil society.

While much lip service has been given and Security Council's time been devoted to discussion of women, peace and security, these efforts resulted in refocusing the application of the resolution away from its original core intent of assuring women's participation in security decisions. Instead, measures in the form of subsequent resolutions have focused on protecting women from victimization with emphasis on prevention of and protection from sexual violence in armed conflict (see Chapter 2). These resolutions on protection of women carried hardly a word about the prevention of armed conflict or women's and little more than lip service to women's role in conflict resolution. Steps toward empowerment have been restrained through a retreat to the assumption that women are but victims of armed conflict rather than agents for avoiding it through conflict resolution and prevention. While any and all intentions to reduce and prevent violence against women are to be supported and enforced, it must be acknowledged that it is largely because women are seen as powerless victims in this continued and constant focus on victimhood that military violence against women within and outside of armed conflict continues at epidemic levels world-wide.

Further exacerbating the problems of sexual violence as a consequence of armed conflict is the undermining of women's daily security by the continued and ever increasing military responses to conflicts, many of which might well be resolved by the implementation of proposals made or negotiated by women, who have in so many instances established communications with most parties to a conflict. Capacities such as those used to establish these communications and conceptualize positive terms of settlement are essential to peacebuilding and maintaining security that are wasted as women are marginalized in formal peace processes. In the name of security, women's potential as peacemakers is repressed while they become less and less secure in their own communities.

Peoples' Action Plans: Civil Society Linking Local Initiatives to Regional Strategies

It is time for women themselves to take direct action as citizens of their communities, regions and the world. It is up to women peace activists and the civil society organizations with which they affiliate to propose and implement Peoples' Action Plans comprised of actions civil society itself can take to actualize the goals of 1325 without depending on the 'political will' of the governments of their nation states.

As several nation States have a stake in the security of any world region, some local initiatives that could be effective at the community level in other nations, might be applied by women's organizations in other countries, making it possible to identify some general principles of local action appropriate to advancing women's empowerment in security matters regionally. While actions should be planned to deal with the particular military-related violence of the particular community, conflicts and other causes of military violence often spill over borders. Robust regional collaboration among local communities might help to prevent the escalation and spreading of the violence. Such cooperation also holds some promise of pushing national governments to act with more intentionality toward authentic implementation of all provisions of 1325. Whatever plans and principles are derived in any community may be of use to women peace activists in many locations in varying political and cultural conditions. While emphasis should be on specific actions suited to implementation in specific localities, the conceptualization of the basic principles of gender equality in all matters of peace and security that should underlie the proposed actions might also be undertaken with a view to the possibilities of the wider application such as characterizes military cooperation at the international level. Some of those principles are to be found in the pillars of the resolution itself and in a concept of national security as the human security of the people of the nation.

Such principles will be encouraging to all local communities, especially those in areas of armed conflict and violence and those who find themselves in what is an essentially a colonial relationship to the nation States that govern them such as Puerto Rico and Okinawa that have suffered under long-term military presence. The security and well-being of these communities are held to be secondary to that of the central state that takes priority over the human security of the people. The affected communities are but instruments for the State security that is conceived so as to protect the interests of the prevailing powers as opposed to the peoples and the vulnerable subjects of the state. Women and most the vulnerable in nations throughout the world still are perceived and treated not as citizens, participants in making the policies that determine their lives, but as subjects whose lives are controlled by the existing powers. They have come not to expect that governments will put a high—if any—priority on their human needs, including their fundamental human security. Peoples' Action Plans would be an assertion of the right to which the international human rights standards accord to citizens of all UN member States.

One major potential of UNSCR 1325 is that in calling for more democratic security policy making by including women is that it holds hope for all vulnerable groups that their human rights and security concerns may no longer be ignored by the states that govern them. Peoples' Action Plans would arise from an alternative notion of national security that observes the meaning of nation as a people or peoples of a given polity or political order. With such a definition in mind and using feminist paradigm of human security as a framework for action planning, peoples' action plans would hold national security to be the human security of the people, all citizens of a nation State, and the daily well-being of all those in the local communities that comprise the nation.

Consideration of community security informs actions by women community activists in several countries where civil society groups have undertaken to apply 1325 provisions locally in the communities in which conflicts actually occur and military violence is committed (see the website of Global Network of Women Peace-builders[1]). Unless and until the fundamental principles of 1325 are fully applied though direct local actions, human security will not be achieved. Empowering women to take action for peace and security in their daily local lives is essential to the realization of the core and original intent of 1325 to serve as a step toward a viable, global peace. Neither nation States nor international organizations can be counted on to take the necessary political actions without women's participation and leadership. Women on the ground can reclaim and implement 1325 by putting it into action in very specific cases in particular localities. So too, they can stand in solidarity and work in cooperation with women in their world regions and all areas of our shared planet.

A Human Security Framework as a Vehicle for Realizing Three Core Pillars of 1325

Women civil society groups seeking to devise implementation strategies directly relevant to the daily security needs of women, their families and communities can work toward achieving the fundamental elements of human security applied to the conceptual frame work of the resolution itself. Each dimension of human security and three specific pillars of the framework of 1325, even its title can be brought to bear on action planning. In each word of the title there is an essential concept relevant to the human security of a nation's people.

Women civil society activists began the whole process that lead to 1325 out of their refusal to continue to be overlooked and marginalized in the questions of war and peace that impacted their lives and those of their families, communities and all the vulnerable of the world. Clearly the term '*women*' is intended to call special attention to the inequality that exist in making and carrying out peace and security policies, as well as to women's particular security needs and their capacities as peacemakers, peacebuilders and providers of daily security for the vulnerable. Most especially, it connotes their intention to take action to fulfil women's rights to participate in all areas of security policy-making and action strategy planning. However, it should also be kept in mind that women's concerns are in many ways the concerns of all the vulnerable and that their exclusion reflects the exclusion of all but a powerful minority in making the polices that determine the security of all human beings, the very survival of the vulnerable and likely of our whole planet. 1325 is a tool for democratizing and demilitarizing policy-making at all levels, local through global.

Peace indicates that the resolution was directed toward reducing and eliminating war and all forms of armed and violent conflict, as well the multiple forms of violence that are integral to militarized state security. Peace is a social order in which it is possible for individuals and communities to actualize the conditions of wellbeing that constitute human security, of which a key element is the realization of universal human rights. The Universal Declaration of Human Rights asserts that 'the inherent dignity and...equal and inalienable rights of all members of the human family is the foundation of...peace in the world'. Among those inalienable rights is the right to participate in making the policies that determine the quality of our daily, ordinary lives and the possibilities of our living in dignity and security. Both dignity and security are systematically denied to women by the militarized state security system.

Security—the final and pivotal concept that titles the resolution— carries the intention not only to prevent military violence against women and to reduce armed conflict. It connotes the core intention to achieve genuine peace by ending organized violent conflict, a major threat to the actual, experienced security of women, their daily well-being and the security of all those with whom they share their lives. Our arguments for peoples' action plans are based on an interpretation of this concept as *human security* as defined by the Network of Scholar of Scholar-Activists on Demilitarization (FeDem). The concept of a four-part comprehensive security paradigm is one of the two dimensions of a possible framework for the design of peoples' action plans. It is proposed as an alternative to the present, violence-prone security system.

A Feminist Human Security Paradigm as an Alternative to Militarized State Security

The paradigm, as described in greater detail in various other publications (among them Reardon cited in Smoker, Davies and Munske 1990 and Reardon cited in Reardon and Hans 2010) asserts that any security system should be designed to achieve and maintain the fundamental sources and requirements for human well-being at local, national, regional and global levels, asserting that if it does not obtain at the local level, it is not assured on any level. In brief, those requirements are: a life sustaining and sustainable natural environment; the meeting of basic physical and social needs; respect for human dignity and human identities through the realization of the international human rights standards; and protection from all avoidable forms and incidents of harm and violence, only one of which is armed conflict.

Meeting these requirements, we argue, should be the purpose and meaning of 'national security'. In the previously cited publications, it is demonstrated that militarized state security erodes and undermines all four human security requirements, even and especially the requirement of protection from harm that is its main rationale. Peoples' action plans should include proposals for alternative approaches to the weapons dependant protection functions of current national security policies. Weapons expenditures drain public funds away from peoples' human and social needs, imposing considerable deprivation of the other three security needs on local communities throughout the world. Should the national governments not 'think locally' before 'acting globally'? Without such consideration, the majority of people on the ground will remain without hope of experiencing authentic human security. This more constructive way of thinking that led the civil society, military and police participants in the security sector workshop conducted by the Global Network of Women Peacebuilders (GNWP) to embrace a more comprehensive concept of security. Human security as the goal and purpose of the security sector features in the workshop conclusions.[2]

The GNWP workshop conclusions and most feminist peace activists assume that women's full participation is essential to the achievement of, indeed any advancement toward, human security. Without women's perspective a truly comprehensive security regime designed to advance all four essential elements of human security is not likely to be devised. Eradicating the major threats to human well-being posed by militarized state security through institutionalizing changes in the conceptualization and means of maintaining national security calls for far more participation by those most excluded from and negatively affected by militarized state security. Such changes will require transforming relationships of civil society in general and women peace activists in particular to the public agencies charged with all four human security elements, most especially to the security sector. The military and the police will need to pursue change within their own ranks so that in collaboration with civil society all may make the conceptual and institutional shift from militarized state security to non-violent human security for the well-being of all nations and the local communities that comprise them.

Women's peace organizations with the knowledge of and commitments to non-violent modes of defence and conflict resolution might help the security sector in re-conceptualizing their roles and practices. Such re-conceptualization, often referred to as 'conversion,' would be directed toward refocusing structural organization designed to deal with various security crises and the security sectors repertory of professional skills of maintaining social order and protecting citizen's rights toward enhancing human security by reducing the incidence of the violence that impedes its realization. In recent decades, some members of the security sector themselves, such as several associated with retired high-ranking army and navy officers have advocated such conversion. So too, some members of both the military and the civil sectors have expressed concern for different training of those members of the military who are now regularly deployed to provide disaster assistance. Such natural disasters as mega-storms and earthquakes now constitute major threats to global security in whatever way it is defined. The conversion of the security sector from militarized to human security as their professional goal has been deemed to be the first among the essential steps in shifting methods and roles of all agents and institutions that now comprise militarized national security systems. The essential shift would be their embracing a more comprehensive and humanly inclusive concept of national security than that which now gives priority to defending the interest of the State over the wellbeing of people. Such was asserted in a session of the aforementioned workshop convened by GNWP that introduced representative of the security sector, military and police to the purposes and provisions of 1325 and UNSCR 1820. Two particular elements of that report that have special relevance to peoples' action plans are this emphasis on human security and its focus on localization as the most effective approach to implementation (see GNWP website for examples of localization in practice[3]).

Local action plans (LAPs) have been drafted by women's civil society groups in Columbia, the Democratic Republic of the Congo, Liberia and the Philippines. LAPs arise from some of the same assertions about the irrefutable need for major local input into all security policymaking. On those grounds alone, women, being the actors who take most the responsibility for human security at local and community levels, would be at least equally represented in all aspects of security policymaking, just as called for in 1325. Such representation is stressed in one of the perambulatory statements, preceding the recommendations. '*Stressing* (sic) the importance of their [women] equal participation and full involvement in all efforts for the maintenance and promotion of peace and security' (UNSCR 1325, 2000).

Three Core Pillars: A Basis of Establishing Goals and Identifying Human Security Obstacles and Indicators

For setting the goals, assessing obstacles and identifying indicators for progress, as well as conceptual basis for planning actions to actualize the purposes of 1325, the three core pillars of 1325, participation, prevention and protection, provide a second dimension to the planning framework (see Planning Matrix, Addendum 1). The two dimensions of the four human security requirements and the three core pillars of the resolution converge in designing measures to assure women greater *participation* in all peace and security matters, advances in the capacities of communities and nations to reduce and *prevent* armed conflict and to *protect* women and the vulnerable from the violence against civilian populations integral to militarized security systems, most especially the many forms of military violence against women (B.A. Reardon cited in Reardon 2015) The process through which the framework is envisioned to be applied is in inquiry into the obstacles to and possibilities for human security, posing assessment questions such as or similar to those put forth below in regard each of the three pillars.

Participation: The inclusion of more women in the military was not an intended aim of 1325, though has been so interpreted by some governments and their militaries. However, it is extremely important that a gender perspective and consideration of the security challenges faced by women and other vulnerable populations be given more consideration in undertaking military action, in the formation of all security policymaking and in planning and executing conversion from militarized state security to human national security.

Women must participate equally and fully in all these aspects and all spheres of the human security paradigm. For in the present time, women are more likely raise the human security questions in policy-making and strategy planning with such questions as: Are those among our community who will be most affected by the proposal adequately represented in this policy discussion? How will the policy or strategy under consideration impact upon the natural and social environments on which the populations to be affected depend? Will it undermine the capacity of the communities in which it will be carried out to meet basic human needs, both physical and social, such as food security and essential health and education services? Does it put any human rights at risk? How will it affect all the community's capacities to protect its people from avoidable harm? Does the proposal itself pose any avoidable harm? If the proposal is deemed harmful in any of these human security realms, can we propose other less or not harmful alternatives?

Prevention: Resolution 1325 was conceived as a peace initiative. The concept of prevention that informs the resolution applies first and foremost to the prevention of armed conflict. A feminist conceptualization does not problematize conflict as such, but rather seeks to eliminate the violence it can produce when alternative conflict resolution is ignored or not given time to mature into settlements. The history of women's peace movements attests to many efforts women have made to prevent and interrupt armed conflict. From the time of the American Civil War to present day political conflicts in the Middle East, Africa, South Asia, Korea and Ukraine among them, women have been actively and courageously involved in attempts to bring the disputing parties together so as to move toward a settlement without the bloodshed and slaughter of armed conflict.

In spite of this clear intent of preventing wars and armed conflicts, this pillar has been limited in the views of many member States to preventing violence against women, assuming that conflict and war can be conducted without inflicting violence on women or on large percentage of civilian populations. Feminists understand that sexual violence is integral to armed conflict and always has been, even before it was recognized as a weapon of war. Preventing war and armed conflict is the most effective way to prevent military violence against women. For this reason, peoples' action plans should put emphasis on alternatives to violence, demilitarizing security and achieving general and complete disarmament as the basis for abolishing war. To achieve these goals, thinking must shift the problem focus from armed conflict per se to the global militarized security system itself.

The *prevention* inquiry opens the possibilities for public discussion of alternative security systems, an inquiry pursued by peace researchers since the end of the Second World War. While the models and proposals this inquiry has produced are somewhat outdated by the changes that have taken place in the causes and nature international conflicts and crises such as terrorism, mass migrations, disease epidemics and climate change, all of which pose sever threats to human security; they deserve study to reveal some of the systemic and particular causes that underlie them and general principles of response to resolve and prevent them. Principles such as, strong international standards for environmental protection, providing universal health care and education to the world's vulnerable populations and, immediately and especially, using law instead of force by establishing permanent peace forces to contain and restrain conflicts threatening to break into violence, compulsory international dispute settlement agencies, institutions for the protection of human rights, plans for stages of a disarmament process running parallel the building of such sustainable peace institutions as an alternative to inevitable war might well make their way into the goal-planning process for peoples' actions to implement 1325.

Questions to be raised in asserting women's perspectives on war prevention might be among others: How can human security requirements be factored into preventing violent conflicts? Do women in the military differ in their approaches to and priorities given to the use of armed force in the pursuit of conflict resolution and the defence of national security? How might women peace activists establish working relationship with military women to cooperate toward ending sexual violence within the military and by the military on civilians; and on identifying and evaluating alternatives to armed force? Would it be to the advantage of greater human security for women to have most armed forces commanded by teams of women and men rather than the present male hierarchy of the chain of command as well gender security officers in all units until non-violence is the norm? How might such more gender-equal military personnel work with women civil society peace activists to extend and strengthen the repertoire of violence prevention measures that will be essential to the preparation of the military to be agents of human security?

Protection: So long as militarized security systems prevail, women and other vulnerable groups will require protection from military violence against women, not only rape but sexual slavery, forced pregnancy and other such bodily assaults. Resolution 1820 put forth as a complement to 1325 was, as previously noted, the first in a series of resolutions on protection and prevention of violence against women in armed conflict. The main drawbacks to these resolutions are a glaring omission and two negative assumptions. The first assumption is that wars will continue to be fought and the second is that the brutality and violations of human rights integral to the institution of war can be mitigated and reduced, but not likely eliminated, by international agreements.

The omission reinforces these assumptions. That glaring omission that underlies States' notion that the *prevention* pillar involves only preventing violence against women is the failure to address and eradicate the problem of *impunity*. This factor has been a major facilitator of all forms of military violence against women. It has shielded perpetrators, especially those who are military, from legal accountability and criminal responsibility. Failure to punish perpetrators that can be identified at *all levels* of national military and international peacekeeping hierarchies contributes to the continuation of the 'regrettable but unavoidable' perspective on military violence against women and to minimizing the magnitude and severity of these crimes. The resolutions regarding 'violence against women in armed conflict' not fully referencing such international laws as those against rape, sexual slavery (see Women's International Tribunal on War Time Sexual Slavery conducted in Tokyo in 1999 by women's civil society groups) and trafficking assure neither prosecution nor punishment, nor do they address military violence against women outside of armed conflict, including and especially that which is epidemic around military bases outside conflict zones, and that against women who serve in military and peacekeeping forces where sexual harassment and assault are common occurrences. Since states have not vigorously pursued justice in these cases, people's plans of action should propose measures to eliminate impunity. Peoples' plans could also deal with protection by such measures as gender training and instructions on the provisions of 1325, 1820 and the other resolutions that deal with violence against women, as well as the laws of war intended to guide behaviours of the military and uphold the integrity and honour most militaries claim to value, and the Nuremburg Principles for individual responsibility for the violation of these laws.

Protection, as with the other two pillars, when viewed within a human security framework is more complex, but also more achievable. Inquiry, for example into ways in which the security sector might provide protection from a broad range of avoidable harms might offer up some promising actions to be integrated into peoples' plans. Starting with the environment as essential to human security, planners might inquire into the sectors potential contribution to dealing with the crises of droughts, floods and famine attributed to climate change and the ongoing issue of long range processes of pollution and resource depletion that are more immediately amenable to improvement by changes in human behaviour. Some sample questions to be raised about each of the four human security requirements are: In what ways do present military activities negatively impact the environment in the locality? Does the priority in the use of resources given to the military deprive members of our community of what it needs for the economic sustainability of our enterprises and that of our families? Have military in or near our community committed any violations of the human rights of the people of the community? Do the terms of their stationing or the ways in which they perform their functions disrespect the human dignity and/or cultural values of the community? Have military personnel imposed avoidable harm on any members of our community? Have women been subject to sexual harassment and assault? Do the military bases in our area provide for our own local security? Are the conflicts that rationalize these bases avoidable or subject to resolution by non-military measures? For ideas about possible specific examples, planners might look into the experiences of communities and women living where there is long term military presence such as Okinawa, South Korea and Puerto Rico, as well as conflict and post-conflict areas.

The Intended Scope, Strategies and Ultimate Goals of the Plans

The guidelines set forth here as a series of generic questions to be considered by any and all civil society groups in any world region intending to take action for achieving the core purposes of 1325 within a process of moving from systems of militarized state security to local/community, national, transnational/regional and international/global systems designed and constructed to achieve and maintain the human security of communities and the persons who comprise them. The focus of this planning instrument will be on the local level with a view toward transnational comparisons and cooperation. Implementation strategies, thus far, have been conceptualized and cast primarily for the national level at which thinking and priority setting are dominated by the drive to strengthen and maintain state security.

It is argued here that plans arising directly from the actual security needs and conditions on local ground on which they are to be implemented are far more likely to be actualized than those arising from national bureaucracy that are *mandated to citizens rather coming from them.* When local community CSOs are integrated into transnational networks in regions that demonstrate a range of common obstacles to peace, security and women's rights to participate in public affairs, there is likely to be more incentive for individual nation states to undertake serious action toward implementation. The actualization of local with parallel regional actions, will vividly demonstrate women's understanding of actual human security issues as they are experienced on the ground and their political capacities to translate that understanding into practical actions. Such common understanding holds promise of advancing the human security of multiple local communities within a given region. So, too, transnational networking can provide a base of peoples' solidarity that could serve to overcome some of the underlying conflicts that provide the rationale for maintaining armed forces and other attributes of militarized security in the regions.

Participation: Inquiry into Security Policymaking as It Affects Local Communities

The various authors in this book have all asserted that women's *participation* in security policymaking and implementation is the first and essential requirement of a process of demilitarizing and humanizing security systems. The effectiveness of proposals to *prevent* armed conflict and provide greater assurance of *protection* of women and all who are especially vulnerable to the multiple forms of violence inflicted through agents of militarized security as well as safeguarding the four fundamental sources of human security will be determined by the fullness and accuracy of the security assessment on which they are based.

The following questions are intended to begin the process of action planning with an assessment of women's participation in peace and security in their own communities and the threats to their human security that endure as a consequence of militarized security systems. The questions are not directed to one particular locality or region. They may be adapted and applied in various forms to the cultural and political specifics and the security needs of any of the various communities that may undertake to devise and apply peoples' action plans. We encourage those networking working with civil society groups in other countries to compare assessments toward the eventual formulation of a regional plan to complement and reinforce local plans. The questions below are intended as a suggestion of one possible process of pre-planning assessment.

How are decisions made about community crises? What agencies and institutions carry the responsibility for the safety and wellbeing of the community? Are elements of human security equally considered with issues of protection from disorder and armed violence? What is the percentage of women in the total personnel of these agencies and institutions? To what extent are weapons an essential tool of maintaining order and security in the community and to what extent are weapons the cause of community insecurity and violence against women?

How might the communal security policies be different were women equally represented in local security policymaking? How might the provisions of UNCR 1325 be applied to increasing women's participation in policymaking both as members of the security sector and representative of civil society? What civil society groups are actively concerned with security issues? How might they strengthen each others' efforts? How might they cooperate and learn from CSOs in other nations in their region? How might they relate to and cooperate with public service agencies, especially the security sector so as advance human security and reduced dependence on armed force? What immediate and longer range changes might be advocated as steps toward greater human security in your community? How might 1325 be a tool for such changes?

Prevention: Assessing Alternatives to Violence and Armed Force to Protect the Nation and Settle Disputes as Steps Toward Demilitarizing Security

The major rationale for the maintenance of the military forces from which stems much violence against women is the necessity of protecting the nation from threats to its security. The goal of demilitarizing security and adopting non-violent alternatives to violence and weaponry in maintaining national security and pursuing national purposes requires an assessment of the actual and constant violence inflicted on women as consequence of militarized security. A detailed assessment of that violence and consideration of the potential alternatives to armed force, with special focus on the forces of the security sector that are affecting local communities, is an essential part of pre-planning assessments.

As the following assessment questions are considered, so too should thought be given to non-violent alternatives to replace the agent or unit of armed force that is the particular source of the violence, and immediate actions and long range functions might be undertaken by civil society itself, for example, a local system of civilian based defence replacing long term military presence that may be stationed in the community. The other constant issue to be kept in mind in regard to each source or agent of military and gender-based violence is the issue of accountability and eliminating the impunity that continues to shield perpetrators from the punishments called for by law, Such laws exist at all levels of society from local to global. Indeed, UNSCRs 1325, 1820 and all those on women, peace and security comprise international law according to Article 25 of the UN Charter. Many plans for alternative security systems involve law as an alternative to force to pursue justice and or to settle disputes. The UNSC resolutions on women, peace and security should be integrated into any new adaptation of those plans and any and all future plans.

Protection: Assessing Violence Against Women and Erosion of the Four Sources of Human Security Arising from Militarized State Security

There is still very little systematic consideration given to the complex and interrelated damage that militarized state security systems do to civilian populations in peace time as well as war. War damage is accepted as an inevitable consequence of warfare as are hardships for civilian populations and war-time violence against women. However, only those affected by such damage outside theatres of war have tried to call attention to the avoidable harm the system itself does on a regular basis in maintaining constant readiness for armed conflict. Those so affected have a special interest in proposing a peoples' plan of action that will call these circumstances to the attention of their fellow citizens outside the affected communities.

While the blinders around the human security conditions of communities living under long-term military presence are worn by most citizens, the damage to entire societies wrought by the present global security system has been continuously and effectively obscured as well. Women have been the majority among the few raising their voices to decry the overall disastrous effects of militarized security on the wellbeing of most of the human family. Since these assaults on human security are rationalized as necessary to protect people from armed attack or foreign domination, peoples' plans must shed light on how little protection this system provides to civil populations in general and to women in particular, and how they have failed to prevent any of the real threats to security in our present world.

The questions below, beginning with consideration of threats to the security of women, address the threats to all the four sources of comprehensive human security.

What forms of violence affect women in your community? Which, if any, result from armed conflict and/or the presence of military forces in the community? (Respondents will find reports on such violence complied by Okinawa Women Act against Military Violence a useful model for this point of assessment; see Akibayashi and Takazato 2010). Which of these forms are attributable to actions by agents of the 'security sector,' that is, military and/or police? Which are attributable to failures of the security sector to protect women and the most vulnerable in the community? Which may be attributable to the manner in which women are treated in the course of seeking protection or justice for a violation of their rights? To what degree are weapons issued to the security sector or guards employed in public institutions involved in these forms of violence? Have the perpetrators been apprehended and held accountable or do they enjoy impunity? What actions might the plan propose to overcome impunity? Is this an area in which civil society and representatives of the security sector might cooperate? Might such cooperative endeavours be included in the action plan?

Has armed conflict or preparation for armed conflict damaged or destroyed any of the natural or humanly constructed *environment* in your community? How might the damage have been avoided? What affect has this damage had on the well-being of the community or any individuals, most especially women? Might the action plan include ways in which civil society could help to reverse such environmental damage? How might civil society and the security sector cooperate on this essential environment clean-up that the responsible governments have neglected? Have any in the community suffered damage to the physical or mental health as a consequence of military activity in our area?

Have the allocation of essential resources and public expenditures to the security sector deprived the civilian population of the satisfaction of *basic needs?* How has such deprivation affected women's capacities to care for their families? How has it affected the well-being of the entire community? How might the action plan address these issues of economic security?

Have members of the community experienced assaults on their *human dignity* through violation of their human rights enacted in the name of national security or in the conduct of military affairs? Have the violators been held accountable? What might feminist peace activists do to instigate a process of legal accountability and when appropriate criminal responsibility? How might the action plan advance such justice and help toward overcoming impunity?

Have adequate measures to avoid armed force been taken in disputes, conflicts and the pursuit of national political goals that affect our community? In such cases, have measures such as recourse to international law, the International Court of Justice or the International Criminal Court (ICC) or mediation, dialogue, various diplomatic procedures or any other forms of non-violent conflict resolution been publicly considered? Do the schools teach citizens about these alternatives to violence or about 1325 and its 'sister resolutions'? Might a call for such education be included in the action plan?

Conclusion

With such an inquiry, as that suggested above for preparation for drafting a people's action plan, the questions now are what should comprise such a plan? How should we produce it? How do we begin its implementation?

In responding to the last question, it is suggested that once a security assessment has been completed, help from as many community organizations as possible willing to share responsibility be enlisted. The distinction between NAPs, LAPs and peoples' plans is that peoples' plans are comprised by actions that citizens and civil society organizations themselves can take, rather than actions government agencies are requested to undertake. It is possible that once actions have been taken, those most effective could be presented to municipal authorities as the basis for local legislation. In the first stages of citizen action essential to initiating such a process, the commitment of cooperating CSOs to those actions would be attested to in their being identified in the preamble as among those calling for the actions proposed in the plan. For, as implied throughout the arguments and assertions presented in this essay, it is not likely that UNSCR 1325 will become the instrument of women's empowerment to bring their wide-ranging peacemaking and building skills to the advancement of human security without the strong support and vigorous efforts of global civil society.

The task is daunting, but no more so than was that of getting the issue from a small group of CSOs onto the agenda of the UN Security Council. We have that experience and those of the 15 years of disseminating and educating about 1325, along with efforts to produce NAPs and LAPs and constant persuading of governments to implement the resolution. With the undertaking of peoples' plans we will have begun a broad process of public education that in turn can be translated into broad public support for establishing gender equality in security policy-making and achieving the shift from militarized state security systems to human security system to strive toward the wellbeing of all the world's peoples. We are, indeed, well prepared to draft and implement peoples' action plans to bring the historic possibilities of 1325 to communities throughout the world.

The Addenda

Two tools are offered here to assist in beginning the process. Appended to this narrative is a matrix based on the two-dimension conceptual framework proposed here; human security assessed and pursued within the main pillars of the resolution and a proposed outline for drafting a people's action plan for the community implementation of 1325.

The *matrix* is to be used as an assessment and planning tool. Peoples' plan drafters might make two copies of the matrix, one on which to note the factors that describe obstacles to human security in the community, and a second to briefly note actions that might overcome some of these obstacles, as a step toward elaborating the actions for inclusion in your community's people's action plan. Both versions of the matrix will also help to demonstrate the interrelationships among the four element of the feminist human security paradigm, and the necessity of each and all. It will, as well, indicate how those security elements are relevant to each of the three core pillars of UNSCR 1325.

The *outline* is offered as one way to organize the content of the plan and suggests some possible elements to consider as content. It is to be emphasized that these tools are offered as suggestion to begin the process of producing a plan that comes from the particular culture and conditions of your community. Neither these addenda nor any NAPs or LAPs you may study in preparation are intended for direct replication. They are learning tools, not models to be reproduced.

May you be creative and relevant in your planning, and vigorous and successful in your implementation!

Notes

1. www.gnwp.org (accessed on 8 June 2016).
2. See www.gnwp.org (accessed on 8 June 2016).
3. www.gnwp.org (accessed on 8 June 2016).

References

Akibayashi, Kozue and S. Takazato. 2010. 'Gendered Insecurity under Long-term Military Presence: The Case of Okinawa'. In *The Gender Imperative: Human Security vs. State Security*, edited by B. Reardon and A. Hans, 38–60. New Delhi: Routledge.

Global Network of Women Peace-builders. 2015. *Recommendations from the "International Workshop on Integrating and Implementing the UN Security Council Resolutions (UNSCR) 1325 and 1820 and the Supporting Women, Peace and Security Resolutions in the Operations of the Security Sector*. Available at: http://www.gnwp.org/news/engaging-security-sector-implementation-women-peace-and-security-resolutions-international (Accessed on 30 May 2015).

Reardon, Betty A. 2015. 'Statement on Military Violence against Women Addressed to the 57th Session of the UN Commission on the Status of Women, 2013'. In *Betty A. Reardon: Key Texts in Gender and Peace*, edited by Betty A. Reardon and D. Snauwaert, 129–39. New York: Springer.

Reardon, Betty A. and Asha Hans, eds. 2010. *The Gender Imperative: Human Security vs. State Security*. New Delhi: Routledge.

Smoker, Paul, R. Davies and B. Munske, eds. 1990. *A Reader in Peace Studies*. New York: Pergamon Press.

The Women's International War Crimes Tribunal for the Trial of Japan's Military Sexual Slavery. 2002. *Proceedings of Women's International Tribunal on War Time Sexual Slavery.* Available at: http://www.asser.nl/upload/documents/ DomCLIC/Docs/NLP/Japan/Comfort_Women_Judgement_04-12-2001_part_1. pdf and http://www.asser.nl/upload/documents/DomCLIC/Docs/NLP/Japan/ Comfort_Women_Judgement_04-12-2001_part_2.pdf (Accessed on 7 June 2016).

Appendix A

Assessment and Action Planning Matrix: 1325 as an Instrument of Human Security			
	Participation	*Prevention*	*Protection*
Environment			
Needs			
Dignity			
Protection			

Appendix B: Outline for Drafting a People's Action Plan

Preamble

This introduction should:

1. Introduce the *drafting organizations or groups* and the perspective on security that informs the plan, "We, members of…" followed by "Keeping in mind that the human security of this community is of paramount concern to its members and should be to all members of public sector agencies…"
2. State the *conditions of violence* that demand women's involvement in security matters, "Considering the following threats to peace and human security of this community…."
   Here enumerate the threats as determined by the assessment inquiry into security threats, conducted in preparation for the drafting.
3. Identify and call to responsibility the public agencies, security sector and other agencies charged with providing some of the source of human security, "We, therefore call upon the following public agencies, in accordance with the provisions and purposes of UNSCR 1325 to enter into cooperation with the women of our organizations to undertake the following actions to reduce violence and increase the human security of this community….."

Proposals for Action

Set forth proposed actions under the categories such as those listed below.

1. Provisions for *women's participation* in decision making with regard to all peace and security matters in the community. Enumerate specific actions to address particular threats to or denial of all the four sources of human security
2. Actions, policies and agencies for the *prevention of armed and/ or all forms of violent conflict.*

3. Actions to assure *protection* of all citizens in general and women in particular from harms to all bases of security in general and protection from violence in particular. Specify types of violence such as: personal and bodily harm such as gender based violence, life and wellbeing threatening lack of health care, denial of education to girls etc. (In this section, it might be useful to reference 1325's 'sister resolutions' regarding violence against women as outlined in the chapter by Swarna Rajagopalan)

4. Suggest steps toward *overcoming impunity* for crimes against women and community well being. If public authorities or members of security sec

Creating Conditions for Change

Here suggest ways in which the changes necessary to effectively implementing the actions and achieving the goals of the PAP. Among them, you might consider:

1. Evaluation and assessment of implementation by setting up *monitoring agency and process* that would be in place for periodic check both scheduled and unannounced.
2. Set up programs for *re-training* in professional skills wherever needed and *gender training* in all public agencies.
3. Propose appropriate programs for *peace and gender education* in all schools, public and private.

Annual Review

Here propose that a body comprised of civil society and public sector representatives be set up to hold hearings in which all involved in the implementation process will be participate in a review and adjustment process aimed at improving and strengthening the plan. Questions such as the following might be addressed by the participants as they review each of the actions that have been undertaken.

1. Was this action accepted and fulfilled by those responsible for it?
2. Was its purpose and process well understood by all involved?

3. What results did it have? Were the results those that were intended?
4. What factors contributed to the results?
5. What, if any, changes might be made in the form of the action, the agents undertaking it or the factors affecting its outcomes in order to increase the possibilities for achieving its purpose?
6. Has it proved ready to present to the municipality for legal confirmation through adoption into our local laws? Would legal adoption strengthen the possibilities for women's empowerment and greater human security in our community?
7. How shall we proceed in the coming year so as to be as effective as possible at achieving the goals and purposes of 1325 through our action plan?

12

Gender Peace and Security:
A Paradigm Shift

Asha Hans

Background

The feminist notion of peace and security envisions a search for equality and justice for all women. This volume has tried to capture these insights on security from varied feminist spaces that are appreciative of women's centrality in peacekeeping. The writings also form a part of a discourse of a search for alternatives to the militaristic-based paradigm of state security and the argument that militarism cannot be addressed without addressing the problem of sexism (Reardon 1985).

In India, which is a focus of this volume, the insertion of gender in the human rights discourse on peace and security has remained on the margins and we the authors believe that it is time to move it to the centre of our inquiries and action. Inclusion of gender in these agendas, we believe, is critical as it is linked to the major issue of armed conflict and its impact on women's lives. Significantly, the disregarding of this important concern of women, we believe, is a consequence of women's exclusion from the political/security discourses and the ignoring of their experience in conflict prevention and ultimate elimination of armed conflict.

The ideological stand on gender equality in security has not been easy to comprehend or adopt globally. In India, the move to include women in this dialogue has been guided by a growing number of women peace activists and organizations who are articulate and continue to place their arguments at regular intervals on this issue. Presently, the larger group of mostly rural women are included on any voice on issues of peace, but their inclusion alone can create a political comprehension and a momentum on women's incorporation in security issues. If these women have to be brought into the discourse and their stand articulated on public platforms, we need to make a serious attempt to include them in our discussions and carve out a niche for them. We need to bring them in to enable us to broaden our knowledge of women's contribution to peace and that can be ascertained by hearing those who have gone unheard. It is women at the grass roots, including those living within the four walls of their homes, who each day question the arming of their villages/ towns, the violence perpetuated against them and their families and the state of conflict itself and based on this situation articulate about creating sites of peace. We can make the process inclusive by listening to these voices and including them in our strategies for building a national consensus on UNSCR 1325 and for enabling us to challenge the notion of women's frailties and fragileness in maintaining peace and introducing alternative security structures. These communications are multiple and can provide a holistic perception of security/insecurity. Understanding their viewpoint is important and requires our attention because they provide a range and history we cannot overlook.

The link between women and 1325 is threefold, relating to the equal participation, representation of women in peace and security and the changing norms of conflict and peace creating a demand among the feminists for bringing in new concepts for ensuring peace. The major assertion emerging through this volume is an attempt to comprehend these linkages and revisit UNSCR 1325 to make it applicable in a radically changing world. The major aim of the book was to assess how UNSCR 1325 can be applied and be used to promote peace through women's full and equal participation. In this endeavour, the writings in the book provide an overall perception that, with the transformations in the international system that have taken place since its adoption in 2000, our interpretations on the resolution has to change. This is possible by adopting a paradigm shift from State security to human security and a new thinking on moving from National Action Plans (NAPs) to Peoples' Action Plan when a non-acceptance of resolution by States is observed.

The following analysis flows from questions raised in the book and the various authors' search for a way forward in the implementation of the resolution, as making an attempt go beyond the existing discourse.

Extending UNSCR 1325

This is the 15th year of UNSCR 1325 and it intersects with 20 years of the Beijing Platform for Action (BFPA). Every writing on the resolution has been a step forward and lays before us new facets that were missing in earlier analysis. In my own involvement with the introduction and implementation of the resolution, the beginning was made at the Beijing Conference in 1995 where the document mentioned in detail the issues of women, peace and security. The process of bringing women in was strengthened at the Hague Appeal for Peace (HAP) meeting of 1999 where an initial step taken at Beijing turned into a movement. It was an ideology developed and endorsed by women activists and peace organizations who had been working together with governments at the UN and outside it. Among these, the HAP led by the indomitable Cora Weiss who had at the 1999 HAP Conference spearheaded the movement for women's inclusion in peace and security played an important part. She was joined by Women's International for Peace and Freedom (WILPF), which was well known because of its leadership in the women's peace movement. My own entry into the peace movement was the association with Elisa Boulding who was the President of WILPF, founded International Peace Research Association (IPRA) and was a remarkable feminist peace activist. The other promoters were Amnesty International standing high for people affected by State violence and the Committee for Refugee Women and Children who had created space for refugee women. Above all were the radical peace activists such as Betty Reardon, my mentor and to whom I owe my understanding on issues of gender and peace education, and who played a strategic role in pushing the agenda for women's inclusion.

The year 2000 was a landmark at the UN, not only for recognition of women's rights but also for breaking into the citadel of its security establishment, the Security Council. With the complete support of some governments in the powerful body, an informal caucus was built by Anwarul K. Chowdhury, the representative of Bangladesh at the UN, and the scene was set for the adoption of UNSCR 1325. The introduction of UNSCR 1325 saw the gendering of a highly masculine body agreeing with the women's notion that security is inextricably linked with gender equality. This value change was not easy to endorse and required strategization, and with the support of Namibia, which introduced the resolution to supporting countries Jamaica and Canada, the demand gained strength.[1] The Security Council adopted the Resolution unanimously on 31 October 2000. The objective of UNSCR 1325 was the recognition of women's role in peacebuilding and it was adopted specifically to address the impact of war on women and ensure women's participation in conflict resolution and peace processes. In its wider sense, it also included putting an end to impunity and prosecute those responsible for genocide, crimes against humanity and war crimes, including those relating to sexual and other violence against women and girls, and exclude these crimes from amnesty provisions. The Security Council also decided that to implement UNSCR 1325 at the national level each country has to prepare a NAP. Till 2016, 57 NAPs have been set up obligating only a very few countries to implement the resolution. However, in the South Asian region, except Nepal, no other country, including India, has taken an initiative.

Post-UNSCR 1325 Resolution, the 'symbol of change', as we observed in the volume, did not fulfil its expectations. It was not surprising that a male-dominated powerful organization such as the Security Council failed to fulfil its pledge to include women. As a diplomat at the UN suggested to the author at the 10th anniversary of the Resolution, UNSCR 1325 has remained a 'soft option'. This perception became its greatest weakness in the years to come compelling writers such as Kara Ellerby to argue that the resolution remains a 'confused and confusing' tool for scholars and practitioners in assessing women's inclusion in peace building (Ellerby 2013).

The formal structures have not recognized the importance of women's contribution and significance of roles played for instance in Bosnia, Ireland, Cyprus, Sri Lanka and even India. Such omissions invariably result in a systemic failure to address the gendered rights of women and post-conflict accountability. In a recent writing on UNSCR, it has been noted that '9 per cent of the delegates of negotiating parties, 4 per cent signatories and 2 per cent of the chief mediators are women' (Hann and Holzinger 2015, 12) Though the representation of women in formal peace-building processes continues to be abysmally low, there exist various instances of women in countries, as mentioned earlier, contributing in informal ways to reconstruction, conflict resolution and peace efforts.

In seeking to end war/armed conflict the resolution assures equal participation of women in all matters of peace and security. The issue and, therefore, the Resolution after 15 years of its inception require an analysis both at the international and national level. Some research and activism has continued the debate on its implementation, while some activists have succeeded in the execution of UNSCR 1325 in their countries through the NAPs. Though seven other resolutions have been introduced, (that is, UNSCR 1820, UNSCR 1888, UNSCR 1889, UNSCR 1960, UNSCR 2106, UNSCR 2122 and UNSCR 2242) the principal resolution still remains UNSCR 1325. The latest resolution, UNSCR 2242, emphasizes leadership, higher financing and partnership with boys and men. Nation States who discussed UNSCR 2242, including India, emphasized its linkage to the sustainable development goals, thus, broadening the concept of peace and letting it filter to all levels of governance (United Nations Security Council 2015). While the issue of peace is broadened, the question before us has been whether these multiple resolutions emerging out of State decision making are strengthening UNSCR 1325 or weakening it. UNSCR 2106 for instance was adopted on 24 June 2013 by the UNSC with an aim to support the recommendations laid out by the secretary general in his March 2013 report on sexual violence in conflict (United Nations Security Council 2013a). However, the women's peace activists who had promoted UNSCR in 2000 indicated concern that with the increase in resolutions around UNSCR 1325 women were not being consulted.[2] There has been also an argument put forward by feminist peace activists that this overlaying of UNSCR 1325 by too many resolutions diverges the issue from demilitarization to violence against women only.

It is important, therefore, that after 15 years if we are to take UNSCR 1325 forward, to enable it to become an agent of change it must be revisited. Transformation is a complex process and one of its important indicators in the course of action is strategic time. The year 2015 provides the precise moment for this as not only does it mark the completion of a decade and half years of UNSCR 1325, but also 20 years of the Beijing review. Furthermore, the UN has released a high-level report by Radhika Coomaraswamy, former Rapporteur on

Violence Against Women, in October on the progress and financing of UNSCR 1325 globally, though not much of the reporting is related to India. One of the positives it notes is the fact that before 2000 only 11 per cent peace accords had mentioned women, after that it increased to 27 per cent. In the six accords where the UN has played a part, the percentage is a high 67 per cent (UN Women 2015, 44–45). The resolution, the report affirms, has a human rights mandate and requires that perpetrators must be made accountable. It also maintains that localization of approaches and inclusive and participatory processes are crucial to the success of national and international peace efforts, and if the resolution is to succeed the Security Council must adopt a gender effect to all its work and the local must be the most important factor. The global study recognizes three constraints on civil society's own effectiveness in this work: lack of resources, gaps between international policies and local realities and finally, lack of trust between governments and civil society (UN Women 2015, 15–16, 22).

Earlier in 2013 the CEDAW Committee had adopted General Resolution 30 in an attempt to strengthen the resolution and directed the States to ensure that NPAs and strategies to implement Security Council Resolution 1325 (2000 demanded) and that subsequent resolutions are compliant with the convention, and adequate budgets are allocated for their implementation (United Nations 2013). 1325 has been carried forward continuously by the UN agencies such as UN Women, as well as civil society, which has geared up with assessment plans and new discourses in 2015. Major amongst the outcome has been the monitoring report by the Global Network of Women Peacebuilders. The report advocated for building the capacity of women so that they can participate in peace negotiations and their implementation, formation of a sub-committee on gender in all peace negotiations to ensure gender inclusion (Global Network of Women Peacebuilders 2014, 61). The organization also supported Women in Governance (WinG)-India to bring out a report on India.

None of these reports could answer many of the issues raised by this book, especially in the Indian context. For instance, how to deal with the changing situation in conflict governance; with the multiple layers of conflict including insecurity posed by economic globalization in women's lives in conflict zones; moving from the traditional concept of security based on militarization by State-armed forces to inclusion of non-state actors and 'terrorism'; and above all bringing into the discourses the demilitarization aspect of the resolution, and what if a NAP is not acceptable to the State.

To overcome the lacunae mentioned above and emerging from the writings in this book, it is obvious we require a different paradigm working at different levels. So as we cross the 15th anniversary of the resolution we have to not only change to the new situation but also reclaim the original thinking on UNSCR 1325 to understand the repositioning from conflict to peace as envisaged in 2000 that demilitarization was at the core of the resolution. Though ending violence is integral to women's security and its removal is extremely important to a state of peace, it must, however, be recognized it is not the fundamental cause for conflict. The foundation of conflict is militarization and unless nations de-militarize conflicts will continue and violence against women will not end.

Removing Barriers to Peace

The path to peace is obstructed by many obstacles that 1325 tried to remove. The major aim was to end conflict that denoted the removal of militarized structures. Modern day militarization, however, is a complex phenomenon with multiple layers. It is constituted of nuclear weapons, non-nuclear weapons, small arms and multiple users such as armed forces, State and non-state security users, police and civilians. The major areas of political conflict in India where weapons are in regular usage by all these actors are on the borders of India. These border areas have been dealt in depth in the chapters by Rekha Chowdhary, Paula Banerjee and Asha Hans. The policy of defending borders is dependent on two factors: high level of armaments and use of specific security laws.

India and the two countries on its borders, China and Pakistan, are all nuclear powers. They are also highly armed in conventional weapons imports and manufacture, or receive armaments in the form of grants. In the case of India, it is the largest importer of arms in the world accounting for 14 per cent in global arms imports (SIPRI 2014, 4).[3] India has abstained from signing the Arms Trade Treaty (ATT), a document that Security Council Resolution 2106 specifically mentions and stipulates that in the Arms Trade Treaty…exporting

States shall take into account the risk of covered conventional arms or items being used to commit or facilitate serious acts of gender based violence' (UNSCR 2106).

A major concern amongst women promoting peace and security issues in India is the huge proliferation of small arms owned and used by non-state actors. The killing by these groups in both North East and Jammu and Kashmir is one of the most complex issues women have to deal with as these actors belong to their own communities. There has been little response from feminist groups even though militarism, whether enforced by state or non-state actors, strengthens gender hierarchies and patriarchy.[4] It also diverges our attention to only State-led militarism and militaristic values of the security system.

The new process of State security systems are linked to heavy domestic militarization that has its other manifestations. The promoters of UNSCR 1325 will have to initiate a discourse on this issue as well as newly emerged or emerging issues such as 'war against terror'. This war as witnessed in India is not a new phenomenon, it has been in existence since colonial times with differential aspects, but little gendered work has been done on this historical aspect of war especially in relation to border conflicts. 9/11 in contrast has initiated a discourse on gender and the war against terror. We as feminists need to take cognizance of this type of warfare, as it has an impact on women. In the aftermath of the terror attack on the US the term 'war against terrorism' began to be used. Later the global terminology of terrorism was used against 'extremist forces' within the country including in the letter by Osama bin Laden reproduced in *The Guardian* (newspaper) where he included Kashmir as one of his targets (*The Guardian* 2002). The security system has come to be defined from a broader perspective in the 'war against terror' with visible as well as tenuous enemies. This has resulted in the terrorizing of the State's citizens and targeting them on political and ideological grounds. It is also a war of semantics, and of fear and disempowerment. It makes no difference between men and women, but has gendered effects. Birgit Brock-Utnem argues that, as in other conflict situations around the world, gendered discourses were used in the US following 11 September 2001 in order to reinforce mutual hostilities. Our acceptance of a re-masculinized society, she argues, rises considerably during times of war and uncertainty where masculine activity remains central as described by feminist investigations (Brock-Utne 2009).

The war against terror is based on a new type of militarized philosophy, that is, a militarization of the mind and, therefore, has different effects. As the UN Human Security Report by Ogata and Sen (2003) states, 'the panic of the war against terror has meant overlooking state terror'.

Besides terrorism, there is also conflict produced by territorial location in terms of strategic importance, for instance international borders and augmented violence due to threats located to territory. Strategic location though defined as 'political' in nature as observed in the chapter on Manipur could nevertheless be economic. These regions are important to the State for the resource as they possess what has set off wars between countries as well as the State and its people. The socio-political nature of conflict has been highlighted in many studies but its link to borders and globalization overlooked women in conflict zones. Wars, especially over resources, provide the core reason for cross-border conflicts. Hydro-carbon deposits and water (both Indus and Brahmaputra) have contributed to their strategic value (Gupta 2013). In the Northeast, the competitiveness between India and China in setting up hydro-electric projects is fuelling insecurity and a higher intensity of conflict, and has resulted in new deployments of paramilitary forces in the region (Hayes 2012, 19). Militaristic security combining with capitalist economies provide an enhanced danger to women especially as both conflict and development induced displacement, run concurrently placing immense pressure on women.

Conflict over water for instance has been in existence since the partition of India and a treaty on Indus waters was signed in 1960 with Pakistan. There are also issues of construction of Baglihar Dam and Kishanganga project in Jammu and Kashmir and many other river water sharing disputes with China, Bangladesh and Nepal (Gupta 2013). In Manipur, the Mapithel Dam located on the Thoubal River in Ukhrul district of Manipur has turned into a site of conflict. The dam site has armed forces deployment of Assam Rifles (AR), India Reserve Battalion (IRB) and the Border Security Force (BSF). The Tipaimukh Hydro Electric project is another site of women's protest. The Dumbur Dam of the Gumti Hydel project in Tripura together with oil and gas finds have sustained a political conflict though the aim is economic control of resources. The Tuli paper mill of Nagaland has also displaced thousands in Nagaland.[5] The economic and the political militarization aspects run concurrently and add multiple levels of oppression on the people. Women I met in the displaced camps in a visit to Manipur and Nagaland in January 2012 spoke of weapons being used to evict them. This easy use of arms on citizens is possible as there are so many armed, security and police forces with weapons. Even when conflict at national level is diffused the guns remain.

As insurgencies continue and with large borders to maintain, conflict flows across borders that increases the stationing of armed force used for both military and non-military purposes. The chief discourse on women, peace and security centring on armed conflict as we understand is linked to the broader perspective of militarization and peace, however, we need to recognize that peace and conflict do not possess unilinear characteristics. In any armed conflict situation, the armed forces, combined with security and police forces create spaces of violence in different sites.

The recent increasing conflict over resources has affected people living on borders. In some places, therefore, the army has taken action due to violence by local security and police forces as in Manipur after the 2004 rape and killing of Manorama by the army (AR; see chapter on Manipur). This act of the women standing up against military rape unfortunately did not decrease the violence against them as new layers of violence were developing and UNSCR 1325 and its sister resolutions needed to take cognizance of it.

Besides increasing use of armaments the second barrier to peace is the use of a legal framework constitutive of suppressive laws. The space of peace for women is shrinking as violence goes deep into society through laws such as those related to the Armed Forces Special Powers Act (AFSPA) accentuation the power of the army through a colonial product in an independent India thereby strengthening the process of militarization (chapter by Amrita Patel). Besides, this national Act linked to the countries' security system, there are many others as observed in this volume that work at tandem within the country strengthening the State security structures (Ritu Dewan). Another significant Act is, the Unlawful Activities (Prevention) Act of 1967 (UAPA) that has been amended twice, with Parliament adopting a third amendment in 2012 to expand the scope of the definition on 'terrorist acts' and include acts that threaten the economic security of

India. In Jammu and Kashmir, the Police Reforms Bill 2013 includes democratic services that refer to use of military and paramilitary forces and the police that are instruments of control (see Ritu Dewan). The Bill permits the state government to declare any area disturbed where police officers are 'always on duty' and the confidentiality clause can override the Right To Information Act, where a six-month deadline for complaint against a police official from 'occurrence of the incident' is provided. There is also the provision of legal immunity regarding decisions taken 'in good faith or intended to be done' and appoint and arm as many civil society committees they want and by extension provides for using any method to stop protests (Government of Jammu and Kashmir 2013). Women find it difficult to respond to violence and law has no answers to end the immunity that enjoy as India has not agreed to the jurisdiction of the International Criminal Court (Saumya Uma).

If the dimensions of conflict have changed we have to go beyond the existing systems of peace promoted through a NAP. In drawing lines around 'conflict' as to what is a conflict area and what is not, actually we need a discourse centred on what sorts of conflicts for instance should fall under this feminist discourse. The government is likely to draw a narrowly defined circle. A feminist instinct is to include larger struggles with the main drivers for conflict being resource-based. This includes struggles linked to displacement due to development, insurgency/conflict due to underdevelopment and communal/religious riots. We can argue in favour of one or the other but the fact remains that there is limited space for women in any decision making and unless that space is not increased the status of women will continue to remain in an unprivileged space.

The most important link to the missing peace discourse globally is related to the specific factor that in this battle it is the 'arms suppliers who continue to sell and profit from weapons that violate human rights and humanitarian law while directly impeding conflict prevention' (PeaceWomen 2015, 10; SIPRI 2014).[6] The Indian arms suppliers Russia and the US have consequently played a key role in conflict and violence intensification against women.

The transition from conflict to peace is possible when we initiate discourses on a culture of peace brought about by reduction of arms expenditure by suppliers, State and non-state actors and by increasing government's social spending to educate women's education and creating awareness on the resolution. In 2015 India stood 9th in the top ten military spending States but is ranked 130 of 188 States of the Human Development Index[7] (UNDP 2015). If human security is a goal this ranking has to be reversed and the country needs to spend more on basic needs of people.

Endorsing a Culture of Peace

We have observed that as a result of the deployment of armed forces in conflict areas in the absence of a legal framework, sexual assault on women continues. This has been raising issues of impunity and remains a major barrier to peace. Conflicts such as in Bosnia, Sri Lanka, Palestine, Ireland, Cyprus, Rwanda and Congo (DRC) highlighted the impact of sexual violence on women[8]. Violence perpetuated by militarization permeates into social structures and spreads across the country. As seen in the chapters by Ila Pathak on riots or Swarna Rajagopalan in her discussion related to conflicts at local levels militarization cannot be isolated to borders. It is in this area where women's silence prevails and it is imperative it be heard but the absence of a common platform of peace makes it difficult. As there has been no formal accountability of the violence committed against women at any level the adoption of UNSCR 1325 in India becomes important.

    Cynthia Cockburn argues that when we are looking for the links between war situated violence and male violence against women in peace times, we need to look for both causality and influence, flowing in both directions (Cockburn 2012). The continuum or lines drawn from home to the battlefield are linked to domestic violence, rape, control and power. In my earlier work on Kashmir I had written of this continuum, which I find today in my work on the North East (Hans 2000, 2010). It stretches from pre-war to war to peacetime and the link to patriarchy is very clear as women find themselves in the centre of violence in all spaces. During war on the end of one continuum is patriarchy where women are targeted as victims, on the other masculinity emerges as an intimidating force. The Hague Appeal for Peace in 1999 had emphasized the role of masculinity on the continuing of violence. As men are mostly responsible for violence within and outside the household, one major issue that has crept up in security concerns is that of linking it to masculinity, which needs to be part of future discourse. It extends from battering within the four walls of a home to the territorial boundaries that enclose a State. This violence is not limited to physical violence by a partner to gun violence by the military but also loss of women's livelihood and increase in poverty as a result of the conflict. This culture of violence in our everyday lives while it is gendered also makes us believe that violence in conflict situations is normal. It makes rape and other sexual abuse during war time not an aberration but a normal continuation of the usual.

As national thinking is rooted in patriarchy, and through its manifestation of inequality, it is a reflection of the expression of an insensitive system that victimizes the vulnerable and makes women who are victims invisible, and consequently excludes them from a legal regime that censures the practice of violence and simultaneously provides immunity to the perpetuators. Within the system the hierarchies are maintained with masculine perpetuators remaining at a higher level whether in war or in normal times. Patriarchy has emerged as a major obstacle to the security of women and is difficult to bring it to an end as it is rooted in social structures. It has survived over centuries because of its flexible construction and ability to survive in militarized and non-militarized situations.

As Reardon comments in her chapter, 'UNSCR 1325 represents a potentially transformative challenge to the patriarchal state and its militarized security apparatus'. It is important that women's support at the local level where conflict is taking place be built through women's solidarity. The hierarchical structure of a State patriarchal system requires a strategy building by women who can then emerge as decision makers and can influence State behaviour. This is the only way that State violence can end, but this is a complex process as the war system itself is changing and affecting civilians much more than before at multiple levels.

In the context of protection of women there are shortcomings in the existing legal framework. Violence against women is a war crime if it is sanctioned by the State as an instrument of war. In this context we need to be alert and prepared to use effective legal instruments for instance to prevent use of rape, which is the most heinous of crimes committed against women. The Rome Statute of the ICC includes rape as war crime. However, its use in India has never been debated either by feminists or civil society. Usha Ramanathan analysing the stand writes:

> India's resistance to accepting the inherent jurisdiction of the ICC is explained, in part, by anxieties about how investigation, prosecution and criminal proceedings in the Indian system may be judged by an international court. The inclusion of 'armed conflict not of an international character' in defining 'war crimes' in Article 8 ICC Statute constitutes another reason for India's concern. Further elements giving rise to India's misgivings are the fear that the Court might be used with political motives, the power conferred on the Prosecutor to initiate investigations pro priomotu and the role allotted to the Security Council. (Ramanathan 2005)

To strengthen the law a recent attempt was made by the Verma Commission in its report to bring these abuses in conflict zones within the criminal law of the country. It had a statement and recommendations on the army-linked laws such as AFSPA. The Commission's statement acknowledged the brutalities of the armed forces against the residents in the border areas that led to a deep disenchantment and the lack of mainstreaming of such persons into civil society. The Commission found that serious allegations of persistent sexual assault on women in such areas and conflict areas were causing alienation. Another issue was related to the borders, which as mentioned above remain targets of extreme conflict and so do the women living on them. The Commission also recognized the linkage between the borders and drug trade and carriers of HIV/AIDS. The Commission asserted that the border regions were highly militarized space where the armed forces, security, [police, insurgence and cross-border armed forces used violence against women, which had been ignored owing to institutional apathy. The committee recommended that every complaint of rape must be registered by the police and civil society should perform its duty to report any case of rape coming to its knowledge (J.S. Verma Committee 2013).

The Verma Committee produced a simplistic solution by emphasizing the role of society and suggesting that both men and women work together to decrease violence in women's lives in AFSPA zones of conflict and end violence against women living in conflict zones. The question of impunity remained unanswered.

To be inclusive and create an environment where a culture of peace exists, we need, I would argue, to analyse how State and social oppression is formulated. It also means analysing the systemic continuum of the private and public sphere of violence, which continuously amalgamates into one. The Constitutional provisions and the ensuing legal framework left gaps that needed a social understanding and response to the silence of women. It is evident from the writings in this volume that change is taking place on the ground and that women are demanding the bringing in of a culture of peace through the use of UNSCR 1325 and its three pillars—participation, protection and prevention. It is time, therefore, for radical change.

Changing a Paradigm: Human Security and a Gendered Plan for Peace and Security

These pillars of the resolution can be developed and a culture of peace introduced by our understanding shift from State security to human security. This is not a new construction as just before the discussions were underway in New York on UNSCR 1325, the participants at the Hague Appeal for Peace meeting in 1999 had begun deliberating on the new security paradigm (Hague Appeal for Peace 2000). Many feminists and other peace advocates welcomed the emergence of the concept of human security as the idea that would instigate the long awaited and much need scholarly and public discourse on alternative security systems. As a feminist perspective of human security, it is an approach that aims to root out violence in conflicts and devise alternative strategies. It defies the notion of discriminatory gender justice, as it exists. The human security paradigm is important as it has the ability to link structures and practices that operate in different need based spheres but have the ability to converge to produce an enabling security environment (Reardon and Hans 2010).

Linking UNSCR 1325 to this discourse, Anwarul K. Chowdhury has argued:

> Security can no longer be understood in purely military terms or in terms of state security. Rather, it must encompass economic development, social justice, environmental protection, democratization, disarmament, and respect for human rights and the rule of law. To attain the goals of human security, the most essential element is the protection and

empowerment of people. As UNSCR 1325 deals with peace & security with special attention to the half of the global population, it is crucially important that the human security concept becomes the key to the resolution's implementation at the national, regional and global levels. (Chowdhury 2011, 4)

The concept of human security, as Reardon argues in her chapter, needs to be the alternative to militarized State security. It can be argued that as in UNSCR 1325 the major objective construed has been to provide the protection of people (specifically women) from harm (especially when related to, e.g., UNSCR 1888) through NAPs that need to be based on the principles of human security. The State is not the only perpetrator of violence, there also exist non-state actors as observed both in the North East and Jammu and Kashmir who are not governed by any laws.

As demilitarization is not only of the State structure but also society, in a world where the State security paradigm exists, the question that confronts women's peace activists is how can a culture of peace be brought in? At a security meeting in Wisconsin there was shocked silence when I argued for general and complete disarmament (University of Wisconsin 1989). I was young and naïve, but I realize now that it was the right path. I still believe that peace is possible by adopting a broader lens of security outside a territorial lens maintained through arms alone. I seek to argue here is that we continue to move forward in our aim for peace and to take seriously Cynthia Enloe's assertion that everything that has been militarized can be de-militarized (Enloe 2000).

The concept of security it is being argued must, thus, change from an exclusive stress on territorial security to a much greater stress on people's security (Derouen and Newman 2011, 242). To attain this goal strategies through people's power have to be adopted. This will not be an easy task as it is not only the State but society that is infiltrated with a culture of force. At this stage the important question confronting peace activists when linking human security to UNSCR 1325 is: Can demilitarization be achieved through a non-violent process? The task can be made easier if the introduction of the new paradigm builds on its publicly accepted history of peace activism. India's independence is attributed to Mahatma Gandhi and the non-violent movement of Satyagraha. Today in India we are far removed from this strategy as unfortunately the non-violent protest by women, whether Irom

Sharmila or Manipuri women (Meira Paebis), have been silenced by a democratic State whose foundation was based on Satyagraha. This shrunken space for protest, as in the case of Irom Sharmila's, is reducing rapidly (Teltumbde 2013, 10). Irom Sharmila's protest began on 2 November 2000, after the AR troops, under the immunity offered by the AFSPA, had shot dead 10 civilians waiting at a bus stop at Malom, Manipur. Sharmila demanded a repeal of the Act and went on her fast unto death.[9] The State used the Indian Penal Code (Section 309) and arrested Sharmila, and her activities were labelled as criminal even though it was a non-violent protest, and force fed her when she used the Gandhian protest method of hunger strike. This has continued for the last 15 years (as many number of tears as UNSCR 1325). To create change it is imperative that we, therefore, re-question the continuing colonial attitude towards non-violent protest as Satyagraha is situated within the core of Indian democracy.

The 'people' promoted change is not likely to occur as State security decision-making forums are out of the reach of people and especially women in India. If we have to use the resolution we must define the strategies for UNSCR 1325 that were conceived primarily as a policy that would assist in inclusion of women in strategic decision-making forums. Secondly, it also aimed at removing violence against women in conflict situations by their inclusion in peace and security policy making. To create the shift to a new paradigm and its vision based on human security the strategies must be inclusive of nature.

In this particular case we have observed throughout the writings in the book that women have been known to advocate peace by creating change through human rights discourses and promoting democratic values. They are known to be promoting values of compassion, justice and a broader security to include their needs such as food shelter, health and education. Women's peace activism has also resulted in the adoption of many international and national legal instruments that contribute to peace and requires the study and analysis of these standards on the ground. In particular make a place at the negotiating tables and other decision-making forums that is rightfully theirs.

It is important here to know the stand of the Government of India in the inclusion of women in decision making where peace activities are concerned. India has a foreign civil service where 18 per cent are women.[10] They are, however, part of the present ungendered security system and have never spoken like Sweden of a 'feminist foreign policy'. As to direct peace negotiations in conflict, Anuradha Chenoy mentions the government's (cabinet committee on security) appointment on 13 October 2010, a panel of three interlocutors to start a peace dialogue in Jammu and Kashmir. One woman was included in the panel of three members. This beginning shows a space for women's inclusion and signifying an opening of the government's stand that women be included in our coalitions of peace so that the spheres of masculinity shrink. Women from Nagaland have set an example for other groups by a continuous negotiation with both the State and non-state actors for their inclusion in peace negotiations (chapters by Paula Banerjee and Asha Hans).

In the case of UNSCR 1325, we need to link our analysis for alternatives by visualizing what the NAP for India has to offer.

National Action Plans and Alternative Strategies

In a message to a workshop on UNSCR 1325 organized by the author in 2011, Anwarul K. Chowdhury wrote:

> As the governments are trying to get their acts together, civil society, on its part, should work together towards the elimination of violence against women and ensure that victims have full access to justice and that there is no impunity for perpetuators...In general, NAPs should be designed to coordinate and strengthen the implementation of UNSCR 1325. They should contain a catalogue of measures, clear targets and benchmarks for full and meaningful implementation. The creation of an action plan provides an opportunity to initiate strategic actions, identify priorities and resources, and determine the responsibilities and timeframes. The whole process of developing a plan is also a process of awareness raising and capacity-building in order to overcome gaps and challenges to the full implementation of UNSCR 1325. (Chowdhury 2011, 3)

The conference decided that to achieve this there would be a need to (a) initiate a discourse on NAP and its process, (b) create awareness on UNSCR 1325 in the country, (c) require a discourse on a regional action plan, taking into account the high level of inter-state conflict in this part of the region and (d) develop a people's action plan.

In the South Asian countries Nepal has already adopted a plan, and Sri Lanka and Bangladesh have started the process. India, which is vying for a permanent Security Council seat might, therefore, in the future agree to develop an NAP. The issue first and foremost is, therefore, to assess women's expectations of the plan in India. The main questions in this context are: Can the State fulfil these aspirations within the security paradigm it promotes? Would demilitarization be the main aim of UNSCR 1325 and form part of the NAP? Would the consultations by the government include women peace activists who can create substantive change or just include women as a symbolic gesture? This would result in women peace activists (as usual) with experiences being left out of the process; Where would UNSCR 1325 be implemented? If Jammu and Kashmir and the North East are not conflicts in the government's perception then how do we define any peace processes where women would find space?

Despite the doubts an NAP is still possible as many non-conflict countries such as Norway, Sweden, Canada and Finland have established them. There might be non-border conflicts where UNSCR 1325 could be used and further research is needed on this. For instance areas under Maoists in East and Central India where the State confronts violence from armed groups.

It is important that the plan for an NAP in India articulate from the beginning that the main objective is the full political empowerment of women that can only be achieved if they are equally represented in security policy and implementation. It should also be recognized that the most effective route to prevention of violence against women is the prevention of armed conflict, a core intention of the original concept of prevention included in UNSCR 1325. If we are to promote NAP we have to be very careful of the process itself and the issues connected with it as just setting them up as experience shows is not enough. Once an NAP is agreed upon the process will be in the hands of the State. In this context we need a plan based on women's thoughts and experiences.

UNSCR 1325 and Developing a People's Action Plan

Women's inclusion as part of the UNSCR agenda will be dependent on our visions and our collaborative thinking. At this 15th year of UNSCR 1325 women's role in peace and security are at a crossroads and we need to design a path that is non-violent and inclusive. This is the moment to take advantage of, as there is the usual the 'anniversary' upsurge that charges energies in the process. This transformation needed for peace is only possible if the peace and women's movement that are currently running along parallel lines join in solidarity. This is an uphill struggle and the contextual feminist viewpoint related to the issue of security within an NAP remains unanswered. From a feminist perspective, the existing security system remains a contested concept (Reardon and Hans 2010). If Security Council Resolutions on women, peace and security are to be implemented, we need to change the interrogation to address the constructions of security: We need to transform our ideas surrounding security by making the definition inclusive of women's visions. We need to ask women in the conflict zones what they consider security. Does security from the perspective of defence and national security have any meaning for them? The indigenous woman whose approach to life is being forced to change, the woman who sees development take a new turn with her secure environment and livelihood destroyed. How do we perceive these women's spaces in this world view? We need to ask what security means to them and where does the concept of State security fit in this paradigm shift. For years we are being told that the people of Jammu and Kashmir and North Eastern states threaten the security of India. We need to ask whose security do they threaten—the woman raped and killed in Delhi, which resulted in large-scale protest by people, the women mass raped in both the regions by the security forces? Where does the newly emerging issue security of people displaced by economic globalization in conflict zones fit in? The State with a top-heavy militaristic structure, which overlooks the needs of its people needs changing as presently it has adopted a State security system that leans heavily on militarization affecting all those who come in its orbit. This structure is neither accountable to its people nor does it have the disposition to end the immunity enjoyed by its broad range of security personal and non-state actors. How then do we ensure women's access to justice? As women are usually placed at the bottom of power structures they remain outside the security decision-making process and cannot change it from within. It is, therefore, imperative that women's inclusion in these decisions making is ensured so as to enable their construction of the value system from war to peace. UNSCR 1325 has transformational capabilities as it re-conceptualizes women's role and fosters women's participation and creates notional changes in the traditional security and peace paradigms.

The process of an argument for a changed world view started after the UN Commission on Status of Women discussions in 2010, on UNSCR 1325 when various women's organizations gathered to celebrate the completion of a decade of the resolution and maintained that the process had not contributed to any great extent to women's participation in peace processes, nor was the protection system in place globally and we needed to rethink (Moser 2010). The year, however, as it remained the landmark year for evaluation of a decade long work, helped in pushing the agenda of women forward in peace-keeping processes. Reviewing the way UNSCR 1325 is being implemented through NAPs there has been a move growing globally that NAPs are not the only method to implement UNSCR 1325. Betty Reardon at the International Studies Conference in 2013 argued that NAPs are 'like foxes constructing a chicken coop.[11] Though the initial aim of UNSCR 1325 was demilitarization, the recent attempts at the formulation of NAPS have been aimed mostly at post-conflict development and reconstruction or a narrower aim that stresses prevention of violence against women in armed conflict. While it is important to create a discourse on UNSCR 1325, we need to make the discourse broader and ask questions confronting us such as whether this is the only method to bring women into the peace and security process? Can the original resolution be explained in the new context or do we add another resolution? Many women have started to feel that NAPs are not the most likely route to achieve peace through UNSCR 1325 as they are being implemented.[12] Some States have even included women in peacekeeping forces (India in Liberia since 2007) and feel there is no more need to implement UNSCR 1325. As Cora Weiss very rightly suggested in a discussion, 'when women gathered around the table to draft what became UNSCR 1325 jobs in the military were not on our minds. We were thinking of women as visionaries for alternative means to resolve conflict not for use of force (7 March 2012)'. In this context, therefore, there is an increasing apprehension among feminists that the basic characteristics of UNSCR 1325 are being overlooked and a time has come to take a strong position.

I would suggest that in implementing UNSCR 1325 we have to move beyond NAPs and think like Elise Boulding who spoke about the wide spread cultures of peace that exist (Boulding 1999). There are three components we need to develop. The first is at the international/transnational level where the women's movement working on the theme goes forward to initiate a dialogue at the UN, especially within the Security Council. The time has come to go back to the roots and evaluate the situation within the main international peace organization. There is an increasing claim by women changing NAPs into transnational efforts with cross-border strategies that are locally derived by women. If we are to move towards the super ordinate goal of peace and formulate plans keeping in mind total transformation, then solidarity among women's groups is imperative. We nevertheless need to raise a campaign for increase of funding to enable poor and rural women who cannot participate in international events to play a part.

Another important strategy is solidarity building at the regional level through collaboration between South Asian countries to ensure that a wide ranging discourse on UNSCR 1325 is started. No initiative on a regional action plan could be taken in South Asia so the question before us is how should we go beyond individual NAPs especially at regional level as Europe has managed[13]? The development within India, a country with a hyperactive State security system can only be replaced if women across the region come together. This process must be an independent women's initiative, as women must have ownership of the process. To achieve this, a regional/transnational women's action plan becomes the key to peace. There is a trans-border women's movement in place that can take up the issue for awareness building on strategic actions defined for an action plan.

At the third level, and the most important, is the shift in UNSCR 1325 to civil society formulated action plans. We feel it is the right moment to think of a people's action plan as an alternative to an NAP (Reardon 2011).[14] Our discussions over the years have prompted not only the bringing together this book but also a chapter on a people's action plan by Reardon. My own assessment, especially from an Indian viewpoint, is that the people's action plan should be originated by civil society and community-based women's groups with the support of feminist groups ensuring that women in conflict zones are not kept out. Women as political agents of change must be high profiled and not as victims of armed conflict who need protection. UNSCR 1325 has transformational capabilities that can assist women in changing the security paradigm. The basic criterion is to prevent armed conflict by our search for alternative solutions and implementation of just laws and move it steadily upwards from the ground level.

There are many examples where people's initiatives have worked. In the Naga peace process in 1997 the ceasefire was reopened as a result of people's initiative. Article 8b of UNSCR 1325 suggests the importance of local women's peace initiatives for conflict resolution that we can adopt. The objective, therefore, before us is the development of a people's action plan in the context of UNSCR 1325. A people's action plan cannot be a few local plans strung together. Local plans do not make a national plan unless there is a mechanism to bring them together. These parameters call for a different structure and require formulation of plans at national and local level. The idea of a people's action plan would be credible if women across the country are involved in its process. It raises a fundamental question about the drawing of lines around the word 'conflict' and what sorts of conflicts fall under the UNSCR 1325 ambit? We as activists scholars must recognize the challenges inherent in both the views and develop a people's action plan by drawing clear goals and objectives. It has become very clear from our discourse that change is being demanded from the women at the grass roots. In this new emerging paradigm high value has to be placed on the local, linked to the national. The demand for a people's action plan has to be a product women's solidarity. At the national level, we need an all-India campaign, which is not difficult if a platform can be built by the women's and peace movement coming together. They could draw up an annual reporting system to the UN. This campaign then would link local to national plans.

Any plan that is formulated would require a conceptual framework and Reardon has provided us with a framework that can be used globally. In the context of India they must be worked out in consultations with women's groups. The monitoring and evaluation of the system must develop indicators that can lay the guidelines not only for the development of a people's action plan but also its conversion into an NAP when possible with women at its core. The action plan aims for a demilitarized State (also society) that is possible through strengthening the delivery mechanism and I would argue that peace education can be this instrument of change.[15] In India, schools do not teach peace issues. Some universities that do so are few such as Banaras Hindu University, Chennai University, Gujarat Vidyapith and Tata Institute of Social Sciences. The author had introduced a paper on gender and peace as part of its MA curriculum. In this context, though disarmament education is important to peace education, the linkage has been tenuous. It still remains a weak factor in India especially in higher levels of peace education and non-existent in school education.

Finally the questions confronting us are: First, why so many women across the globe are putting energy into UNSCR 1325? As a peace activist, I can only argue that it is a revolutionary resolution as it directs us from the State security paradigm to a gendered security one and believes that women's voices count. It stands on the belief that women's experience of conflict and their attempts at preventing it transform the system to one based on peace. Simultaneously linked to the above is a corollary (also raised by Soumita Basu) as to why so few women are paying attention to UNSCR 1325 in India? The fact that it commits governments to the centrality of women's role in decision making regarding peace is a path that has been un-tread as security is considered the sole right of the State and so remains problematic to commence. The 15th anniversary of UNSCR 1325 should make the women's movement realize that we need to create new opportunities for alliance building on the issue. We hope the book will start a dialogue on what does SCR 1325 means not only in India but in countries affected by conflict and how best it can be utilized.

Notes

1. Namibia's inclusion was important as the Windhoek Declaration and the Namibia Plan of Action were a follow up of the BFPA and called for mainstreaming of gender perspectives in peace operations and processes (United Nations 2000).
2. Personal communication, 5 July 2013.
3. India's imports of major arms increased by 111 per cent between 2004–08 and 2009–13, making it the world's largest importer. Its imports—14 per cent of the global total—were almost three times larger than those of China or Pakistan, the second and third largest arms importers and regional rivals of India. Russia supplied 75 per cent of Indian arms imports, the USA 7 per cent and Israel 6 per cent (SIPRI 2014, 6).

4. The only study directly linked to patriarch on UNSCR 1325 is by Puechguirbal (2010, 172–87).
5. For details on economic resources, see Government of Nagaland (2004, 89–92); Government of Tripura (2007, 33–66); Government of Manipur (2006, Chapters IX and X).
6. The figures for India include expenditure on the paramilitary forces of the BSF, the Central Reserve Police Force, the AR, the Indo-Tibetan Border Police and, from 2007, the Sashastra Seema Bal, but do not include spending on military nuclear activities. In terms of GDP per cent, it has fallen from 3.7 (1988) to 2.4 per cent (2014) but still constitutes 9.1 per cent of government expenditure (SIPRI 2015).
7. India's military expenditure has risen from168 billion Indian Rupees in 1988 to 3,008 billion in 2014 (SIPRI 2015) and its place in the development index is 130 of 188 countries (UNDP 2015, Annex 1).
8. The Women in Conflict Zones Network run by Wenona Giles of York University, Canada brought together women from Sri Lanka and Bosnia/Kosovo. Cynthia Cockburn has worked with women's groups ranging from Cyprus, to Ireland, to Bosnia-Herzgovina and Palestine. Information of author as member of WICZNET.
9. IPC Section 309 Attempt to commit suicide: Whoever attempts to commit suicide and does any act towards the commission of such offence shall be punished with simple imprisonment for a term that may extend to one year (or with fine, or with both).
10. Female diplomats have held the highest posts: three have been foreign secretaries (Chokila Iyer, Nirupama Rao and Sujata Singh), one permanent representative to the UN (in Geneva) and representative to the disarmament negotiations (Arundhati Ghosh), and one was deputy national security advisor (Leela Ponappa).
11. Personal communication, 24 May 2013.
12. Conference on gender, peace and security organized by Sansristi, Bhubaneswar, 13–14 March 2011 and 18–19 April 2013.
13. Most regional action plans are in Europe or European promotes (in West Africa).
14. In Bhubaneswar, India on 27 and 29 March 2011 under the aegis of Sansristi, a gender resource centre, a small group of activists, writers and scholars met to discuss UN Security Council Resolution 1325 and its relevance in the Indian context. The objective of the conference was to assess how 1325 applies to the Indian context and how it can be used to promote peace. Focus on the understanding and interpretation of UNSCR 1325 included intervention on the resolution as a tool for demilitarizing security and this was possible through the development of a people's action Plan.
15. Teaching peace in conflict regions is becoming more common. Courses were done in erstwhile LTTE territory in Sri Lanka (inclusive of gender and conflict) specifically for women and also in Jammu and Kashmir in India. As Harris and Lewer who were involved in the LTTE course argue, it 'provides local stakeholders with educational space…help develop peace-building activities by offering people the necessary knowledge with which to analyse and think about the causes, management, resolution and transformation of violent conflict in a depoliticized, safe and educationally rewarding context' (Harris and Lewer 2008, 127).

References

Boulding, Elise. 1999. *Culture of Peace: The Hidden Side of History*. Syracuse, NY: Syracuse University Press.

Brock-Utne, Birgit. 2009 (2008). 'Gender Perspective on Peace Education and the Work for Peace'. *International Review of Education*, 55 (2–3, May): 205–20.

Chowdhury, Anwarul. 2011. 'Message by Ambassador Anwarul K. Chowdhury, former Under-Secretary-General of the United former Ambassador of Bangladesh to the UN and President of the UN Security Council in March 2000'. In Workshop on Women and Peace Towards a new Decade of Security Council Resolution and Searching for Alternatives to State Security, organized by SANSRISTI, Orissa, India, 13–14 March, 3–4.

Cockburn, Cynthia. 2012. 'Don't Talk to me About War: My Life's a Battlefield'. 25 November. Available at: https://www.opendemocracy.net/5050/cynthia-cockburn/%E2%80%9Cdon%E2%80%99t-talk-to-me-about-war-my-life%E2%80%99s-battlefield%E2%80%9D (Accessed on 2 January 2014).

Derouen, Karl and Edward Newman. 2015. 'Postscript Challenges and Opportunities for Forwarding Gender, Peace and Security'. In *Gender, Peace and Security: Implementing UN Security Council Resolution 1325*, edited by Theodora Ismen Gizelis and Louise Olsson, 232–44. New York: Routledge.

Ellerby, Kara. 2013. '(En)gendered Security? The Complexities of Women's Inclusion in Peace Processes'. In *International Interactions: Empirical and Theoretical Research in International Relations*, 39 (4): 435–60.

Enloe, Cynthia. 2000. *Maneuvers: The International Politics of Militarizing Women's Lives*. Berkeley, CA: University of California Press.

The Guardian. 2002. 'Full Text: Bin Laden's "Letter to America"'. *The Guardian*, 24 November. Available at: http://www.theguardian.com/world/2002/nov/24/theobserver (Accessed on 10 October 2013).

Global Network of Women Peacebuilders. 2014. *Security Council Resolution 1325: Civil Society Monitoring Report 2014*. Women Count. Global Network of Women Peacebuilders. Available at: http://www.gnwp.org/resource/women-count-%E2%80%93-security-council-resolution-1325-civil-society-monitoring-report-2014 (Accessed on 7 June 2016).

Government of Jammu and Kashmir. 2013. *Draft Jammu and Kashmir Police Bill*. Department of Home. Available at: http://jkhome.nic.in/home.pdf (Accessed on 22 June 2014).

Government of Manipur. 2006. *Draft Human Development Report*. New Delhi: Planning Commission of India.

Government of Tripura. 2007. *Tripura Human Development Report*. Available at: https://india.gov.in/tripura-human-development-report-2007 (Accessed on 14 June 2016).

Government of Nagaland. 2004. *State Human Development Report*. Kohima, Nagaland: Department of Planning & Coordination.

Gupta, Arvind. 2013. 'IDSA Keynote Address'. In *National Seminar on Federalism, Foreign Policy and Border States: Dynamics from North East States of India*.

Sikkim University, 22–23 March 2013. Available at: http://idsa.in/speech/ SikkimUniversity_agupta (Accessed on 7 June 2016).

Hague Appeal for Peace. 2000. *The Hague Agenda for Peace and Justice in the 21ˢᵗ Century.* Available at: http://www.haguepeace.org/resources/HagueAgendaPea ce+Justice4The21stCentury.pdf (Accessed on 4 January 2014).

Hann, Ursula and Astrid Holzinger. 2015. *Symposium Report: Enhancing Women's Share in Peace and Security.* Vienna, Austria: Austrian Federal Ministry.

Hans, Asha. 2000. 'Women Across Borders in Kashmir: The Continuum of Violence'. *Canadian Woman Studies,* 19 (4): 77–78.

———. 2010. 'Human Security the Militarized Perception and Space for Gender'. In *The Gender Imperative: Human Security vs State Security,* edited by Betty Reardon and Asha Hans, 384–409. New Delhi/New York: Routledge.

Harris, Simon and Nick Lewer. 2008. 'Peace Education in Conflict Zones: Experiences from Northern Sri Lanka'. *Journal of Peace Education,* 5 (2, September): 127–40.

Hayes, Ben. 2012. *The Other Burma? Conflict, Counter–insurgency and Human Rights in North East India.* Amsterdam: Transnational Institute.

J.S. Verma Committee. 2013. *Report of the Committee on Amendments to Criminal Law.* Available at: http://www.ncte-india.org/Commission.asp (Accessed on 25 June 2014).

Moser, Annalise. 2010. Women Count: Security Council Resolution 1325: Civil Society Monitoring Report. New York: Global Network of Women Peacebuilders.

Ogata, Sadako and Amartya Sen. 2003. *Human Security Now.* Commission on Human Security. New York: United Nations.

PeaceWomen. 2015. 'In Focus: How Arms Transfers Can Violate Human Rights and International Human Rights'. In *Pieces of Peace: Peace Through Gendered Conflict Prevention,* 10–11. Available at: http://wilpf.org/wp-content/ uploads/2015/08/WILPF-PeaceWomen_Pieces-of-Peace.pdf (Accessed on 7 June 2016).

Puechguirbal, Nadine. 2010. 'Discourses on Gender Patriarchy and Resolution 1325: A Textual Analysis of UN Documents'. *International Peacekeeping,* 7 (2): 172–87.

Ramanathan, Usha. 2005. 'India and the ICC'. *Journal of International Criminal Justice,* 3 (3): 627–34.

Reardon, Betty A. 1985. *Sexism and the War System.* New York: Teachers College Press.

Reardon, Betty. 2011. Keynote Address on Women Peace and Security in Proceedings of the Workshop on Women and Peace Towards a New Decade of Security Council Resolution and Searching for Alternatives to State Security organized by SANSRISTI Bhubaneswar, Orissa, India 13 and 14 March 2011, 12–15.

Reardon, Betty and Asha Hans. 2010. *The Gender Imperative: Human Security vs State Security.* New Delhi/New York: Routledge.

SIPRI. 2014. *SIPRI Fact Sheet.* Available at: http://books.sipri.org/files/FS/ SIPRIFS1403.pdf (Accessed on 20 January 2015).

———. 2015. *Military Expenditure Data Base.* Available at: http://www.sipri.org/ research/armaments/milex/milex_database (Accessed on 20 January 2016).

Teltumbde, Anand. 2013. 'Criminalizing People's Protests'. *Economic and Political Weekly,* XLVIII (14, April): 10–14.

United Nations. 2000. 'General Assembly Security Council'. Doc No. A/55/138-S/2000/693.

United Nations. 2013. *CEDAW Document C/CG/30 General Recommendation No. 30 on Women in Conflict Prevention, Conflict and Post-conflict Situations.* Available at: http://www.ohchr.org/Documents/HRBodies/CEDAW/GComments/ CEDAW.C.CG.30.pdf (Accessed on 20 January 2015).

UNDP. 2015. *Human Development Report Work for Human Development.* Available at: http://report.hdr.undp.org/ (Accessed on 7 June 2016).

UN Women. 2015. *Preventing Conflict, Transforming Justice, Securing the Peace: A Global Study on the Implementation of United Nations Security Council Resolution 1325.* Available at: http://wps.unwomen.org/~/media/files/un%20women/wps/ highlights/unw-global-study-1325-2015.pdf (Accessed on 7 June 2016).

United Nations Security Council. 2013a. *S/RES/2106 (2013).* Available at: http:// www.un.org/en/ga/search/view_doc.asp?symbol=S/RES/2106 (Accessed on 12 June 2014).

United Nations Security Council. 2015. 'Security Council Unanimously Adopts Resolution 2242 (2015) to Improve Implementation of Landmark Text on Women, Peace, Security Agenda. 7533rd Meeting of the Security Council'. Available at: http://www.un.org/press/en/2015/sc12076.doc.htm (Accessed on 14 June 2016).

University of Wisconsin. 1989. 'Summer Institute on "Regional Conflict and Global Security: The Nuclear Dimension', University of Wisconsin, July 28–August 4.

About the Editors and Contributors

Editors

Asha Hans, PhD, is Co-chair, Pakistan India People's Forum for Peace and Democracy; former Professor of Political Science, and Founder Director, School of Women's Studies, Utkal University, India. A leading campaigner of women's rights, she has participated in the formulation of many conventions in the United Nations. She is the President of Sansristi—a gender resource centre. Her recently published books include *Disability, Gender and the Trajectories of Power* (2015) and *The Gender Imperative: Human Security vs State Security* (with Betty Reardon, 2010).

Swarna Rajagopalan, PhD, is a political scientist who works as an independent scholar and writer. She is also the founder of The Prajnya Trust—an NGO working on peace and gender. She has written on a range of gender and human security-related topics and is the Co-editor (with Farah Faizal) of *Women, Security, South Asia: A Clearing in the Thicket* (2005).

Contributors

Paula Banerjee is Professor in the Department of South and South East Asian Studies, University of Calcutta, and the Director of Calcutta Research Group. She has worked extensively on UNSCR 1325. Her latest books are *Borders, Histories, Existences: Gender and Beyond* (2010) and *Women in Indian Borderlands* (co-authored with Anasua Basu Ray Chaudhury, 2011).

Soumita Basu is Assistant Professor of International Relations at the South Asian University, New Delhi. Her primary research interests are the United Nations, feminist international relations and critical security studies. She is Associate Editor of the *International Feminist Journal of Politics*.

Anuradha M. Chenoy is Dean, School of International Studies, former Chairperson of the Centre for Russian and Central Asian Studies, Jawaharlal Nehru University (JNU), and Director of UGC Area Studies Programme of Russian and Central Asian Studies. She has done short term consultancies with many international organizations, such as, UNESCO (United Nations Educational, Scientific and Cultural Organization) International Committee of the Red Cross (ICRC), Expert Group on Women, Peace and Security of UN Women South Asia, and civil society organizations, such as, Action Aid, Asia Europe People's Forum, WISCOMP (Women in Security, Conflict Management and Peace) and so on. Author of the acclaimed *Militarism and Women in South Asia* (2002), her latest book is co-authored with Kamal Mitra Chenoy and titled as *Maoist and Other Armed Conflicts* (2010).

Rekha Chowdhary, former Professor of Political Science at University of Jammu, was selected for the ICSSR (Indian Council of Social Science Research) National Fellowship in 2013. She was a Fulbright Scholar at the School of Advanced International Studies (SAIS) Johns Hopkins University, and a Commonwealth Fellow in Queen Elizabeth House (QEH), University of Oxford. She has published widely on issues related to Jammu and Kashmir.

Ritu Dewan is President of the Indian Association of Women's Studies (IAWS), and Director, Centre for Development Research and Action, Mumbai. She was, until her retirement, the first-ever woman director of the Department of Economics, University of Mumbai, and the founder-member of the first centre of gender economics. She is also a consultant to UNDP (United Nations Development Programme), UN Women, ILO (International Labour Organization), World Bank, Kashmir Foundation of Peace and Development, Government of Maharashtra, and so on. Her other honorary posts include National Executive Member of the Pakistan India People's Forum for Peace and Democracy, Honorary Advisor to the Kashmir Foundation for Peace and Development Studies, and member of the board of trustees of the Centre for Budget and Governance Accountability (CBGA).

Amrita Patel is presently with the Women and Child Development Department, Government of Odisha. She is a scholar in women's studies and has conducted research work on women's perspective of displacement and migration, gender budgeting, land rights of women and violence against women, amongst other development issues affecting women. Her interests are policy analysis and evidence-based advocacy.

Ila Pathak was Professor of Indo-English Literature and a Bachelors of Law. She was a pioneer for women's rights in India. Co-founder of Ahmedabad Women's Action Group (AWAG) in 1981, and former President of WILPF (India) and Vice-president of WILPF International, Ila died on 9 January 2014.

Betty A. Reardon was among the members of women's civil society organizations (CSOs) who initiated the movement for UNSCR 1325. A feminist, peace educator and the Founding Director of the International Institute on Peace Education (IIPE), she has published widely in theory and practice of peace education, the relationship between sexism, and militarism and feminist perspectives on human security.

Vibhuti Ubbott is Lecturer of Political Science, Jammu and Kashmir Education Department and has a PhD from the University of Jammu. She has been working on issues related to gender with focus on Jammu and Kashmir.

Saumya Uma works as Assistant Professor and Assistant Director of Centre for the Study of Social Exclusion and Inclusive Policy, National Law School of India University (NLSIU), Bengaluru. Her work, since 1994, largely consists of research, writing, speaking, capacity-building, critiquing and advocating for law and policy reforms through the lens of gender and human rights. Her publications include, *Rights of Adolescent Girls in India: A Critical Look at Laws and Policies* (2012) and *Pursuing Elusive Justice: Mass Crimes in India and Relevance of International Standards* (co-edited with Vahida Nainar, 2013).

Index